The Music Diva Spectacle

The Music Diva Spectacle

Camp, Female Performers, and Queer Audiences in the Arena Tour Show

Constantine Chatzipapatheodoridis

Bristol, UK / Chicago, USA

First published in the UK in 2021 by
Intellect, The Mill, Parnall Road, Fishponds, Bristol, BS16 3JG, UK

First published in the USA in 2021 by
Intellect, The University of Chicago Press, 1427 E. 60th Street,
Chicago, IL 60637, USA

Copyright © 2021 Intellect Ltd

All rights reserved. No part of this publication may be reproduced,
stored in a retrieval system, or transmitted, in any form or by
any means, electronic, mechanical, photocopying, recording, or
otherwise, without written permission.

A catalogue record for this book is available from
the British Library.

Cover designer: Alex Szumlas
Copy editor: Newgen
Production manager: Sophia Munyengeterwa
Typesetting: Newgen

Print ISBN 978-1-78938-436-9
ePDF ISBN 978-1-78938-437-6
ePub ISBN 978-1-78938-438-3

Printed and bound by Short Run.

To find out about all our publications, please visit
www.intellectbooks.com
There you can subscribe to our e-newsletter,
browse or download our current catalogue,
and buy any titles that are in print.

This is a peer-reviewed publication.

Contents

Acknowledgments	vii
Introduction	1
1. Time Goes by so Slowly: Madonna's Camp Revivals	40
2. LaLaLas and WowWowWows: Approaching Kylie Minogue's Extravaganzas	74
3. We Flawless: Beyoncé's Politics of Black Camp	102
4. Highway Unicorns: Camp Aesthet(h)ics and Utopias in Lady Gaga's Tours	133
5. Dressed for the Ball: Audience Drag in the Arena Space	171
Conclusion	195
References	201
Index	229

Acknowledgments

The process of writing this book has truly been a memorable journey. Starting with little steps in the form of term papers for my master's program and then becoming a venture into the world of spectacle as part of my doctoral dissertation, it has been quite a fulfilling as well as challenging experience to watch it evolve through each stage.

This journey has been the product of individual effort as well as support coming from family, friends, professors, colleagues, institutions, and people I have met along the way. First of all, I would like to express my immense gratitude to my thesis supervisor, Professor Zoe Detsi, who not only believed in me and this project but, most importantly, kept pushing me toward the path of critical exploration while making sure I didn't deviate from the set track. Her continuous support and professionalism are values that have greatly honed my work ethic. I would also like to thank the members of the co-advising committee behind this project, Dr. Christina Dokou and Dr. Konstantinos Blatanis, who alongside Professor Detsi kindly offered their expertise by paying attention to every little detail of the work and sparking stimulating debates—an invaluable help indeed. May our academic paths always cross!

I am also heavily indebted to the foundations that financially supported this project while still at an early stage. First of all, the Hellenic State Scholarship Foundation significantly facilitated the research process and helped me attain both professional and personal goals. Speaking of journeys, I owe a lot to Fulbright Foundation Greece for giving me the opportunity to travel to the University of Alabama in 2016 via the newly founded Doctoral Dissertation Research Programme. My sincerest gratitude goes to Artemis Zenetou, Els Siakos-Hanappe, Mike Snyder, and Angie Fotaki for promoting an inclusive ethos through their work at Fulbright. My heartfelt appreciation goes to Dr. Tatiana Summer and Dr. Joel Brouwer without whom my access to the campus and resources of the University of Alabama would have been impossible. Last but not least, I would personally like to thank my mentor and friend Professor John Howard with whom

I was lucky enough to reunite during my stay at Alabama and who subsequently agreed to join my dissertation defense committee.

I am also blessed to have been given access to America's most important queer archives. I would like to thank the personnel, volunteers, and fellow researchers I met at New York's The Center (The Lesbian, Gay, Bisexual and Transgender Community Center) and Fort Lauderdale's Stonewall National Museum and Archives. I am also eternally grateful to the European Association for American Studies for awarding me with the Transatlantic Travel Grant and thus allowing me to travel to San Francisco, have access to the museum and collection of the GLBT Historical Society archives, and, of course, experience the city's vibrant culture. Thank you to all individuals, groups, and organizations for preserving and promoting queer histories and for inspiring a future project and dream of mine.

My purest feelings of love and devotion are reserved for my academic home, the School of English, Aristotle University of Thessaloniki. Thank you for giving me the best undergraduate years as well as warmly accommodating my graduate steps along with quite a few interesting side projects. A huge thankyou to my professors Tatiani Rapatzikou, Savas Patsalidis, Giorgos Kalogeras, and Domna Pastourmatzi and especially my diploma thesis supervisor Yiouli Theodosiadou, as well as to all the personnel in the administration offices, the library, and the technical support center for making my academic journey a veritable adventure.

Last but certainly not least, I am eternally grateful for the "invisible heroes" behind this incredible journey and practically behind my whole life. Thank you to each and every single close friend of mine who has been guarding my steps, pushing me to unexplored corners of my mind, tolerating my quirks and mood swings, and, most of all, showing me that although at times I may be traveling alone, I never feel lonely. The ultimate and deepest thankyou of all, of course, goes to my family whose unconditional love and endless support keep shaping the best of me.

Introduction

Dorothy Gale singing "Over the Rainbow" in *The Wizard of Oz* has constituted a defining moment both for Judy Garland's career and her subsequent queer consecration as a gay icon. Longing for a land where the impossible can happen, little Dorothy managed to appeal to the queer psyche by offering a liberating songtext whose open-endedness could easily accommodate queer people's desire for freedom of expression. The song was backed by the film's colorful spectacle esteemed for its time proportions that aided in vivifying the liberating effect. *Oz*'s onscreen transition from black-and-white monotony to technicolor-imbued imagery marked a connotative passage from secularity to dream and from seclusion to openness. Coupled with Dorothy's otherworldly, albeit friendly, encounters in the Land of Oz, the transition's queer message was indeed hard to miss. "Over the Rainbow" became Garland's signature song as she went on to be established as one of the most iconic figures of American queer culture and perhaps one of the first to exert a wide queer appeal of considerate magnitude and longevity. More specifically, gay men's attraction to Garland's star icon was not simply directed toward the star herself but was part and parcel of what the Garland experience enclosed: namely, the opportunity to find, in a very practical sense, the dreamland she was musing about. At a time when queer socialization was mostly under the radar, Garland's appeal openly helped semantify queer bonds and culture sharing among gay men to the point where a cultural stereotype was birthed: "friends of Dorothy" became a euphemism for homosexual men, exposing and specifying what had then been clandestine.[1] Years later, impacting the queer community of New York City, Garland's funeral service on June 27, 1969 followed by the Stonewall riots on June 28 instigated rumors that connected these two events. Though that idea seems far-fetched, one cannot overlook the fact that what was possibly a coincidence was indeed a temporal landmark enveloped with queer affect, which was triggered by the grief over the death of the icon as well as the aggressiveness of the Stonewall incident.

Almost 70 years after Dorothy's musical call to the Land of Oz, Kylie Minogue appears on a glittery crescent moon prop to perform "Over the Rainbow" during the Dreams segment of her *Showgirl: The Greatest Hits Tour* (in 2005). Kylie, whose notoriously lavish extravaganzas have for years attracted international audiences, has emerged as a contemporary gay icon catering to her queer market as well as serving as an advocate of the modern LGBTQ+ movement. Her choice to include Garland's classic in the concert setlist of her greatest numbers is a self-conscious one that aims at bringing together the queer past and present. Minogue and her creative team are well aware of both Kylie's and Garland's queer appeal; the idea to have the former quote the latter is a musical nod to the cultural canon of queer iconicity and repertoire. Such acts of intergenerational homage and cultural exchange are frequent among divas who generally share the target groups of queer audiences. In fact, since pop culture serves as a plateau of sharing and intertextuality whereupon producers and consumers of culture navigate accordingly guided by tastes, desires, and sensibilities, it is conditional that the linking lines between producers and consumers are dynamically formed out of the specificity of the cultural codes they (wish to) share. The line established between divas and queer audiences, for that matter, relies on culturally specific information available to queer groups and, at the same time, generates new relational codes that preserve and forge the said link. Kylie's tribute to Garland is a demonstration of knowing her audience by addressing all these elements that constitute Garland's as well as her own relationship to queer culture.

Divas and queer people have long been affiliated. The cultural production of queer communities manifests a wide range of divas coming from the popular fields of music, cinema, and television, among others. They have been upheld as inspirational figures of power, success, and glamour and have served as models for sexual, gendered, and emotional identification. As a matter of fact, queer people's fascination with divas has almost become a truism, since their relationship, being of reciprocal interest and respect, has been widely solidified through years of mutual cultural exchange. Divas have variously fed the queer imagination while, in turn, their followers have invested in their icons in terms of cultural power, finance, and sentiment. Delving deeper into the practices and productions of queer communities in North America, for example, we find an array of famous women who have each been a commonly agreed-upon adored icon. First and foremost, the silver screen has functioned as the primary source of diva fascination, introducing glamorous women, femme fatales, virgins, and whores to the queer public (Babuscio; Halperin; Harris). It is noteworthy how queer culture absorbed and reiterated the drama around the personae of Marlene Dietrich, Marilyn Monroe, and Joan Crawford, to mention just a few; or how fictional characters, such as Norma Desmond, portrayed by Gloria Swanson in *Sunset Boulevard* (1950), and Margo Channing, played by Bette Davis in *All About Eve* (1950), have left their imprint on camp culture with their distinct acting style. Theatre has also given life to notorious heroines who have been embraced by American queer culture; consider fictional characters from highly popular dramatic and musical texts, such as Tennessee Williams's Blanche DuBois (*A Streetcar Named Desire*) and Alexandra Del Lago (*Sweet Bird of Youth*), or Christopher Isherwood's Sally Bowles from *Goodbye to Berlin*, who rose to Broadway popularity with *Cabaret* (1966) and was subsequently immortalized on screen through Liza Minnelli. Last but not least, the domain of music, which is the focal point of this book, offered queer culture a great many entertaining divas. The musical personae of Diana Ross, Cher, Whitney Houston, as well as more contemporary ones such as Christina Aguilera and Ariana Grande have generated some of the most popular music diva models whose extravagant theatrics have found inroads into queer cultural expression.

The American queer paradigm of diva adoration, as perhaps the most densely annotated one, is only an indicative case. As a matter of fact, the circulation of cultural data between divas and queer groups has been a model materializing across the globe. With cultural specificity always factored in, the diva–queer group relationship model is to be found in most of queer localities, thus manifesting itself as a transcultural mode of appeal that nurtures and is nurtured by local cultures. Each queer locale has its own pantheon of adored divas who abide by the specificities and desires of their accustomed queer culture.[2] However, soon one notices that, on a global level, the diva models and their appeal tactics tend to overlap in terms of persona structure, image politics, and fan reception. From dramatic flair to assertive narratives of femininity and from pathos to glamorous aloofness, world divas share an expressive network of assets. As interaction between cultures, especially in the digital era, progressively leads these models to convergence, it is important to underline that a shared global diva culture cultivates a global audience, the aspects of which, though varied, are, by extrapolation, led to convergence as well. In this light, what is the receptive ethos of a global queer audience and, more importantly, how does this impact on or align with queer politics, localities, and personhood?

To explore this argument further, I turned to specific international diva cases, including Madonna, Kylie Minogue, Beyoncé, and Lady Gaga, who, despite embodying Western standards in terms of politics, image, gender, and sex, exert global appeal in the sense that they allow for identification flexibility as they target a broad-radius audience market. The drive for this work lies at the dynamic links connecting these divas with global diva-adoring queer audiences. Questions emerge as to what is comprehensive of the physiognomy of queer audiences, what the culture enveloping them is, as well as how this culture has gone global. Other questions pertinent to this are how the diva worship model has become popular among queer groups, what role glamorous femininity (within the broader context of how femininity is constructed) plays in the narratives of queer expression and fan attachment, and, most importantly, how the relationship formed between divas and queer fans materializes. Always attentive to essentialist slips, it is imperative to note at this point that divas do not exclusively appeal to queer cultures since they embody consumerist fantasies that appeal to a broader audience market at once. They are indivisible from the capitalist plurality that gives birth to them. However, the cultural channel connecting them with queer groups that allows the flow of code-sharing makes the divas' queer appeal all too specific to ignore. What is it ultimately about divas that queer culture finds so fascinating and ever-inspiring? What does the figure of the diva stand for in the camp imagery of queer practices, and how is her spectacle attuned with queer sensibility? All things considered, why does queer indulgence in diva culture (still) merit analysis?

I will pursue the aforementioned arguments within the framework of the diva spectacle, which I consider to be a rich ground that can best accommodate a critical analysis for the study of culture-sharing processes, namely production and reception. Since most scholarly approaches of the diva culture are usually applied from a visual culture studies perspective, meaning that analyses are concerned with the political and aesthetic construct of the persona as this appears in audiovisual media, my decision to follow a cultural reading via a performance studies route is governed by the need to examine both divas and audiences at their meeting point. In light of this, the diva concert tour show is a potent field of study that can provide a spherical and invigorating understanding of both divas and queer audiences, simultaneously attending to matters of production and reception. I see tour shows as the spatial and temporal moment wherein the relationship between the star diva and fans fully materializes. As opposed to the study of sound, image, or text produced by the diva persona through the mediums of song and music video, the study of a concert show allows for a kaleidoscopic approach that not only includes the aforementioned media but also expands on live performance as a spatiotemporal event. Adding to that the fact that tours from the divas examined here are of international coverage, the materiality of space juxtaposed to the distant and immaterial nature of the digital media is of key importance in observing the diva concert experience.

In order to address the aforementioned questions, I have opted for specific divas' international tour shows to be the primary material for my analysis. Live performances are fecund terrain for critical study not only as regards the subject matter of this project, which is diva camp and queer audiences, but also in the general sense of mass entertainment, cultural production, and the politics of representation. More specifically, diva shows are creative amalgams fused out of different genre-strands of performance, including the rock music concert and musical theater, and also draw from the performative traditions of burlesque, disco, and even the house and rave scenes. Therefore, contextualizing them within the broader field of performance,[3] my analysis centers on the live interpretation of divas' songs and is mostly concerned with staging, showcase, and delivery. I am also paying attention to genre specificities in tandem with the performed acts by looking into them in relation to their historical roots and (re)signification within the diva show. For instance, delving into the disco scene, which is among the most frequent sources of citation for the diva stage, is of primary importance in understanding both its performative lexicon and aesthetic structures as well as its origins in queer entertainment.

In selecting the examined material, I have set a timescale of approximately ten years, so as to draw from plenty of cases that can corroborate the basic premises of the diva adoration model: namely, consistency, reiteration, and circulation. What primarily governs this decision, though, is to cover a period of time—starting as early as 2005 with Kylie Minogue's *Showgirl Tour*—that takes into account the emergence of digital culture and, in particular, the rise of online social media as the leading channel of pop culture dissemination and distribution. While the internet has significantly affected the way music is produced and consumed, live concerts are still privileged to be a reliable source of finance for artists as well as to maintain an aura of authenticity due to their "liveness"[4] and the ability to bring performers and audiences in proximity. As Alice O'Grady indicates,

> [f]or artists the live event has become the latest weapon in the arsenal against the ubiquity of file sharing, downloads and easy access to music via Spotify and YouTube but, in return, audiences expect the live sound to be as close to the recorded version as possible, and they want a show. (117)

One cannot simply overlook the impact digital culture has brought on audience reception as well, since live performances have also increasingly become mediatized events shared by both artists and audiences online, thereby making the newness of each spectacle readily available on the global web.[5] Audiences' recorded material—raw footage, that is—may even provide access to shows or parts of a show that would otherwise be unavailable to audiences as artists will not always record and release concert footage for commercial use. As a matter of fact, this study has largely benefited from unprofessional online material when attendance was impossible, thus proving that digital culture can serve as a critical archival tool.

In processing my case studies, I am applying a camp reading of divas' shows. Of course, the diva spectacle by and large can be characterized as camp in the way, for instance, musical theater and disco are, since not only does it fuse a variety of flamboyant theatrics, but it also generates camp meanings through its acts; it toys with gender and sexuality as well as presents the stage as a camped-up environment which unfolds around the diva. We will see, for example, how Kylie Minogue and Lady Gaga create over-the-top stage acts or how Beyoncé manages to feminize her performances through camp kinesis. Apart from approaching the tour shows holistically, taking into account their main structure, overarching themes, and motifs, as well as social, political, and historical details undergirding them, what I will primarily be focusing on are specific acts within the shows where a camp synergy is at work. By that I mean the effect accruing from a very particular performance, gimmick, or narrative that successfully foregrounds the principal attributes of camp: namely, (gender) playfulness, exaggeration, flamboyance, irony, parody, retromania, and nostalgia, to name just a few.[6] An essential component of the show, the acts are rather important in binding the show together and offer a kaleidoscopic view into the stage of the diva and her various personae, allowing her to smoothly transition from setting to setting and from role to role. Thus, a critical approach of them is mandatory in helping us understand where the diva camp lies and then extend to the way this becomes communed to audiences.

Aside from utilizing past and present bibliography on camp in order to explore the case studies, I have also drawn from a variety of secondary sources. First and foremost, reviews by professional concert and music critics found on online magazines and newspapers have significantly aided in approaching a concert show. Since attendance was not always an option in order for me to account for the presentation and appeal of a show, I resorted to concert reviews that I believe are comprehensive not only in illustrating aspects of a show in detail but also in annotating audience reception. For that reason, I have turned to reviews from a variety of local posts in order to establish as more of a plural and less homogenizing view as possible with regard to the global audience proxy. Furthermore, I have approached creative and stage directors, choreographers, and producers involved with the show-making process. Albeit not novel, live music performance is a research field that remains underexplored, considering the cultural and artistic capital that goes into it. As such, the mechanics and structures of a live show are currently shared only by those engaged in its production and critical analysis, thus mainly making available readings of the actual staged performance. I wanted this project to delve deeper into the operations of the spectacle and that partly led me to approach key figures associated with my case studies. Though establishing contact with some of them has been challenging, I have managed to secure interviews with vogue instructor Jamel Prodigy (aka Derek Auguste), who has been active in the New York ball scene and has collaborated with pop artists such as FKA Twigs, as well as Kylie Minogue's long-term art director William Baker, whose contribution to this project was essential in not only helping to explore the persona of Kylie but also detailing the process of creating a live show.

Last but not least, I would like to specify my usage of terms regarding queer groups and culture. I use the term *queer* to refer to the culture in the general sense, including homosexual, bisexual, transsexual, and transgender groups or cultural practices historically associated with these groups. While the term *gay* may be used interchangeably with *queer*, I try to limit its usage where needed, as *gay* often implies *gay male* and may eclipse other identity categories within the queer spectrum, especially if one takes into account how gay men usually come across as more privileged and visible.[7] As far as identity politics is concerned, my usage of the *LGBTQ+* umbrella term, where applied, will specifically indicate Western groups identified with the said movement and culture, since the birth of a coherent and politicized *LGBTQ+* culture has its origins in the Western world. That is the reason why I do not use the umbrella term to refer to non-Western communities and groups; *queer*, as a more open term, is used instead. Also, practices like Pride, for instance, are treated within the *LGBTQ+* context as they are largely performed under a very specific sociopolitical discourse, if not agenda. Conversely, practices such as drag or vogue are addressed as *queer* since their performance is not necessarily attached to a community identifying as *gay* or *transgender* but is more broadly connected to queer culture. Finally, *queer* is also employed for those historical aspects of the culture that were prevalent prior to the gay liberation movements. *Homosexual* culture is acknowledged as an umbrella term that encompasses queer activity, practices, and lifestyle prior to the politicization of sexual identities, yet it largely fails to embrace concepts of bisexual, pansexual, or transgender expression, let alone it being a carrier of clinical/pathologic connotations. Once again, *queer* emerges as a valid general term that covers for all principally because it resonates with the nonnormative character of the aforementioned categories.

In structuring the chapters of this book, though all of them center on the camp of divas and its onstage exposition, I also set diva camp as the axis around which other critical conundrums revolve. The first chapter explores the camp of Madonna in relation to the performative construct of the diva-persona. With her performances raising some very important questions with regard to a variety of subject matters, from feminism and pornography to activism and then some, Madonna has for years stimulated research interest with her controversial acts as well as her political advocacy. While one could argue that a Madonna studies analysis seems anachronistic since most academic interest on the artist peaked in the periods of the 1980s and 1990s and gradually faded into the 2000s, the truth is that her performances are still fecund ground for research, especially when factored in are issues of ageism and the music industry as well as nostalgia indulgence and the social media era. Regarding live touring, not only have Madonna's notorious showcases managed to preserve her status of an ardent arena performer but have also continuously stirred new interest in her persona. As evident in her tour acts, the artist is constantly reinventing herself by changing looks and seeking new music and dance styles. At the same time, though, she cannot help but be locked in her own name brand and the performance features that originally propelled her to stardom. As a result, she often ends up toying with generic themes and narratives already found in her work. This approach is simultaneously indicative of an exhaustive (self-)referential pool as well as a need to nostalgically appeal to her fans through her own image. This is exactly where I trace the roots of her camp appeal and production. Coupled with her drawing from queer scenes and sources, such as vogue and S&M, a fact that still raises questions on cultural appropriation, Madonna's camp is a consciously queer(ing) approach of performance that wishes to maintain her icon within the diva tradition of queer culture.

Focusing on Kylie Minogue, the second chapter approaches the artist's camp performance of femininity. Kylie is renowned for her Vegas-style extravaganzas that bring into the arena large groups of queer audiences, especially gay men. Her persona and stage are built upon a camp imagination, with her hyperfeminine posture being surrounded with ornate onstage details and embellished with vibrant soundtracks. The latter, in fact, are patterned out of the sounds and sensibility of the disco and dance/house scene, which have been fundamental in formulating queer musical and aesthetic taste. Kylie's showgirl persona embodies the performed tradition of burlesque, as she toys with her onstage identities and offers a titillating look into her theatrical world. She establishes herself as an object of desire by traditional Western standards, but simultaneously undermines this position by drawing attention to the fictitious nature of her gender performance. Simultaneously, she fulfills a gay male fantasy by overtly drawing from existent camp culture and also by equally laying emphasis on the spectacle of the male body. Studying Kylie's stage brings attention to an array of conundrums concerning the subject matter of camp and queer culture in general. The camp-macho binary is one of them as it foregrounds notions of effeminacy and machismo permeating gay male culture. Also, Kylie's relationship with Baker, her creative director who overtly builds the artist's spectacle upon/through specific queer angles, raises questions with regard to authorial intent and Kylie's own agential role in her spectacle. As case studies, Kylie's shows and persona have not spawned academic interest until recently simply because much of her persona was either compared to her contemporary Madonna or presented a lack of political valence. By looking on and around the Kylie spectacle, I wish to delve deeper into a largely underexplored stage persona, who for four decades now shapes and is shaped by queer culture.

INTRODUCTION

In the third chapter, I center on the icon of Beyoncé Knowles and her stage interpretation of camp. Currently, the persona and performances of Beyoncé are at the epicenter of pop culture studies with cultural scholars approaching the icon from numerous standpoints, specifically addressing matters of race and gender more often than not. The artist's recent projects have vigorously brought matters of racial representation and feminism center stage, reinvigorating critical dialogue as regards racial and feminist discourse going mainstream. Criticism, in fact, seems polarized, since the artist is either hailed as the new assertive role model of a Black woman who is fully in control of what image she is conveying to her audiences, or being criticized for commercializing a feminist/fauxminist aesthetic to promote her work. It is true, however, that Beyoncé is a highly popular artist whose trend-setting and audience-appealing tactics bespeak of savvy marketing. At the same time, her performance art is effective in foregrounding a racial-cum-feminist identity politics. This intersectional position created by her performance is also where her camp is located. Drawing from both Black and White queer culture, her exposition is one of Black camp, a critical performance that simultaneously assaults ingrained notions of Whiteness and celebrates Black vernacular traditions. As a matter of fact, Beyoncé's case reveals a necessity: namely, the specification of Black camp, which in part serves as a critical reminder of a dominant White gay culture and the need to envision Black queer production in camp's rigidly White past.

The fourth chapter of this book will approach the camp performances of Lady Gaga. Since her debut as an international act in 2008, the artist has attracted critical interest with her outrageous shticks and performance art. The cultural phenomenon that is Lady Gaga would seem a rather well-examined area of research since scholarly debates have been extensive in investigating her persona. Covering a wide spectrum of critical topics, from postmodern art and the avant-garde to materiality and body politics, Lady Gaga's performances have been provoking, socially conscious as well as controversial and at times incongruous. Her embodiment of a queer aesthetic has also been of utmost importance in her work as she goes on to become a vessel filtering and producing queer art. As a result, a vibrant queer fandom has formed around her icon and, being aware of that, Lady Gaga has willfully directed her performances toward gender-fluid concepts and a politics of inclusion; as matter of fact, she has been vocal about sexual minorities worldwide both on- and offstage. Therefore, one would imagine that to talk about Lady Gaga's camp performance is redundant. Yet, I argue that much of cultural analysis on the artist has been concerned with her early projects and predominantly with her video and celebrity iconography. Her live stage still remains a terrain for critical investigation, especially when it comes to structure and audience immersion. Drawing from musical theater, performance art, and an array of queer scenes, Gaga's stage is the camp spectacle par excellence that plays with generic conventions in being a faux-concert: namely part-theater, part-gig, part-showcase. Simultaneously, her live performance is supported with dramatic action, placing the artist in theatrical tasks, arcs, and settings, thus enhancing the dramatic nature of her persona. My intent here is to present a kaleidoscopic insight into Lady Gaga's stage camp, updating current views regarding her queer reconfiguration of the staged self as well as exploring in depth her affiliation with queer groups.

The decision to approach the said performers and their tour shows is governed by the logic that, apart from their large queer fan following, their live stage houses a plethora of queer references, be they acts that directly draw from the artistic repository of queer culture or showcases that bear strong queer resonances as well as praxes that are energized with the poetics of camp to which queer fans actively respond. This is why in the final chapter of this book I am focusing on the cultural body of the audience, always in relation to the diva spectacle. The primary scope of this chapter is to theorize and explicate the praxis of what I identify as *audience drag* and pay attention to its roots in drag culture. Drag as a queer praxis, namely one that is performed within the circles of the community and serves as an entertaining device parodying (hetero)normative culture, can be traced to as early as the nineteenth century, more specifically in London's molly houses. Subsequently, American drag balls and individual drag shows started populating queer nightlife and eventually gave shape to the drag scene we currently know. Audience drag, as a derivative practice of stage drag, is addressed as part of drag's transition into a more visible, if mainstream, circle. I also address this praxis in the context of fandom since it stands for an embodied performance that materializes fans' adoration of the diva. In addition, the transformation of the fans into the performing persona in the public space of the arena inevitably invites questions of space and, more specifically, the spatiotemporal concept known as "the event." In light of this, the public/private and stage/street dichotomies importantly affect drag performance and will be given attention to in relation to the figurative and literal openness that audience drag enjoys in the arena space. Ultimately, this chapter approaches audience drag as camp fandom precisely because it employs a queer performance that brings together divas and fans, creating a temporary colorful realm of gender-fluidity, queer visibility, acceptance, and belonging, a queer utopia perhaps, that reifies notions of community within the safe environment of the diva spectacle.

INTRODUCTION

The camp of the diva: Theory and praxis

In order to theorize the relationship between divas and queer fans, I will delve further into the cultural body of camp, a distinctly queer aesthetic, if sensibility, that has been the quintessential component behind the diva adoration pattern. Although cultural theory on camp has been extensive, its subject still remains a contested topic among its critics. Fabio Cleto attempts a succinct, yet densely configured definition: "Tentatively approached as *sensibility, taste*, or *style*, reconceptualised as *aesthetic* or *cultural economy*, and later asserted/claimed as *(queer) discourse,* camp hasn't lost its relentless power to frustrate all efforts to pinpoint it down to stability" (2, original emphasis). Drawing from postmodern theories on subjectivity and textuality, Cleto carefully approaches camp as a mode of perception/expression that entered gay male culture by means of *adoption*, meaning that it did not originate in the said culture and its points of origin are rather obscure to trace:

> Being *affiliated* (the term coming from the late Latin *affiliatus*, "adoptive son") with homosexual culture, camp is not the direct and legitimate offspring of a homosexual selfhood active with the *properties* of "biological paternity." The origins of camp are elsewhere—where, we can't say—and only through a cultural process, so to speak, of *adoption*, camp has been brought to its supposed or reclaimed "homosexual paternity."[8] (5)

Homosexual men nurtured and circulated camp by infusing it with queer qualities, that is with a perception of reality—a heteronormative reality—through the eyes, psyche, comprehension, and living of queer subjectivity as this accrues from the historical and collective social life of queer people. Camp, thus, can only be thought of as an effect of cultural synergy that, whether it has come to be solely affiliated with homosexual men or not (which is arguably the case), fuses heteronormative reality with queer signification, hence *queer discourse*, as Cleto underlines.

When talking about camp as part of gay male culture, one has to consider that perspectives on it have largely been formulated out of a Western and predominantly White experience of homosexuality. American culture and theory provide much of our understanding on camp, inevitably filtering it through a narrowly focused lens. Though theorists of camp in later years have been rather flexible with and alert to camp's Western/White background, they managed to do so by contesting previously theorizing attempts that appeared monolithic as regards camp's cultural formation. Initially, Susan Sontag's seminal essay "Notes on 'Camp'" brought the subject of camp in the academic limelight and eventually triggered a critical engagement with its politics and poetics. Sontag's "Notes" accounted for a homosexual subculture that was by and large American, which, by extension, relied on the European past and its cultural production.[9] Perspectives on camp prior to Sontag can be traced in Christopher Isherwood's novel *The World in the Evening* wherein he vaguely divides camp into low and high art—the former emulated by "a swishy little boy with peroxided hair, dressed in a picture hat and wearing a feathered boa, pretending to be Marlene Dietrich," the latter being associated with "the whole emotional basis of the Ballet, for example, and of course of Baroque art" (110). Isherwood's referential field too has its basis on Eurocentric ideals of art evaluation, beauty, and class, and connects the image of the swishy boy camp's exposition with male homosexuality. With Isherwood's quote serving as an influential starting point of camp's literary existence as well as Sontag's detailed essay, which functioned not only as a discursive pool to draw from but also as a template for contestation and debate, much of what was written about camp up until the end of the 1980s could not help but account for a camp culture of White male homosexual production.

It was not until the 1990s that theories on camp acquired a more nuanced perspective by dissecting the dominant discourses of Whiteness and maleness permeating its canon. By then, also, camp's artistic tools had entered the market sphere of mainstream culture, thus becoming a widely shared aesthetic enjoyed outside queer subcultures. Easy as it is to think that pop and straight culture simply appropriated camp from its subcultural zones of production, the truth is that queer people were also keen on projecting their culture onto more visible and even marketable avenues. According to Alexandra Chasin, "[t]he 1990s was a banner decade for gay men and lesbians. Representations of gay men and lesbians on television, in newspapers and magazines, in courts and in legislatures, in the workplace, and in pride marches and other public forums, increased dramatically" (29). In explaining how exclusion from mainstream culture can be corrected by simply entering the market with financial power and enfranchisement, Chasin argues that gay and lesbian groups were given a spot in the marketplace by being acknowledged as social consumers with "gay dollars" and, thus, had their identities consolidated by means of finance (29–39). This was rather expected considering how the political agenda of gay and lesbian movement in America invested in enfranchisement, which was seen as the vehicle to social visibility. Daniel Harris corroborates that

> [t]he selling of gay culture was a synergistic arrangement, a marriage of convenience, a profitable intersection of interests, one that, far from resisting, homosexuals have fought long and hard to bring about, doing everything possible to make themselves more appealing in the eyes of advertisers. (6)

Ever since, queer culture has become increasingly monetized, inviting main-stream market into its lifestyle and practices. As a result, queer-inflected cultural productions like camp were now widely available for consumption, enjoyment, and utilization.

At the same time, camp and its mechanisms became more open to criticism, which is how cultural theorists were given more ground to work on and, by extension, challenge the dominant patterns behind its production and annotation. Turning to queer and feminist theory, critics such as Moe Meyer and Pamela Robertson ascribe deconstructive qualities to camp by applying it on their cultural analyses as a critically postmodern tool with a subversive and radical edge. In seeing camp as "political and critical," contrary to Sontag's critique,[10] Meyer defines camp "as the total body of performative practices and strategies used to enact a queer identity, with enactment defined as social visibility" (5). The writer contextualizes camp within the postmodern condition and pop culture, underlining its appropriation from dominant culture and, therefore, it being simply derivative when co-opted by non-queer hands (13–15). On a feminist note and raising critical queries not only over camp per se but also over its scholars, Robertson tackled male homosexual essentialism by claiming female agency in the production and reception processes of camp, a topic previously undertheorized, at best, and ignored, at worst.[11] The writer witnesses a pattern governing camp that deems female subjectivity as a victim of misogyny and castigates camp theorists' analyses on it as rather insufficient:

> [G]ay men appropriate a feminine aesthetic and certain female stars but [...] women, lesbian or heterosexual, do not largely appropriate aspects of gay male culture [...] Women, by this loic, are objects of camp and subject to it but are not camp subjects. (*Guilty Pleasures*, 5)

Significantly so, Robertson's astute critique underscores the complexity behind the relationship of camp and female representation and, inevitably, that between gay culture and divas, which is a highly ambivalent one.

Regarding diva worship, camp has almost by definition been ambiguous, as it has been adoring, deriding, but, above all, scrutinizing female stars. Indeed, camp culture is itself a close study of divas and female behavior, which, to a great extent, can only be characterized as compulsive. Hollywood divas, for instance, have primarily served as objects of scrutiny and emulative desire for the pre-Stonewall generations of gay men. Daniel Harris maintains that

> over the decades gay men became so adept at communicating their forbidden desires through camp allusions that a sort of collective amnesia has descended over the

whole process, and we have lost sight of the fact that our love for performers like Judy Garland was actually a learned behavior. (21)

The writer adds that gay inclination to diva worship is still misconceived by many as "an innate gay predisposition" (21), predominantly because the diva cult has been culturally entrenched and perpetually disseminated among generations of gay men. Stonewall is set here as an alleged threshold that marks the beginning of a change of attitude toward the diva cult due to the fact that the forthcoming generations claimed more assertive identities—the 1960s liberation movements certainly played a key role in that—ones that seemed to be dissonant with the insecure, disenfranchised, and self-loathing queer psyche ensuing from the repressive conditions of the closeted self. According to Harris, "[b]y the early 1960s, some gay men had begun to express repulsion for our obsequious fawning over celebrities" and "[b]y the 1980s and 1990s, the pantheon of immortals, while still treated reverently by many gay men, had become fair game for ridicule," demonstrating that "the diva had come to be perceived as the emotional crutch of the pathetic old queen" (21–22). This is how the writer imagines diva camp's transition from reverence to ridicule, coming to a seeming oblivion. However, Harris does not account for the fact that as a more self-conscious and socially visible gay identity emerged, different routes of identification, pleasure, and affect were sought. For, while the cinema diva adoration may have grown irrelevant, unable perhaps to widely captivate post-1980s generations, especially millennials, the adoration pattern itself remains dynamic and queer culture's connection to it has found a new focus of interest, one that is reflective of current cultural tastes, sexual and gendered expressions, and emotional states of the modern queer self.

This new focus, I would like to argue, nests now in the domain of music. Music divas, as matter of fact, seem to have emerged as this modern cultural symbol, advocate, or, plainly, focus of enthusiasm of queer culture. Seeing how queer culture in the United States develops through its practices, lifestyle, and cultural profile, music divas have become dominant models of camp pleasure in a way that is at points fundamentally different from past diva models, but, at the same time, bearing referential similarities with them. One would see, for instance, how pop music personae nowadays—compared to previous Hollywood divas and models—endlessly inspire drag performances, continuously inform and update camp lexicon, and virtually saturate queer realities not only in America but globally as well. The reasons behind this transfocalization of interest certainly vary, as we shall see shortly, and, of course, it should be noted yet again that American queer culture is taken here as a point of reference as well as an indubitable influential source that feeds global perspectives. International diva acts, such as the ones serving as case subjects in this research and other notable personae, including Adele, Lana Del Rey, Nicki Minaj, Katy Perry, and then some, have in their own way infused their audiovisual performance and songtexts with a camp aesthetic, incorporating elements of irony and parody, and reenacting overtly histrionic/dramatic femininities, which seem to resonate with queer culture's contemporary physiognomy. Simultaneously, though, the camp of these divas appears heavily derivative when it comes to structural motifs, themes, and cited sources, which is rather indicative of two items: first, diva worship is a repeated pattern that sees old divas, serving as imitative and inspirational templates, pass the baton to new ones, thereby establishing a sort of camp lineage; and, second, by buying into diva narratives, queer culture endorses and preserves diva culture, and, conversely, divas acknowledge their queer appeal and accordingly invest in it.

Music divas have always been a vital cultural component of queer communities. Their musical personae backed with songtexts that could usually engage queer audiences in their affective narratives or erotic undertones have provided firm basis for identification and enjoyment. In addition, their extravagant image and often pompous delivery, attributes that rendered their personae otherworldly, larger-than-life characters, established them as emblematic figures in camp culture and spawned genre- or scene-related archetypes. The opera diva is a noteworthy example here. Prima donnas like Maria Callas and Joan Sutherland have fascinated the queer imagination with voice and posture alike. In his work "Diva Worship and the Search for Queer Utopia," Craig Jennex adumbrates the relationship of opera female performers with their gay male audiences, arguing that a strong queer following of the opera diva ultimately resulted in the birth of the "opera queen" stereotype, which primarily reflects White, middle-class gay male taste and has been quite persistent (346). Drawing from previous works of Wayne Kostenbaum, Mitchell Morris, Paul Robinson, and Michael Bronski on opera divas, camp, and homosexuality, Jennex explains that opera occupies an upper tier in the culture of camp because of its structure to braid together typical theatrical elements with emotional exaggeration—elements that have rendered it "one of the most ostentatious art forms in the history of Western classical music tradition" (352).[12] In this deliberately over-theatricalized environment the diva becomes a grandiose figure, an emotionally tantalizing dramatic character in the body of a vocal virtuoso, exhibiting simultaneously acting and singing adeptness. What perhaps underlines best the queer/camp appeal of the opera diva is her superlative acts of dramatic transgression, all lavishly cloaked in period costumes and marvelously climaxing in high notes.

Although queer people—specifically gay men—have been ardent followers of the opera genre, the truth is that the adoration of the opera diva has been narrow in scope. Traditionally, the uniqueness, if bizarreness, of opera meant that it was predominantly available to its connoisseurs while the prestigious costly productions remained rather inaccessible to lower-income audiences. This helped preserve the eclectic aura around opera and along with it an elitist culture. Under this premise, it is well understood that opera divas catered to a very specific audience of queer men who, in turn, took pride in their attachment to them and sought to connect with other queers. Specifically, Jennex touches upon the sexual culture that was presumably flourishing in the opera houses, which meant that attendance was clearly a chance for interaction (347). "Participation in opera culture," Jennex expands, "allowed gay men with the necessary capital an opportunity to perform their non-normative identities in ways that created a queer space in what is conventionally identified as a heteronormative experience in Western culture" (347). It is important thus to remind ourselves, as the writer does, what the context surrounding the diva icon is and how this engages the queer audiences clustering around her. As we shall see further on in this work, the politics of space and, by extension, admittance to or exclusion from it have played and still play a key role in the formation of divas' queer audiences, demonstrating that the relationship between them does not solely rely on fans' adoration of the diva.

Another quintessential and surely more accessible music figure than her operatic counterpart is that of the torch songstress. With a chic, ultra-feminine profile and a highly emotional repertoire, the figure of the torch songstress, which originated at the end of the nineteenth century and peaked in popularity in the decades of the 1930s and 1940s—consider the cases of Billie Holiday and Sarah Vaughan—became the symbol of unrequited love. John Moore defines the torch song as "a lament sung by a woman who desperately loves a commonplace or even brutish man. The latter treats her badly, leaves her or no longer cares for her. Occasionally, he ignores or rebuffs her tentative advances. And yet she remains inexplicably enslaved to him" (32). The torch songstress's unreciprocated pathos would serve as an emotional state that queer men, specifically, could relate with at the time, since their expression of love interest toward a man often entailed risk and usually remained unfulfilled due to social limitations. In that sense, torch divas offered empathy to queer men, yet in a highly dramatic, often grandiose way reminiscent of opera and Hollywood scenarios. Moore implies that this pathos was rather a driving force for torch divas, whose immersion in their drama enclosed "a hint of narcissism which suggests that in some way they [were] rather enjoying their emotional agonies" (33). As such, their pathos is a stage act, a performed melodrama that adds to their already delicate profiles qualities of vulnerability, instability, and obsession with/over a male figure, qualities that both subvert—because they are acted out—and legitimate—because they are acted upon—their performance of femininity.

Torch divas emulated cosmopolitan models of femininity, embodying mostly a modern and urban aesthetic in attire and behavior, which underlined their personae as elegant, yet particularly aloof. John Moore explains that

> visually, the torch singers are linked through images of urban sophistication. These images—projected by the singers on stage and constructed for them in promotional material—are deliberately contrived to convey the impression that these women are urbane, worldly-wise, but hence rather world-weary, and possessing a deep sadness edging toward despair. (33)

Moore adds that there was also a sense of exoticism surrounding their personae mainly due to the use of cosmetics and lavish costuming (39), which fulfills the camp imagination of viewing femininity as an unrealistic object of appeal. Torch songstresses are in part perceived by the camp eye as living ornaments, distant, peculiar, and narcissistic, which underlines their ontology as rather passive, considering their mania for unrequited romance. Queer audiences at the time could empathize with the torch diva because their social, emotional, and cultural self was conveyed through, and projected upon, such personae. This, of course, represented only part of the queer self as it is often male-centric and cannot be sufficiently accounted for, especially when we take into consideration queer resonances in other contemporary figures and genres, such as the erotically tinged music and profile of the blues singers.[13] In the history of camp, torch songstresses were largely eclipsed by Classical Hollywood divas who usually monopolized camp interest at the time. Yet, they have managed to leave their imprint on music culture and further become citational models for future artistic ventures. The camp of the torch diva, as a matter of fact, has been influential on the British soul diva tradition best reflected in the personae of Adele, Amy Winehouse, Duffy, and Paloma Faith.

Progressively and more specifically with the advent of the freedom liberation movements of the 1960s, a new diva model emerged, that of the disco diva, which has been fundamental for queer culture and the camp canon. The rise of disco in the early 1970s saw many African American and Latinx female artists dominating the scene, while audiences were racially, ethnically, and sexually mixed. However, as Gillian Frank argues, disco songs performed by women resonated among gay men, whose empathetic response derived from their own narratives of oppression or coming out (284).[14] In fact, the writer points out that "disco music rose to cultural prominence within the gay community at the moment of their political and cultural ascendance" (285). Disco divas also brought sexuality center stage, lyrically, sonically, as well as spatially, as indicative of the 1960s and 1970s sexual *zeitgeist* that impacted on pop music. Discotheques would become safe spaces of sexual expression embellished with titillating anthems and centralized around the orgasmic voice of the diva. Judy Kutulas argues that "[d]isco divas created a fantasy woman in songs like 'Dancing Queen' and 'Hot Stuff,' a woman whose desires completely coincided with men" (188). Similarly to torch divas or, basically, to every diva model, disco queens emulated unrealistic standards of femininity. Considering they were predominantly women of color, they were burdened with an additional semiotic load of hypersexual and exoticized femininity. Queer men and particularly queer men of color cross-identified with them primarily because their intersectional social position, nuanced with racial/ethnic and sexual markers, was likewise perceived as exotic, deviant, and usually threatening. Hence, the site of and around the disco diva, be it material or aural, could embrace queer expression and encourage bonding very practically so. Tim Lawrence witnesses a change in social dancing during the rise of disco that saw audiences migrating from the heterosexual couple dancing of the dancehall tradition to solo and group dancing, which laid emphasis on the movement of the body (234). Sound-wise, the repeated beats and lyrics of divas' songs played by the DJs proposed an alternative temporality in which progressive linearity was replaced with cycles of aural pleasure—a queering of time (Lawrence 238–39).

Indeed, the disco diva has generated a culture or, better, established a cult. Her image is permeated with ambiguities, though, since she embodies a very physical notion of corporeal pleasures and, simultaneously, exists in an extra-social sphere, a pedestal, or even altar—an apt religious metaphor comprehensive of diva worshipping. Her body and image, as two very semantically charged sites of femininity, become highly coded in terms of gender performance because of their inflated, unreal proportions. Kutulas underlines that "[d]ivas' clothes, hair, and presentation reinforced the fantastic and sexual elements of their reputation" (188); she adds that "[t]he disco look was apolitical," opposing the wokeness and, at times, radicalness of its era (188). Their camp appeal largely emphasized surface over content and aesthetics over politics, favoring the erotics of the image and a complete detachment from reality—as the combination of disco with narcotics culture offered at the time—over an active engagement with their sociopolitical reality. Disco divas occupied a liminal position between reality and fantasy, reenacting their divine status as musical goddesses.[15] They worked toward a synesthetic effect that tilted more toward sonic pleasure than visual—in fact, they rarely performed live[16]—thus placing emphasis on their ethereal profile. It was this theatrically fabricated and highly performative construct of the disco divas that ultimately foddered camp culture and went on to dominate the queer club sound as well as spawn imitative templates for female impersonators.[17]

While the cases of the opera diva, the torch songstress, and the disco diva would steadily inform camp culture, it was the new diva model of the 1980s that rose to prominence, the cultural impact of which heavily shaped current perceptions of female performers and diva adoration. By shifting balance away from the Classical Hollywood model that stood central within camp corpora, yet by then already considered outdated, the 1980s music diva patterned herself after previous diva models, especially the disco queen, and became the object (or subject) of camp appeal. Of key importance was the fact that the new diva was backed by the rise of music television, a major turn not only in conceptualizing, (re)imagining, and popularizing music cultures but also in understanding notions of performance and performativity of gender identities within the domain of music. Divas making their debut at the time, such as Madonna, Cyndi Lauper, Annie Lennox, Whitney Houston, and Kylie Minogue, were introduced to their audiences as audiovisual personae whose musical production was highly mediated through dramatic narratives. Becoming the new medium for experiencing music, the music video triggered a paradigm shift in the way music audiences perceived notions of performance and persona.[18] In a way, the format of the music video allowed artists to experiment with their onstage/onscreen personae, enacting a variety of roles in different settings and, thus, inhabiting multiple identity positions. Audiences were being exposed to role-playing as an important mode of expressing their own identities in a rather flexible way. More specifically, for queer audiences, Steven Drukman explains that "[m]usic video, a performative form that, by its very nature, exposes identities as necessary fictions, is already imbued with camp" (88), adding that camp plays a key role in queer spectators' fascination with the performative forms of music due to its particularly diverse changeability of roles (88–89). The idea that the music of divas was being visualized in a playful, usually colorful and, above all, theatrical fashion certainly allowed for a diversity of images and personae that helped view identity as role-playing and bolstered spectators' notions of self-expression.

It is important to note here that music television perpetuated what had already been a cultural standard: namely that music is gendered and genres appeal to audiences by this logic, assuming masculine and feminine traits and aesthetics and thus creating gendered dynamics.[19] For instance, genres such as rock would often uphold an aggressive masculinity that is perceived as authentic and politically active, whereas teen pop would usually be interpreted as feminine, nonserious, and apolitical (Biddle and Jarman-Ivens 3). Queer audiences seem to have challenged gendered dichotomies as they would usually cross-identify with genres; for example, pop artists and divas, in particular, have been rather popular among gay male audiences, while hip-hop artists and rock divas were rather popular with lesbian ones. Yet, cross-identification risks turning into another generic stereotype that tends to homogenize and generalize assumptions over what is possibly a collective inclination toward a music genre. Simplistically and erroneously so, this framing forces a heteronormative understanding of gendered musical taste according to which lesbian taste overlaps with that of heterosexual men and, accordingly, gay men's with that of heterosexual women, thereby reiterating binary perceptions already dominant in popular culture.[20] Indeed, pop divas may have grown immensely popular with gay male audiences, but one should not assume that every gay man adores pop diva music, or, conversely, that divas only appeal to gay men and heterosexual women. Stan Hawkins argues that "in recent years numerous pop representations have deviated from the rigidity of heterosexual norms, with the emphasis falling on the theatrics of sexual subjectivity" ("[Un] Justified", 200). As models of postmodern culture and identity, pop divas favor gender-fluidity and sexual assertiveness because practically they are constructed as commercial artists with a crossover audience market and their cultural production has to be understood as inclusive as possible.

At the time this new diva model emerged, an out and proud queer culture was still at a niche state. The fact that pop divas brought gender and sexual multiplicity into mainstream circles certainly encouraged queer visibility. Divas' camp, a largely esoteric and secretive pleasure up until then, which was discursively extracted from codes and subtexts found in cultural corpora, progressively became ubiquitous in music culture. This was quite affirming for queer audiences and producers who were being accredited with artistic contributions to divas' enterprises in the sense that they were witnessing their cultural praxes moving mainstream-wise. Alternating between images, divas served as multicultural mediators that, among other things, incorporated more vividly queer signifiers of lifestyle and expression. Madonna, for instance, is the case par excellence as she managed through constant reinvention to simultaneously address a variety of audiences, queer among them. Citing mostly from Latinx, African American, Catholic, and queer culture, Madonna's persona exemplified the new diva model who was elastic in accommodating multiple roles at once. Madonna's camp lies at the kernel of transformation seen as playful art. In this light, divas like her were more open, commercially so, to culturally diverse presentations of persona as a means of approaching their audiences. As such, queer culture heavily informed divas' perception of gender performance and, by extension, endorsed their flamboyant interpretation of gender, especially their notion of femininity. In addition to that, queer praxes gradually populated the divas' stage and video performance, a fact that partly rendered the culture itself more visible and solidified divas as queer allies in terms of promoting non-binary sexual options and gender diversity.

At the same time, divas bringing attention to queer culture inevitably raises questions of cultural appropriation. Praxes, styles, and fashions of queer culture, including, to mention just a few, the practices of drag and camp, queer talk, or the subcultural activities of the leather and S&M scene, somehow found their way into divas' art presentations. The work of Madonna, Cher, and Annie Lennox, for example, has undeniably borrowed from queer culture's artistic resources.[21] Borrowing has always been of ambiguous character, pointing to issues of authorship, authenticity, and representation and the way these influence the final outcome of a cultural product. One would argue that divas' borrowing from queer culture is nothing but appropriation since they may often illegitimately decontextualize cultural images and practices for the sake of spectacle. On the other hand, in today's culture, as we shall see more in depth in the following chapters, cultural practices are widely shared in mass consumption, thus largely existing in an already decontextualized (or recontextualized) state, with little policing over who does indeed appropriate or pay homage to cultural authenticity and why. Divas may resort to queer references as a means of queer-baiting, but they may also acknowledge the act of citation as a tribute to their queer following; in fact, the former does not cancel out the latter. In turn, queer audiences can either endorse or disapprove of divas' citational practices—although a strategically marketable targeting on the divas' end ensures endorsement in the overwhelming majority of cases. Philip Auslander emphasizes that audiences play a key role in cocreating a pop persona that will be accustomed to their appeals and attuned with their sensibilities, arguing that "[they] try to make performers into who they need them to be, to fulfill a social function" ("Musical Personae", 115). Queer audiences, to a great extent, will allow divas to engage with their culture because they need to validate their cultural praxes as contributive to the divas' creative processes. The latter may also be assigned with the role of cultural ambassadors or advocates, as has been previously mentioned, thus reifying their social role as allies.

Divas wishing to cater to their queer market have more willfully directed their persona and spectacle toward a queer aesthetics and politics. While previous models appeared less engaged, creating a spectatorial distance and setting themselves as objects of appeal, contemporary divas allow themselves to be more interactive with audiences and seem to be more in charge of the character-persona they inhabit. Their camp appeal might derive from audiences viewing them as objects of camp, hence it is only a matter of reception, but can also be a self-conscious employing of theatrics aimed at generating camp pleasure, which will be filtered by the audiences as such.[22] Also, by immersing themselves in the practices of queer culture, collaborating with queer artists, or, of course, being queer themselves, divas become connoisseurs who will eventually get to implement their cultural knowledge into their personae and performances. For instance, the divas treated as case subjects in this research have all involved queer producers, stage and art directors, choreographers, and stylists in their performance projects, thereby adopting a queer aesthetic that seeks to enervate their spectacle with cultural components of the queer community. Moreover, many a time they are active partakers in the queer movement, thus ascribing a sociopolitical role to their persona. From HIV/

AIDS activism to gender diversity awareness strategies, divas have occasionally aligned themselves with various social strands of the queer movement—perhaps another marketing trick, albeit one with sociopolitical valence.

Above all, though, in their personae and praxis, divas enclose the qualities of transformation and resistance that soundly resonate with their queer audiences. Divas' life and career narratives abound with discourses of challenging phases, survival skills, comeback stories and image reinventions. The star narratives of the artists examined in this work, including Kylie, Beyoncé, and Lady Gaga, align with those of Elizabeth Taylor, Diana Ross, and Judy Garland that so endlessly fed the camp canon of yesteryear. In other words, the challenge of survival and the need to adapt to adversities usually constitute the social reality of queer life when placed in a heterosexist and patriarchal context in which discrimination over, fear of, and, at times, violence against the queer self require from the latter to be constantly defiant and agile. Referring to Judy Garland, Richard Dyer underlines that the diva's star appeal is based on a combination of strength and suffering to which queer audiences respond (*Heavenly Bodies*, 144–45). Rich in themes of empowerment and assertiveness, diva narratives are variable and polysemous, and the qualities they carry can address the socio-psychic basis of queerness that experientially accrues from the said queer *modus vivendi*. Always aware of possible essentialisms behind this argument, it should be noted that throughout the global history of queerness, there have been patterns of frequency and consistency shared alike by most queer individuals: deviance from conventional social genders that leads to discriminatory practices, whether these entail violence, hierarchy, or invisibility, is arguably encountered in most societal structures. As queerness and the social living of it become a point of reference in the life of a queer individual, it is understood that, on a collective level, the sensibilities and perceptions of queer people, *mutatis mutandis*, are more likely to converge. The fact that diva worshipping is a practice encountered across a variety of queer cultural models, each, of course, pertaining to cultural and local specificities, demonstrates that star narratives encompass thematic strands and emotional maps that resonate within queer imagination worldwide.[23]

Along with the identification through empathy that has been fundamental in establishing solid queer fandom around the personae of some of the most popular divas, it is also a poetics of attitude that equally informs the divas' appeal to queer imagination. Whereas empathy addresses the queer emotional basis connected to vulnerability and the feeling of being misfit in a heterodominant reality, expressing thus some sort of passivity, attitude reflects an active means of coping with that reality. Sassiness, aloofness, as well as the fads and quirks of divas constitute some of the characteristics that add up to their attitude, instilling in their praxis an extraordinary quality. As celebrities, divas' private lives are constantly in the spotlight and therefore developing an attitude partly demonstrates their response to their inquisitive and hectic lifestyle, which by extension demands from them to behave in a very specific and, at times, staged manner.[24] Of course, attitude may also be a derivative of luxury and leisure along with a sense of superiority and vindictiveness, qualities largely found in camp culture as well.[25] In all cases, its expression points to a sarcastic weapon against uncomfortable, hostile situations or extremely trivial conventions. As a result, queer audiences often revel in divas' sassy demeanor and may usually internalize and reiterate that certain attitude both as camp pleasure and a form of counterresponse. The welcoming of divas in queer culture and their worshipped status within camp traditions attest to them being collectively agreed-upon models of empathy and attitude, variously fulfilling queer fantasies, desires, sentiments, and mentalities. To identify, thus, with a diva is a practice entailing the individual's own interpretation and engrossment of the diva's star narrative.

In light of that, pop divas and their managerial teams have nowadays come up with novel promotional strategies as a means of meeting their audiences' desires. Though the music video has remained a primary tool in visualizing music material, the culture of music television so prevalent in the pre-millennial years has been eclipsed by digital culture to a great extent. The relationship between divas and audiences is now largely formulated through online media, thus reinvigorating the ways artists and fans communicate, importantly, expanding target markets and commercial impact. As with seemingly every aspect and product of pop culture, divas too have social media presence and their work is mainly distributed via the internet. The usage of socials such as Instagram, Facebook, Twitter, and Tik Tok, among others, has become a mandatory outreach, giving audiences a sense/illusion of proximity with their adored artists. Advertising through online media has also expanded divas' market radius, allowing for global coverage instantly and more easily. With regard to queer audiences, divas are keener on virtually exercising their social role as queer allies by taking to social media and publicly voicing their support. Their celebrity status may often serve positively in broadly raising awareness on issues of gender (in)equality and freedom of expression, since they may utilize their influential personae to promote campaigns as is frequently the case with Madonna, Kylie Minogue, and Lady Gaga. They may also directly address queer audiences, thereby forging their affiliation with them and creating a sense of exclusivity; for instance, in promoting her *Rebel Heart* album (in 2015), Madonna partnered with gay dating app Grindr to host a contest out of which winners would get the chance to chat with her through the platform. Last but not least—and this is what this study pays attention to—live performance remains steadily one of the most effective, perhaps even traditional ways of divas approaching audiences, which compensates for the immateriality and distance media culture creates. As live touring artist, divas are aware of that and have notoriously upped the ante in terms of live performance output. Let us turn to the character and structure of the touring diva spectacle as well as the queer fan cultures that gravitate toward them.

Queer audiences: Global gay culture, the arena tour spectacle, and fandom

Inasmuch as this work concerns itself with international divas, it is important to underline that their affiliation with queer culture and, by extension, notions of gender performance, sexuality, queer aesthetics, and politics enclosed in their personae and work meet a global audience, which is diverse and idiosyncratic by default. In arguing that divas are mediators of queer culture, one has to identify this culture as predominantly Western and, in particular, Euro-American oriented. Therefore, what instructs their personae and performances are perspectives of a Western queer culture that, compared to others worldwide, has occupied more of an epicenter in terms of visibility and documentation. This immediately raises questions of power dynamics in relation to the nature of the divas' character and spectacle vis-à-vis local receptions. More specifically, European culture as exemplified and perhaps monopolized by the region's most economically and culturally influential countries, such as Germany, the United Kingdom, France, and Spain, has served as home for a nascent queer lifestyle and political movement—a proto-queer culture, so to speak. European LGBTQ+ communities currently have a vibrant presence in most European cities and queer tourism and entertainment seem to flourish in metropoles, such as Berlin, Barcelona, Milan, and Amsterdam. In a similar vein, American popular culture, as today's dominant global trend-setter,[26] has lately been more queer-inclusive, paying particular attention to issues of visibility and representation; consider how the film, music, television, and comic book industries are increasingly featuring queer narratives, characters, and styles, which serve as fodder for mainstream productions and are then circulated globally. The advent of social media has also contributed in disseminating these perspectives of queer living, sometimes ignoring the plurality of queer communities worldwide. Developing in conditions of rapid economy and neoliberal politics can be understood as the principal reason why Western queer culture has emerged as a dominant paradigm. This allowed certain queer groups to exercise their cultural power through investment, literally and figuratively buying their way into today's mainstream culture, and, consequently, (over)projecting specific aspects of queer living.[27]

As our understanding of a now thriving global gay culture is heavily informed by the Euro-American paradigm, non-Western queer communities are balancing between local politics and the sociopolitical vocabulary brought along by global gay culture.[28] Dennis Altman argues that:

> The assertion of "Asian" and "African" values as a counter to what is perceived as imported Western individualistic values is a growing part of nationalist ideologies in a number of countries, and often includes claims that homosexuality is a "Western import", despite evidence of well-established pre-colonial homosexual cultures and practices. (180)

The lexicon of LGBTQ+ identities along with the political nuances they carry has served as a comprehensive and rather instructive agenda for local nascent LGBTQ+ movements worldwide that seem to adopt and recontextualize them as best fitting their cultural specificity. At the same time, though, it has opened roads to the idea of a governing global gay culture, the practices and values of which seem to have taken over. Proposing Argentina and Mexico as two non-English-speaking countries whose queer activism was initially part of local struggle and movements, Altman underlines that "commercial pressures and American influence were too strong, and gradually both a gay movement and a commercially gay world emerged in these places, superficially at least with strong American influence" (71). Demonstrative of that is also the fact that Pride celebrations are more and more becoming integral to world queer movements, thus placing the Stonewall riots, the event that was shaped out of queer struggle in America and largely concentrated the gay liberation pulse around it, at the center of global queer history.[29] Stonewall's importance accrues from and frames the very idea that queer communities rising to resist police harassment and social marginalization are after all a deeply democratic one in their potential to appeal to every oppressed queer individual. However, its emergence in contemporary global gay culture as the epitome of queer struggle risks foregrounding the American experience as archetypal and may, by extrapolation, obstruct local political fruition.

As best indicating the politics and practices of global gay culture, Prides are indeed noteworthy modern structures that have managed to gain crossover political validation in terms of visibility and longevity. What perhaps makes the tradition of Pride events so widely received is their colorful presentation of a community that celebrates freedom of sexual and gender expression. In most parts, though, Prides' promotional success is market-driven as they constitute lucrative financial cores with the ability to attract large consumer audiences. Apart from groups and organizations joining the, more often than not, week-long celebrations culminating around the march, usually setting up fanfare and LGBTQ+-related market fora, Prides can also boost local economies since they serve as magnets for queer tourism. Also, more and more small businesses and large companies are joining the fair with sponsorships and Pride-exclusive campaigns, marking the events as inextricably capitalist-bound.[30] Encouraging as it is to acknowledge that Prides are now even blooming in countries where sexual conservatism dominates political and social thought, their consumerist character and their emphasis on a celebratory culture risk mitigating their political potential. Worse, in countries where the queer movement still needs to go through a process of sociopolitical osmosis, Prides and, by extension, local queer communities will usually be at the recipient end of criticism, ridicule, or even violence.[31]

The reason why I have drawn attention to the sociopolitical and economic discourse of Prides is to establish a coherent context around the idea of global gay culture not only as a signifier of Western values, histories, and expressions but also as a carrier of a social stigma associated with notions of promiscuity and camp. First of all, what is inherent about global gay culture is an erroneous assumption that it is a gay male culture. Gay men often come across as disproportionately visible, emerging as perhaps the most privileged group in the LGBTQ+ community—especially when markers of Whiteness and class are factored in—and serving as a sort of prototype for gendered and sexual evaluations. Even the use of the term "gay" in what is defined as *gay* culture, an umbrella term that stands for LGBTQ+ culture in general, may imply that it is a culture centered on and around gay men.[32] At the same time, precisely because global gay culture implies male homosexuality, gay masculinity may usually become the primary target of derision. Images of Prides that usually circulate media, especially those occupying a more conservative place on the political spectrum, lay emphasis on a rampant culture personified in the figures of the muscle man and the drag queen. Though these figures represent only certain aspects of queer culture, they attract criticism because of their hypersexualized and highly gendered profiles. As two polar ends of the popular, if stereotypical, images of gay men, that is, the hunk and the camp, muscle men and drag queens exemplify, respectively, the notions of virility and campness, which, in their extremes, are interpreted as threatening by heteronormative culture: the former because it foregrounds a sexually aggressive culture associated with virile masculinity; the latter because it embodies the flamboyant and hysterically effeminate side, markers of both decadence and promiscuity.

To return to the primary focus of this work and connect it with Pride, I see the diva spectacle, which largely relies on queer aesthetics and, at times, itself is a derivative of queer culture, as a praxis crossed with markers of Western-ness as well as preconceptions linked with queer expression. The stage of the diva can indeed serve as a rich ground to construe the social dynamics of queer culture as this is orchestrated around the body of the divas and always in relation to audience reception and global/local perspectives. First and foremost, the diva spectacle must be contextualized within the category of the pop music concert, the *raison d'être* of which is entertainment. Its scope, most of the times, may appear limited within its own nature as a showcase of theatrics, erotic appeal, and shock value, which are employed to address the audiences' sentiments. As such, there is a default principle in its celebratory nature that establishes it as nonserious and lite in content, hence apolitical. This framework, in fact, follows a strand reaching back to the generic division between rock and pop music discussed earlier here. More importantly, this division is gendered since rock exemplifies a masculine ideal as opposed to pop's feminine character. Think of the way shows by artists such as Roger Waters (Pink Floyd), U2, and Red Hot Chili Peppers are filtered in the public mind compared to those of divas examined in this project. The diva spectacle is obviously more elaborate and flamboyant, completely atunned with an effeminate/feminine aesthetic and thus severing most of the ties with the masculine-framed rock concert show. In light of this, one may find it hard to ascribe political character to the showcases of artists like Kylie Minogue or to consider them provoking in any terms other than erotic or glittery.

Yet, I would like to argue that to assess the diva spectacle as apolitical is to ignore its plurality. Juxtaposing it to the alleged authenticity and hegemonic masculinity of the rock concert may lead to a sexist evaluation of the female-led concert as incapable of concerning itself with anything other than the presentation of female sexuality, let alone politics.[33] A reason may be that, structurally, a diva show lays emphasis on aesthetics. Diva concerts are built around the idea of a musical show that is usually extravagantly staged; light show installations, huge screens with backdrop extra-concert footage,[34] titillating dancer/posers, lavish props, and often unconventional constructions—as we shall see in more detail in the following chapters—comprise the diva stage, turning it into an arena-size theatrical production. A comparison between the concerts of Janet Jackson, Katy Perry, Mariah Carey, or Jennifer Lopez to those of rock artists such as Metallica or Muse, as well as pop male artists such as Justin Timberlake, Bruno Mars, and Maroon 5, leads us to tracing numerous differences in terms of visuals, supporting props, and costuming, with the female concert coming across as notably more colorful and theatrical than its male counterpart. Even concerts by male artists, including U2, Roger Waters, and Michael Jackson, who have time and again come up with daunting productions, seem aesthetically toned down as opposed to the extravagant spectacle divas offer. Arguably, from their very structural core, female and male concerts follow a gendered division: the former, being ornate and fashioned around the female star, abides by traditionally feminine/-ized characteristics of ornamentation, whereas the latter sticks to simpler structures, implying that emphasis should be given to the aural and lyrical content of the show.

The plurality of the diva show, though, lies precisely at its theatricality. The extravaganzas created by divas enable dramatic fluidities on stage, thus allowing divas to morph in and out of roles. Built with thematic sections, the shows unfold into acts that see artists and their surrounding crew in new settings. Tour shows, including those of Madonna or Lady Gaga, usually even exhibit narrative structures as well, a fact that brings their concerts closer to a musical theater experience. In a way similar to their music videos, diva shows lay equal emphasis on aural and visual showcase. In this way, they can accommodate an array of narrative arcs and themes wherein divas have the opportunity to not only be creative but also address various topics through performance. Madonna, for instance, has frequently featured political commentary in her backdrop visuals, while Lady Gaga has employed performance art to touch upon body politics and discrimination. More importantly, their alternating between images embodies a postmodern approach of identity understanding, cultivating into their audiences the idea that insofar as identities are constructs, they are, to a great degree, performed.[35] Considering that divas' audiences largely consist of queer groups, this idea becomes important in promoting an ethos of sexual and gender diversity. Taking also into consideration that a lot of thematic acts pay particular attention to queer expression, drawing from queer scenes and citing related material, the diva show ultimately becomes inclusive, transforming into a space that fosters the notions of queer representation and collectivity.

Since the performed show is part of a world tour, its main concept, content, and ethos are brought in front of an audience that is highly diverse in terms of ethnicity, race, religion, sexuality, and gender. Though some changes regarding the setlist or stage of the show may occur from time to time, the core structure remains unaltered.[36] Therefore, practically the same show is presented to all audiences. What significantly varies, though, concerns reception, not production. A Buenos Aires audience, for example, may demonstrate different responses to a show than a London one, simply because each locale is crossed with different markers of social identities and politics. For instance, Madonna's *Confessions Tour* (2006), which featured the notorious act of the singer performing hung on a crucifix, caused quite a stir to much of her Catholic audience in Rome as well as the Vatican. Conversely, Beyoncé catered specifically to her New Orleans audience by inviting on stage a local act as part of her *Formation Tour* (2016). Locales play a key role in world tours, and divas, being aware of their shows' content, may even seek to create a memorable occasion or even controversy, as was the case with Madonna, so as to benefit from publicity. On the other hand, their laying emphasis on the specificity of locales, either by focusing on cultural aspects or even by pushing local boundaries, can often help bring attention to sociocultural aspects that would have otherwise remained unaddressed. Queer culture is one of them since queer expression is central for both productions and audiences. Beyoncé's guest act for the New Orleans show, for that matter, was Big Freedia, a transgender artist from the local rap/bounce scene who performs in drag and helped bring important focus on local queer representation (see more on the third chapter). Exposing audiences whose composure remains attached to a largely heteronormative and patriarchal parent culture to notions and presentations of queerness, be it manifest through camp or explicit sexual diversity, diva shows contribute to queer visibility on a global level. The fact that such aspects of the shows challenge local perceptions regarding not only gender and sexual expression but popular entertainment as well, instills into the diva spectacle a quasi-political character.

In light of this, divas' queer audiences are welcomed into a performative environment that encourages diversity and expression. This is rather important considering that these shows are also played in areas that have traditionally been antithetical, socially, politically, or even legislatively, to queer communities. The shows of Madonna and Lady Gaga in Moscow, for instance, have strongly been opposed by Russian conservative groups because they allegedly promoted homosexuality (see Chapters 1 and 4, respectively). Despite attracting conservative criticism, in most parts diva concerts provide queer groups with a sense of inclusion and belonging. Reception of divas from local queer audiences is not simply positive but vibrantly supported since divas offer open spaces for expression and support to their queer audiences. In a way, the shows create isles of queer temporality and spatiality, allowing for identification and affect, at least for the duration of and within the contours of the concert. Yet, one must always be attentive to the means under which these spatiotemporal occasions are created: namely, pop culture market economy. For Jack Halberstam, "'queer time' is a term for these specific models of temporality that emerge within postmodernism once one leaves the temporal frames of bourgeois reproduction and family, longevity, risk/safety, and inheritance," while "'[q]ueer space' refers to the queer place-making practices within post-modernism in which queer people engage and it also describes the new understandings of space enabled by the production of queer counterpublics"[37] (*In a Queer Time and Place*, 6). As is also the case with Prides, diva shows are driven by consumerist operations; hence, their opening of a queer space and time is also underlined with a capitalist ethos and does not successfully abide by Halberstam's concept, in which a process of rupture with the normative is necessary to attain queer spatiality and temporality. Queer audiences are by no means radically breaking any ties with normative reality around them in attending a diva gig. On the contrary, as consumers, they actively partake, along with the non-queer members of the audience, in the capitalist processes that give birth to divas and spectacles.

They do, however, manage to create spaces of identification and belonging, perhaps in a utopian way and momentarily so, by way of escapism, allowing themselves to enter the camp reality of the diva spectacle and express their queerness through their interaction with divas and other queer individuals at the said time of the concert. Indicative of that is audiences' camp response to diva spectacles. By attuning themselves with the aesthetic character of the show and with the diva character present on stage, audiences engage in a camping-up of their performance of gender as a means of, first, validating their connection with the performing diva and, second, affirming their own identity. Their position as receivers and producers of camp adds to the idea of queer temporality and spatiality as they seem to actively perform a queer tradition. In fact, their becoming connoisseurs and performers of camp in light of the diva spectacle transcends the temporal and spatial liminality of the concert show and establishes a continuity of queer praxis through the performance of camp. As has been explicated earlier, divas' praxis has a firm basis in the culture of camp and has come to embody a popular manifestation of it. Being simultaneously producers and objects of camp, divas infuse their spectacles with gendered theatrics, offering ironic twists and toying with familiar tropes and narratives to a queer effect. In the receiving end, queer audiences do not necessarily identify with the performing divas, but rather with the colorfully queer(ed) reality surrounding them during the particular special event. In critically approaching the process of identification of gay male culture with divas, David Halperin explains that the term itself is not particularly helpful in our understanding of the diva adoration pattern (258–59). Instead, the writer argues, "[w]hat we may be dealing with, in the end, is a specific kind of engagement that somehow mobilizes complex relations of similarity and difference," a process that "produces fields of practice and feeling that map our possibilities for contact or interrelation among cultural forms and their audiences, consumers, or publics, and that get transmitted from one generation to another" (259). I would like to extend the argument further and propose the diva show and the body of the audience as an actual field of practice—and praxis, in the dramatic sense—that reifies the relationship between divas and queer audiences.

Performing camp, rather than merely absorbing it, is key to this very reification. Halperin follows a traditional school of thought in approaching camp through film divas whose audiences were mostly receivers of camp—and if they were producers, they would either be sharers of cultural knowledge/data or they would be actual performers found in the well-known circles of glamorous impersonation. I argue that what the camp tradition of the music diva has provided is more access to the performative aspects and mechanics of camp, in part due to adding to its popularization and also because of a more engaged artist–audience interaction. Another reason is that camp is not anymore the arcane culture shared by the queer few that it used to be, but is widely perceived and enjoyed by many—even non-queer—consumers. It is my contention that its praxis still remains grounded on a queer subject, though, and its reiteration or performance requires from its producers to actively adopt its aspects, be they mannerisms, aesthetics, discourse, or style; hence an immersion in and continuation of the act of queering—perhaps playfully so—cultural texts, images, even identities. Diva fans, for instance, transforming into the diva herself in a praxis that draws from the field of impersonation, best demonstrates this immersion into the mechanics of camp. I identify this praxis as *audience drag*, a camp reconfiguration of the gendered self into the onstage diva persona that sees audiences employing the art/craft of drag and the cultural knowledge around the diva as a way to express not only queerness but also fandom and collectivity.

By proposing audience drag as a contemporary camp praxis, this study wishes to move away from previous theoretical models of camp whose reception—mainly in the film diva tradition—was largely viewed as passive. Drawing from the field of popular culture and fan studies will help toward approaching audience reception of diva camp as actively partaking in the circulation, performance, and preservation of the diva worship tradition. Contrary to the idea of passive audiences as inherent to understandings of mass entertainment most famously theorized by the Frankfurt School,[38] Lawrence Grossberg argues that "[a]udiences are constantly making their cultural environment from the cultural resources that are available to them. Thus, audiences are not made up of cultural dopes" (53). This idea nests within fan cultures, which, albeit completely aware of their status as pop culture consumers, are seen as moving beyond the seemingly nullifying effect of mass culture in consciously approaching their objects of adoration and critically navigating through ideological fixity. John Fiske underlines that "[f]andom offers ways of filling cultural lack and provides the social prestige and self-esteem that go with cultural capital" (33). Though fandom is inevitably circumscribed with capitalist/consumerist grids, one cannot doubt that it is a mode of expression that allows space for socialization and an acceptance of the queer self through the processes of collectivity and culture-sharing.

Currently, fan cultures appear to be more engaged in cultural production themselves, being active cocreators of pop texts, images, and lifestyles, especially considering the pool of cultural knowledge they have access to through digital culture as well as the prospects for connectivity and instant gratification the latter provides. Their complete immersion in the world of their adored star, as often signified through fan-operated websites or fan-made merchandise, marks the nature of the fans as prosumers, namely both consumers and producers. In their exploration of the concept of prosumption, George Ritzer and Nathan Jurgenson hold that perceptions on popular culture not only migrate from traditional views of consumers as passive but, most importantly, challenge the very notion of the consumer by introducing that of the prosumer, who willingly buys into as well as (re)produces and shares popular culture.[39] Fans engaging in creative processes related to a star persona reinforces and perpetuates their established bonds with the latter, a fact that further acknowledges fans as equal contributors to pop culture. According to Detlev Zwick et al., "the ideological recruitment of consumers into productive co-creation relationships hinges on accommodating consumers' needs for recognition, freedom, and agency" (185). Demonstrative of that are fansites that do not simply update their viewers on an artist's news, but actively organize and engage fan communities in conversation as well as other more tangible projects, such as tributes or artworks, which validate their relationship with the artist. At the same time, artists highly benefit from fans' investment in and circulation of their persona, capital, and appeal, since fan communities often enthusiastically advertise their adored star across all forms of media in a way that requires little to no effort. As Ritz and Jurgenson indicate, "prosumers seem to enjoy, even love, what they are doing and are willing to devote hours to it for no pay" (22). The constructedness of a star persona after all can be an open-ended process, thereby inviting fans to make sense of their relationship while it is progressing. As a result, the practices that fans engage in not only fortify their relationship with the star but also ascribe them with a sense of cocreation and inclusivity in the cultural body of the star persona.

The post-passive model of the fan as prosumer is vital in our understanding of contemporary fan cultures, in general, and diva fans, in particular. In knowingly immersing themselves into the cultural body of the diva through practices such as audience drag, fans not only get to apply, share, and demonstrate their cultural knowledge but also manage to claim quasi-authorial positions in the way pop culture shapes their identities. Diva worship in its Classical Hollywood stage, for instance, generated a gay male-centered camp culture that allowed closeted gay men to utilize diva trivia as shared codes that helped them identify (with) each other and establish bonds. As Harris notices, though, "[b]ecause gay culture is becoming less closeted [...] the need to seal our furtive communal bond through the secret handshake of Hollywood trivia is disappearing," adding that "[l]iberation is destroying the need for celebrity culture as a group marker, as a way of expressing tribal inclusion in a private membership club of the cognoscenti" (33). This, however, is demonstrative of a self-conscious queer fan culture that does not solely rely on practices like diva worship to make sense of their communal world and identity. For queer audiences now, diva camp is transparent, meaning that they can see through its mechanisms as well as the pleasures and possibilities it offers. Its consistency and prevalence are indeed less indicative of a need to utilize its codes toward communing one's covert queerness, as it used to be, but gravitates more toward an acknowledgment of divas as relevant with and contributive to the formation of queer culture as we currently know it. One will notice how divas still occupy much ground in everyday (Western) queer culture and discourse—from the bar scene to internet memes to the local community center to daily discourse—thereby maintaining their role as cultural mediators that promote inclusion, community, and bonding. Diva camp has in a sense become a joint in the cultural body of queer communities, sort of an established tradition that is, which currently operates on a global level.

NOTES

1. Cf. Daniel Harris's essay titled "The Death of Camp: Gay Men and Hollywood" as this appears on *The Rise and Fall of Gay Culture*.
2. Consider French diva Dalida who was adored across France and whose tragic figure left its own mark on the local queer community.
3. Performance here is directly connected to Schechnerian and post-Schechnerian conceptualizations of the term (and, by extension, its research field) to include the staging and attendance of social events, such as theater, concerts, sports, and rituals, among others, in which performance encompasses dramatization, audience reception as well as spatiotemporal effects at work. For more, see Richard Schechner's *Performance Theory* and Nathan Stucky and Cynthia Wimmer's edited volume *Teaching Perform-ance Studies*.
4. Discussing the concept of liveness, Auslander stands critical with the binary opposition of live performance and mediatized culture, arguing that traditional views prioritizing the live over the mediatized form/event by valuing the former as authentic over the latter's artificiality seem to invoke clichés and appear obsolete in the modern media-saturated environment (*Liveness*, 2–3). It is true though that when it comes to music concerts, the notion of liveness still relies on this presupposition and both performers and audiences do not seem close to abandoning the physicality of the live performance.
5. O'Grady notes that:

    > [P]erhaps due to the improved and increased remote accessibility to such events, attitudes to authenticity of "being there" are undergoing a paradigm shift. We want to experience the event for ourselves, physically, but at the same time we want to record our presence and broadcast it so that others can observe our participation. (120)

6. Although each one of these attributes may vary depending on the context surrounding camp, it is for the sake of brevity that I choose at this point not to address them more in depth but rather explore them throughout this research. These characteristics are drawn from the large literature on camp and can be found explicated mostly in, but not limited to, in the works of Sontag, Newton, Dyer (*Culture of Queers*), Babuscio ("Camp and the Gay Sensibility"), Meyer, Robertson (*Guilty Pleasures*), Cleto, and Shugart and Waggoner.
7. Here, I concur with Simon Watney's argument in that:

> The great convenience of the term "queer" today lies most immediately in its gender and race neutrality. This is only to remark that for many young Americans the term "gay" is widely understood to mean "white," "male," "materialistic," and "thirtysomething." On the contrary, "queer" asserts an identity that celebrates differences within a wider picture of sexual and social diversity. (52)

8. Cleto here explicates the notion of paternity, arguing that "those who have spoken on behalf of camp as a gay property and offspring [...] assume *male* homosexuality as the real 'parent' and 'owner'" (5, original emphasis).

9. From literature to art to ballet, European culture has been populated with camp figures, discourses, and images opulent with absurd taste and queer erotics: for example, the Mannerist movement in painting, Beau Brummell's style, Jean Cocteau's writings, Serge de Diaghilev's aesthetic impact on the Russian Ballet, among others (Core 9–11). See also Sontag's Note 13 and 14 in "Notes on 'Camp'" for more examples (qtd. in Cleto 57).

10. In Note 2 in her essay, Sontag argues that "[t]o emphasize style is to slight content, or to introduce an attitude which is neutral with respect to content. It goes without saying that the Camp sensibility is disengaged, depoliticized—or at least apolitical" (qtd. in Cleto 54).

11. Drawing from the seminal works of Joan Riviere's "Womanliness as Masquerade" and Esther Newton's *Mother Camp: Female Impersonators in America*, Robertson, relying on camp's "affinity with feminist discussions of gender construction, performance and enactment," argues how misogyny can be averted when dealing with camp by revisiting camp performance as gendered play (*Guilty Pleasures*, 6).

12. See more on Wayne Kostenbaum's *The Queen's Throat: Opera, Homosexuality, and the Mystery of Desire*; Paul Robinson's *Opera, Sex and Other Vital Matters*; Mitchell Morris' "Reading as an Opera Queen;" and Michael Bronski's *Culture Clash: The Making of Gay Sensibility*.

13. Consider the popularity blues singers such as Bessie Smith, Ma Rainey, and Gladys Bentley had and how their songtexts enclosed queer undertones and sexually charged lyrics, with marked lesbian erotics, as opposed to torch songs, the concerns of which were "entirely romantic, and [did] not include the earthiness of playful eroticism of contemporary blues lyrics" (J. Moore 32). For more, see also Angela Davis' *Blues Legacies and Black Feminism: Gertrude "Ma" Rainey, Bessie Smith, and Billie Holiday*, and James Wilson's *Bulldaggers, Pansies, and Chocolate Babies: Performance, Race, and Sexuality in the Harlem Renaissance*.

14. Frank elaborates that:

> Gay men interpreted popular songs such as Wilson Pickett's "Don't Knock My Love," the Pointer Sisters' "Yes We Can," Aretha Franklin's "Respect," MFSB's "Love Is the Message,"

INTRODUCTION

and Gloria Gaynor's "Never Can Say Goodbye" as reinforcing gay pride and affirming gay identity, romance, and sexuality. (284)

15. Consider the case of Amanda Lear whose excessively stylized femininity and the mystique around her romance with David Bowie often led to misconceptions of her as transsexual, though those were the attributes that propelled her to cult stardom.

16. Kutulas supports that:

> The flamboyance of the style appealed to some in the audience but put off others. Yet most people didn't see disco divas perform live; disco was dance music, not concert music. There were not intimate concert experiences where fans might get to know performers they felt they already knew thanks to liner notes and lyrics. Disco women were all surface glitz; they otherwise conveyed little sense of individuality or personality. (189)

17. According to Kutulas "[d]isco queens served as models for cross-dressers. The sexual ambiguity and role reversals implicit in disco further distanced it from 'real life' which meant that the sexual power of disco queens of either gender was somewhat illusory" (189). See also Brian Currid's " 'We Are Family': House Music and Queer Performativity", and Nadine Hubb's "'I Will Survive': Musical Mappings of Queer Social Space in a Disco Anthem."

18. See more in Simon Frith, Andrew Goodwin, and Lawrence Grossberg' s (eds). *Sound and Vision: The Music Video Reader*.

19. Biddle and Jarman-Ivens argue that "musical genres are gendered spaces and operate according to highly codified conventions. Genres create gender formations by creating *points de capiton* ('quilting points') within their space between signifiers and gendered meaning" (9).

20. Andrew Ross notes:

> Denied the conventional "masculine" and "feminine" positions of spectatorship, and excluded by conventional representations of male-as-hero or narrative agent, and female-as-image or object of the spectacle, the gay male and lesbian subcultures express their lived spectatorship largely through imaginary or displaced relations to the images and discourses of a straight, "parent" culture. (323)

21. Consider, among others, Madonna's "Express Yourself" (1989), "Vogue" (1990), and "Justify My Love" (1990), Cher's "If I Could Turn Back Time" (1989) and "Walking in Memphis" (1995), and Lennox's "Why" (1992) and "Little Bird" (1993). For Madonna's "Vogue" and her cultural interaction with ballroom culture, see the first chapter.

THE MUSIC DIVA SPECTACLE

22. Philip Core argues that "camp is in the eyes of the beholder" (7), meaning that one can only interpret a system of signs, postures, images, objects, and icons as camp. It can also be argued, though, that one can direct the process of interpretation by intervening into camp's coding process. This is more feasible when talking about performances of camp, wherein acts can be controlled, dramatized, staged, and generally orchestrated to one's will.

23. World divas with strong queer following such as Dalida, Maria Callas, and Selena seem to have exemplified this pattern through their tragic icons and life narratives.

24. Consider the case of Britney Spears' infamous breakdown in 2007 and her sassy response in her comeback album *Blackout* (2007).

25. For instance, the practices of "throwing shade" and "reading" (or put-down) have been common within camp culture, requiring wit, smart-strike focus, and swiftness, in order to be as effective as possible. Eloquent queens will take a jab at each other or third parties in verbal battles that prove how each has honed the craft of vindictive camp talk. Camp talk has time and again come across as crude and virulent, yet it has also forged effeminate men who practice it with an aggressive quick response and disarming humor that accrues from their oppressed position within patriarchy-ordered social structures. See more in E. Patrick Johnson's *No Tea, No Shade: New Writings in Black Queer Studies*, and "SNAP! Culture: A Different Kind of Reading;" as well as Marlon B. Ross's "Camping the Dirty Dozens: The Queer Resources of Black Nationalist Invective."

26. Richard Pells enumerates the reasons why America has emerged as a global cultural phenomenon and capitalist power, among them being the wide coverage of American media conglomerates; the effective establishing of English as the language of mass communication; the size of American population and its key role in creating a solid domestic market with expansive potential; and, last but not least, the ability of the American market to draw ideas from foreign cultures and fashions, repackage them, and sell them back (144–45).

27. By no means does this argument wish to overlook or downgrade the political struggle of Western queer culture to social and civil achievements. At the same time, one has to take into consideration that certain privileged groups among queer communities, especially White, middle-class gay men and lesbians, managed to largely formulate today's queer culture due to financial, social, racial, and political benefits. For further reading, consider Steve Valocchi's "Individual Identities, Collective Identities, and Organizational Structure: The Relationship of the Political Left and Gay Liberation in the United States," and "The Class-Inflected Nature of Gay Identity," as well as Chasin's *Selling Out: The Gay & Lesbian Movement Goes to Market*.

28. In querying whether same-sex discrimination in many countries is produced either by nationalism or globalization, David Murray makes an accurate point when arguing that "[o]ne could make a very good case for stating that it is homophobia that has been successfully globalized, not global gay consumer culture" (5). As he explains:

INTRODUCTION

> We should also be suspicious of the claim that homophobia is simply produced in relation to the rise of gay and lesbian activism around the globe which in turn results from the arrival of the foreign sociosexual category "the homosexual" via various modalities (tourism, migration, media, the Internet). (5–6)

"In other contexts," he adds:

> [T]he rise of "gay identity" constructed through transnational commodity aesthetics, political activism, and new modes of electronic communication has come to represent, for some, a more cosmopolitan and modern nationalism but has simultaneously created a backlash against this figure who represents, for others, "foreign" sexual values imported through foreign non-governmental organizations and popular culture. (8)

29. It should be noted that Stonewall was one of the many aspects of political gay struggle in America, not *the* one. As Altman argues:

> Modern gay liberation was not born alone at the Stonewall Inn, as current mythology (and several films) encourage us to believe. There were simultaneous developments of a new sexual radicalism in California, while the 1968 students movements in Paris and Italy saw the emergence of radical homosexual groups, which drew on the heady mix of radical Freudianism, Marxism and anarchism that characterized that period. (53)

30. Consider campaigns from sporting and fashion industries such as Adidas and H&M, which largely publicize partnerships with LGBTQ+ individuals in light of Pride events.

31. The Russian LGBTQ+ community, for instance, has been facing discriminatory constitutional laws on the grounds of amorality; Moscow has consecutively banned gay prides for the past ten years (Amnesty International). In Turkey, Istanbul Pride has been banned since 2015 for security reasons as authorities are concerned over public outbursts against LGBTQ+ members (Dittrich). It goes without saying that in countries where homosexuality is still penalized, such as Kenya, Nigeria, or Uganda, Prides imagine a utopian action as these areas are still home to homophobic violence; Uganda's LGBTQ+ activist David Kato, for that matter, was brutally murdered in 2011 for promoting homosexual lifestyle and rights (Gettlemen).

32. Many lesbians identify or come out as *gay*, despite the fact that *lesbian* has been established as the equivalent of *gay* for homosexual women. This is indicative of the fact that *gay* has been widely used, presumably because of its practicality. The history of the word is marked with the homosexual male subject and, in fact, demonstrates that homosexual identities are built around this presupposition. For more on the history of the terms, see

Philip Herbst's entries of *gay* and *lesbian* in Philip Herbst, *Wimmin, Wimps, and Wall-flowers an Encyclopædic Dictionary of Gender and Sexual Orientation Bias in the United States.*

33. Of course, this is also perpetuated with musical genres per se and their lyrical content. The tradition of rock music abounds with politically charged songtexts as a means of addressing a more mature and socially engaged audience, while pop music, the primary target market of which is young audiences, usually employs narratives of romance, sex, and fun.

34. Examining concert shows both by female and male artists, I have found that prerecorded material with narrative content featuring the artist and functioning as backdrop video for the concert appears more in divas' shows and seems to add metatextual information on their performing persona. In this way, divas underline the fictitious character of their persona and undergird their live show with narrative power.

35. Following the Butlerian notion of performativity, according to which "performativity must be understood not as a singular or deliberate 'act,' but, rather, as the reiterative and citational practice by which discourse produces the effects that it names" (*Bodies that Matter*, 2), Matt Hills explicates his theory of music fans performing their "fan identity" by distinguishing between *performance* and *performativity*: the former "presupposes a willful and volitional subject," whereas the latter "in no way presupposes a choosing subject" (158). I expand on this point of fan's gender performance through the praxis of *audience drag* in the last chapter.

36. For example, when being part of a festival showcase, the duration of the show may be reduced. Also, changes in stage structure are often venue-specific, depending usually on capacity. Production teams of a tour typically come with alternative planing of a show (A show, B, show etc., where A stands for the designed prototype) so as to meet the prerequisites of a festival or venue event (W. Baker).

37. Halberstam sees *counterpublics* as "spaces created and altered by certain subcultures for their own uses," such as the appropriation of underground porn theaters by queer men seeking pleasure (*In a Queer Time and Place*, 186). The writer argues that "there should be a collective project(s) that is rewarded not by capital or visibility, not by the market, but by an affective connection with those people who will eventually be the vessels of memory for all we (now) forget" (187).

38. Richard Butsch argues that "[t]he concept of mass […] is a term of the twentieth century, when social critics became less concerned with crowds and more with an inert mass and isolated individuals" (2). Social theory connected to the Frankfurt School framed a passive consumer audience who fails to critically filter its cultural surroundings. Horkheimer and Adorno, as the School's prominent figures, saw mass consumption and the culture industry perpetuating passive consumers, arguing that

> [a]s naturally as the ruled always took the morality imposed upon them more seriously than did the rulers themselves, the deceived masses are today captivated by the myth of

success even more than the successful are. Immovably, they insist on the very ideology which enslaves them. (134)

Elsewhere, Adorno reiterates that the culture industry is ultimately deceptive in "imped[ing] the development of autonomous, independent individuals who judge and decide consciously for themselves" (106).

39. Originally drawing from Alvin Toffler's concept of prosumption for which the writer proposed "the rise of the prosumer" as indicative of a capitalist state that sees the processes of production and consumption as ultimately integrated (265), Ritzer and Jurgenson argue that prosumers are willing to simultaneously produce and consume in what appears to be reproductive cycle that ignores effort value parameters (22). The writers apply this model on web usage, indicating that websites like Amazon, Wikipedia, and Facebook are, to a great and controllable extent, user-operated in the sense that users are free to sell and buy products, read and edit information, present and view visual material—in a sense simultaneously produce and consume culture (19–20).

1

Time Goes by so Slowly:
Madonna's Camp Revivals

Madonna's great period was 1983–1992. She absolutely changed the world. There's no doubt about it. And since then, it's cringe-making [...] It's embarrassing [...] But what Madonna did was to allow young women to flirt with men, to seduce men, to control men. She showed that you could be sexy, but at the same time, control the negotiations, control the territory between male and female.
(Camille Paglia, *Reason*)

It's crazy, what's happened in my life and what I've been through. If I really think about it, I've had an amazing life. And I've met so many amazing people [...] I feel like I've survived so much. And sometimes I miss the innocence of those times. Life was different. New York was different. The music business was different. I miss the simplicity of it, the naiveté of everything around me.
(Madonna, *Independent.ie*)

Madonna's emergence to stardom in the early 1980s coincides with American popular music taking a turn to the phase of New Pop, a novel condition defined from the rise of MTV and the music video medium, which becomes the primary format of music reception. Simon Reynolds and Joy Press describe New Pop as a deconstructive force (317), picking up the baton from previous music movements, such as the early 1970s glam rock and the 1960s countercultural bohemia in the American and British terrains, which fervently opposed traditional rock (and roll) values. The 1980s, however, lacked the political valence of the preceding decades, which makes the phase-turned-era-turned-culture of New Pop all the more questionable and its politics of subversion, as Reynolds and Press put it, "precarious and complicated," to say the least (317). Being a decade of a general social backlash, the 1980s witnessed, among other things, Ronald Reagan and Margaret Thatcher's ultraconservative Right-oriented policies and neoliberal tactics, vacillations of the "second wave" feminist movement, and the AIDS crisis afflicting the gay community before turning to a trans-communal epidemic.[1] It is quite ironic, then, how currently Madonna misses "the simplicity" and "innocence" of those times. In rosy retrospection, those times may really appear sugar-coated, but the feeling was rather different when her inflammatory actions of, say, kissing the effigy of a Black Jesus or exposing wedding lingerie on stage, were met with harsh criticism. For Camille Paglia, probably Madonna's most ardent academic defender who now opts for disdain, this was when the performer changed the world. She may have pushed boundaries in terms of gender and race—"Express Yourself" (1989) was undoubtedly a call to arms—but her feminist/humanist cause was always contained within and curtailed by a neoliberal consumerist ethos as well as a self-centered drive for profit.

Arguably, Madonna's challenging of social notions and cultural clichés with overt visual and conceptual expressivity has remained keen throughout her 30-year-long career in the entertainment business. Her envelope-pushing attempts were and still are the axis around which her work rotates. What has changed, though, is the chronological and sociopolitical context wherein this work is placed. For instance, the *Spinal Tap*-like documentary *Madonna: Truth or Dare*, with a camera following the artist on a daily basis on- and offstage during her *Blond Ambition World Tour*, in 1990, can also be read as a racy reality show, long before reality TV even existed. A celebrity discussing openly her sex life to the point of even releasing a soft-porn coffee-table book boldly titled *SEX*, featuring photographic material with her in all kinds of sexual fantasies, was groundbreaking in a post-1980s context when music artists could only be erotically envisioned by their audience either through their music video narratives and live performances, in which sexuality was always contained, or via tabloid culture. One can imagine that an entire erotic novella created and embraced openly by Madonna herself was surely a provocative move, not to mention an ideal media magnet in light of the *Erotica* album. Currently, though, responses vary when Madonna openly provokes the public with overt sexuality, especially when one takes into account that she is a middle-aged performer in a youth-targeting business; for example, consider social media criticism on the artist's age that followed her live-streamed French kiss with hip-hop artist Drake during one of her Coachella showcases.[2] Ageism aside, women showing flesh in music performances has currently become a/the norm compared to Madonna's 1980s and early 1990s peers. What is then the point of a derrière-exposing Madonna now?

Concerning her feminist advocacy, Madonna's artistic endeavors have been meticulously examined by scholars and music critics mostly in terms of gender norm subversions. Academic literature and press on Madonna entail some of the most crucial conundrums permeating the ontology of her persona(e) and performances, including the always problematic binary of the Madonna/whore complex along with issues of censorship (Pisters), voyeurism and exhibitionism (Herr), fetishism and objectification (McRobbie, "Second-Hand Dresses"; Peñaloza), cultural appropriation (hooks, *Black Looks*; Robertson, *Guilty Pleasures*), women in business (Gairola), and, currently, ageism (McMahon; Naiman; Sullivan). Interestingly, there is no clear-cut division in these debates that would allow reading Madonna monolithically. Throughout her career and the long-lasting influence of her icon, she has indeed pushed the envelope as regards sex or artistic expression on stage; yet, she has time and again sustained and encouraged ideological power structures, most notably, White patriarchal supremacy, according to bell hooks (hooks, *Black Looks*, 157), or the inevitably capitalist-bound nature of her work. Thus, it is intriguing to explore how the approaches behind all these–isms reveal the profound and productive, but still intricate and problematic character of the Material Girl.

In this light, Madonna's camp is another question that is tangential with the abovementioned topics and is what this chapter seeks to problematize further. With critics of camp long debating on Madonna's oeuvre (Robertson, *Guilty Pleasures*; Shugart and Waggoner; Hawkins, "Draggin Out"), it would be axiomatic to argue that the performer's show is camp-fuelled. As totalizing as this argument may sound, one cannot help but acknowledge that the icon of Madonna has been structured upon and cemented with camp qualities. In this perspective, critics have attempted to examine grounds of camp production and reception inhabited solely by gay male subjectivity, thus offering alternative readings against camp's gay essentialism. For instance, in *Guilty Pleasures*, Robertson points out the misogynist aspects of camp and recuperates female agency behind camp practices. The camp of glamorous divas has been attractive to gay male subjectivity, yet it has always worked restrictively against women, putting them on a pedestal of dubious worship and attributing passive qualities to them. Robertson challenged this very thesis of gay male camp through Madonna and other Hollywood stars by highlighting the subversive feminist nuances in their performances of female masquerade. Regarding Madonna's agency behind the production of camp, the critic suggests that it functions on two parallel lines:

The first predominantly heterosexual pop and/or postmodern style of camp applies to Madonna's career as a whole—in her extraordinary self-marketing, her changing images, and her retro-cinephilia. The second, more explicitly homosexual and

> political style of camp inheres primarily in Madonna's explicit references to gay subcultures, especially drag and voguing, in her stated identification with gay men, her flirtation with lesbianism, and her AIDS charity work. (119)

Robertson provides accurate remarks regarding Madonna's career up until *Guilty Pleasures* was written. Twenty years later, however, there are instances where the political nuances of female/feminist camp are still ambiguous. When it comes to camp's high appeal to queer audiences and female divas exploiting it toward lucrative ends, it becomes rather problematic to sanction such production regardless of it being female- or male-authored.

Madonna is indeed a woman in power who is now in control of her own image and artistic creation. Robertson does not fail to see this, too: "no analysis of feminist camp would be complete without an acknowledgement of Madonna's role in bringing camp to the forefront in a transnational consumer society" (119). Helene Shugart and Catherine Egley Waggoner support that "although Madonna has had and continues to have camp moments, her performance is not consistently camp" and this "may well be a function of the fact that she was and continuous to be an innovator with regard to disrupting the confines of female sexuality in popular culture" (136). In agreement with Robertson, Shugart and Waggoner underline Madonna's agency behind her icon and camp in an effort to emphasize the feminist politics in the artist's projects. However, both analyses see Madonna as the sole proprietor behind her production of camp. Madonna may now manage much of her work's final outcome, always in line though with music market needs, yet there is still at work a complex power and business network around her. For one thing, queer culture, the primary source of camp production, comprises a large part of this network and its contribution is to be found in Madonna's fields of fashion and music production, artistic creation as well as audience attendance. The point of this argument is not, of course, to downgrade the feminist valence inherent in Madonna's camp, but rather to reclaim and reimagine the queer roots of camp as cooperative in the star construct that is "Madonna."

The Madonna reader has always had to deal with ambiguities regarding the persona that eventually led to polarities. Is she Madonna or whore? Is she ultimately in control of her objectification or is she the pink-ribboned package of pop consumerism? Is her artistic palette indeed driven by cultural appropriation or simply cultural borrowing or, worse, copying for lack of original creativity? Is "Madonna" a camp object or an object of camp? Or, no object at all? Despite the either/or nature of these questions, there is not a single correct answer; in fact, every answer seems valid because Madonna's icon remains fluid. Each of these, though, especially those concerning the very essence of her camp, must be treated contextually. For example, the controversy that the release of the video of "Justify

My Love"[3] generated in 1990 resulted in it being banned from music television due to its risqué depiction of S&M and queer action. Consider now the 2012 video of "Girl Gone Wild," which features Kazaki, an all-gay-male Ukrainian group, dancing semi-naked in tights and high heels next to Madonna. MTV critic Jocelyn Vena reviewed the video as "the perfect homage to the singer's foxy 'Sex' book and *Erotica* days of the '90s. Crunchy, sexy and edgy, the 'GGW' clip is certainly the perfect response for anyone yearning for *that* Madge of yesteryear" ("Madonna Owns", original emphasis). For, in 1990 Madonna fans might have never seen "Girl Gone Wild" uncensored or even aired, but in 2012 the video moves from "crunchy" to iconic. Cultural criticism changing with time allows for new spaces to revisit Madonna's camp, with questions arising as to whether her political risqué camp retreated into a celebrated iconicity, a mere nostalgia, and, by extension, whether the said camp nostalgia should be treated that simply.

Madonna's tour history attests to such nostalgia and celebration. Unlike her albums, videos, and singles that incrementally build on her icon, her tours offer a rich and condensed projection of who "Madonna" is supposed to be. Within a span of two to three hours, the shows are capable of (re)introducing, glamorizing, and verifying Madonna as the Queen of Pop in a self-referential and icon-affirming spectacle. Through the processes of sampling and (re)mixing Madonna's songs (or her songs with other artists' songs) into brief medleys, the shows are created to be reflective of club culture. Intertextuality and pop culture references lie at the core of her spectacle. Typically, each one of her tours' audiovisual staging (with the exception of *Confessions Tour* that I will shortly address) positions Madonna within current trends, thereby affirming her designated place in the pop world. Her *Sticky & Sweet Tour* (in 2008–09), for example, opened with Madonna sitting on a throne under the sonic influences of Timbaland and Kanye West, whose music projects were both on the spotlight at the time. As Madonna's icon is being further ingrained in the spectacle fair year by year, her tours indulge more and more in a celebratory excess of her icon and its longevity.

Simultaneously, the camp pastiche of her stage derives its power from the past and explodes extravagantly into the present. In every tour show, Madonna makes sure to cite from queer culture. As is the case with Hispanic and Black culture, the artist makes sure she flaunts her queer affiliations by presenting herself amidst queer-inflected scenes, thereby reaffirming her lasting relationship with the culture's histories and origins. In doing so, she cements her gay icon status, one that exhibits and promotes aspects of this long-established intertwinement. Of course, the relationship between Madonna and queer fandom is one of mutual adoration: in response, queer groups comprise many of her arena audiences and are a considerable cultural and economic factor endorsing her artistry and contributing to her legacy.

Nostalgias on a dance floor

Madonna's prefame story has been retold many times throughout her career, because, according to her, "it is good to look back and tell a story of how a girl from Detroit came to New York" (Hiatt). In her personal realization of the American Dream, it is admitted that her gay dance teacher Christopher Flynn played a key role in exposing Madonna to gay culture.[4] Ever since, her support for and by the community has been keen while one could argue that the development of her career and status as a gay icon are inextricably linked. In addition to that, her longevity in the entertainment industry has bound Madonna, the individual, and "Madonna," the icon, into a single person, at least in the public mind. Her identity as "Little Nonnie" Ciccone, the teenage girl from Michigan, has long been surpassed by her status as Madonna/"Madonna." Philip Auslander

> see[s] the performer in popular music as defined by three layers: the real person (the performer as human being), the performance persona (the performer's self representation), and the character (a figure portrayed in a song text). All three layers may be active simultaneously in a given musical performance. (*Performing Glam Rock*, 4)

Auslander's explication of the pop performer is vital in our understanding of the Madonna/"Madonna" symbiosis. The fact that the audience has to deal with two or more aspects of the performer's identity instills into the persona various facades of mystique. Essentially, this layered subjectivity, this power to don different masks and to build each time a different narrative around them, is where the power of Madonna's diva camp exists.

As Madonna's artistic palette is growing, so is her need not only to reinvent herself but, most importantly, to reaffirm herself as the chameleonic persona who skillfully evades fixity. The first two decades of her career saw Madonna emulating different personae, such as the "Marilyn Monroe" or the "Marie Antoinette".[5] In the years after 2005, however—with the exception of the "Madame X" persona for 2019's namesake album—instead of reinvention, she has settled for either revisiting past personae or acting out "Madonna" in various settings and scenes. For instance, *Confessions on a Dance Floor* and its accompanying *Confessions Tour* saw Madonna drawing heavily from the 1970s music scene, paying homage to ABBA, and recreating a *Saturday Night Fever*-ish aesthetic. Unlike, however, Mistress Dita, her alter-ego dominatrix from her *Erotica* days (*circa* 1992), or the geisha persona from the *Ray of Light* album (in 1998), the performer in the *Confessions* era rather opted for a Madonna-goes-disco project, which can either be viewed as an inability to creatively reinvent her persona or, quite the opposite, as an attempt to place her icon on the imaginative forefront through the disco scene. "Madonna" is a red-hot, politically charged persona that can no longer be contained inside other personae. Indeed, her icon ends up copying itself in true Baudrillardian fashion, drawing referential power from itself. In fact, her persona, which more often than not stands synonymous with controversy, can simply rely on its own power to provoke. Her mechanisms of metamorphosis are now no secret to her audience. It is Madonna, the provocateur, the always Catholic-inspired, the mother, the activist, the business woman, the Kabbalah devotee, the feminist, the poly-sexual, behind the mask. The project-like quality behind her reinventions immediately renders such acts as strictly professional. In this light, her inspirations are nothing but a careful study of her social surroundings that aims toward artistic and, by extension, lucrative goals. As her artistic trajectory from 2005 onward reveals, the performer did not really embrace any other persona, neither on- nor offstage, but her own. Rather, she acknowledges the legacy she has so far created and chooses to alternate either between acts she's already familiar with—consider the geisha-inspired martial arts segue of "Bitch I'm Madonna" for the *Rebel Heart Tour* and the kabuki-inspired performances of "Frozen" and "Sky Fits Heaven" for the *Drowned World Tour* (in 2001)—or between scenes that will be host to her own persona—as is the case with *Confessions Tour's* disco or with *MDNA Tour's* rave. As a result, "Madonna," the icon, becomes transparent and will no longer share the spotlight with any other personae. If it is an act, then it is certainly one of solipsism.

This, of course, does not seem to prevent audiences from worshipping her; in fact, it is exactly why they do so. After all, it is a Madonna show and in her performances egocentrism is *raison d'être* in the sense that she occupies the epicenter. Yet, Amy Robinson argues that "Madonna has provoked immense pleasure in her fans by courting their identities as a component of her own. At various stages in her interviewing career Madonna has claimed to be Black, a man, working class, and a lesbian" (340). What she did, though, was create sites of representation as a means of allowing a wide range of audiences to identify with her. In terms of camp, audiences acknowledging such artifice neither obscures the cultural nuances imprinted on Madonna's manifold identity, even when cultural appropriation is at work, nor reduces the level of pleasure derived from the act of identification with each one of them. Identity, be it gendered, racial, or ethnic, is consciously perceived aesthetically in its performative nature within the context of camp. According to Jonathan Dollimore,

[camp] is situated at the point of emergence of the artificial from the real, culture from nature—or rather when and where the real collapses into artifice, nature into culture; camp restores vitality to artifice, and vice versa, deriving the artificial from, and feeding it back into or as, the real. The reality is the pleasure of unreality. (225)

In this sense, to take pleasure in Madonna's camp is not simply to acknowledge the artifice but to embrace and enjoy its staged alternative dimension as such, abiding by the rules of role-play governing her camp performance.

The *Confessions Tour*, as a case in point, an extraordinary set of show that diverges from a typical concert show (even from a typical Madonna show), offers a retro-stylized reality with its revival of disco. The tracks in the *Confessions* album are structured in a DJ-composed set: in sequential order, the ending of one song is at the same time the beginning of the next one. Stuart Price, producer of the album and musical director of the tour, also mixed the music of the show to appear as in a continuous flow. This is the reason why the show is not open-ended or flexible and provides restricted time to interact with the audience. Contrary to most concert shows, *Confessions* shifts attention from audience participation to audience immersion; it only devotes little time for sing-alongs, mainly toward the "Hung Up" finale, and out of the 22 songs performed, there are only three ballads to tone down the show's energy. Emphasis is instead laid on the disco revival as an experience to be lived like an authentic vivid night at a discotheque. Mash-ups and medleys add more to that, thus enhancing the show's conceptual form as a gigantic disco dancefloor. In addition, following the formula of "Hung Up", Price's sampling and remixing did not make any musical references to contemporaries, but included only past songs of Madonna meddled with hits from Donna Summer, ABBA, and the Trammps. Strobe lights, synthesizer beats, disco balls, '70s attire, and Madonna's toned Fonda-esque posture recreate disco in its dazzling extravagance. It is not a plain tribute to a bygone era, but a meticulous simulation of a past form of entertainment. The camp of disco's nightlife adoration is reterritorialized in the *Confessions* stage whose time-bending reality resonates all through the sound of "Hung Up"'s ticking clock, suggesting that "time goes by so slowly."

Before delving into the tour's segments and acts, it is vital to understand the political and historical underpinnings of disco. The scene has been strongly associated with the queer community, appearing in the public mind as stereotypically gay, not only because its generic formation owes its existence to the community but mainly due to its clientele's frivolous attitude and image-conscious profile (Frank 292). This flattening understanding was not erroneous in its entirety, though, due to the fact that the colorful façade of disco was at the time juxtaposed to the edgy authenticity of rock music, a scene and genre oriented around the heterosexual White male consumer.[6] Politically, according to Gillian Frank,

> two trends led to the association of music with identity politics and to later conflicts between disco fans and rock fans: the emergence of the youth movement in

the 1960s with rock as its music and the emergence of the gay liberation movement
in the same period with disco as its music. (280)

Observing the anti-disco backlash of 1979, Frank explains that disco, largely
perceived as "gay and elitist" (278), threatened core values of American rock,
including heterosexual masculinity. The homophobic sentiments that disco
inspired in fans of rock coincided with the late 1970s anti-gay campaigns that
sought to curb gays' sociocultural ascendance and put them back into the closet
(Frank 285–6). Eventually, the social implications of disco were harnessed and
soon its momentum was stifled, making room for its offspring that was the dance/
house scene.

Culturally, disco exhibited racial and ethnic diversity before crossing over to
mainstream American market. Nadine Hubbs explains that "[h]istorical accounts
locate disco's origins in Manhattan clubs whose clientele were African American
and Latinx, and gay—meaning: gay men" (232). The collective aspect of the
dancefloor along with the anthemic nature of survival and the undisguised sexuality upheld in the songs of predominantly Black female artists, such as Gloria
Gaynor, Diana Ross, and Donna Summer, instilled into queer subcultures a sense
of belonging and social visibility. Taking into consideration post-Stonewall identity politics, such plurality was cemented into one coherent community flourishing
in discotheques that developed a common awareness. What appears problematic, though, in the accounts of disco's social containment is the invisibility of
lesbian entrepreneurs and producers.[7] Homosexual men *qua* men still had more
socioeconomic privileges than lesbians, a fact that granted them access into
entrepreneurship, which, by extension, allowed them to expand and thrive in the
nightlife entertainment. Frank supports that "disco allowed gay men who owned
discotheques and who served as disc jockeys and producers to become highly visible and respected within the music scene" (284). In addition, they established
an everlasting relationship with female performers, especially from the African
American community, as is evidenced from the epicenter the figure of the disco diva
occupies in camp culture. However, the popularization of disco, mainly through
John Badham's landmark *Saturday Night Fever* and its accompanying best-seller
soundtrack by the Bee Gees, "made disco safe for white, straight, male, young, and
middle-class Americans" (Frank 288) but, at the same time, curtailed its racial and
ethnic inflections. Disco's subcultural queerness was now boxed in a homogenized
perception of gayness as effeminate aestheticism, which was further regulated into
metrosexual heterosexuality, considering the straight star image of the Bee Gees
and Travolta's impactful character, Tony.

In its revival of disco, accordingly, the *Confessions Tour* stages a celebratory
homage, ensuring at the same time that its queer nuances are highlighted. The

show's fierce opening sees a whip-wielding Madonna landing on the stage inside a giant disco ball and soon sexuality becomes an integral theme for the show. The BDSM-inspired scene includes leather-clad dancers simulating horses—the segment is appropriately named the Equestrian—and is embellished with electronic sounds reminiscent of Giorgio Moroder's productions. Establishing a direct connection with the past, Madonna mixes one of her songs with Donna Summer's signature hit "I Feel Love", "an all-time gay classic, a totem of the pre-AIDS era," as Jon Savage and Ewan Pearson put it, whose repetitive beat and vocals manage to "obliterate the tyranny of the clock".

For the next segment, the Bedouin, Madonna tones down the beats in favor of more politically charged performances. Among these, the performance of "Live to Tell" stands out not only due to its subsequent controversy but rather for the camp effect it eventually creates. Run by the interlude's confessional tone, Madonna, dressed in red velvet clothing, emerges again on stage hanged on a massive mirrored crucifix and wearing a crown of thorns—indeed, a campification of Catholic Christianity par excellence. Behind her, counting numbers list African children orphaned by AIDS annually. Toward the end of the song, Madonna steps down from the cross while images of African children and quotes from the Bible appear on screen. The provocative performance of "Live to Tell" infuriated the Protestant, Catholic, and Muslim world, with religious leaders from Rome and Moscow accusing Madonna of blasphemy, urging boycotts against her concert and calling for her excommunication.[8] What is explicitly ironic about this performance is Madonna's invocation of her political persona that puns with Catholic imagery. Essentially, her "performing Jesus" act, in concert with her background of charity work and controversial past acts, deflects attention from the actual political content, the AIDS-infected African children, and transfocalizes onto Madonna, the provocateur. Furthermore, the decision to stage such performance within a high-grossing entertaining tour risks flirting with the postcolonial stereotypical framing of a helpless, AIDS-afflicted "Third World" by standing in juxtaposition to it as a more often than not costly American spectacle. For, audiences may applaud the artist's political message, but, in the pleasure of camp, content is obscured by artifice—style over content, in Susan Sontag's terms—as soon as Madonna moves onto her next act. It would be erroneous to claim that the specific performance is not politically aware with regard to the African AIDS crisis. Yet, the fact that the artist chooses to do it on a far-from-negligible, productively expensive, and highly coded prop reorients the political nature into the edifices of the iconic, itself raising important questions with regard to the political nature of Madonna's icon.

The artist's icon is egotistically political in its power to engage its viewer in the process of decoding what is seemingly hidden behind its artifice. In this sense, Madonna offers up herself for deconstruction, consumption, and satisfaction. To take pleasure in the specific performance is to ultimately fetishize Madonna for what she is expected to sell: controversy and iconicity. She reaffirms her position as a pop fetish[9] through the campification of Catholicism, which she has continuously been doing throughout her career as part of her ironic/iconic engagement with religion. Most importantly, the specific performance of "Live to Tell" is permeated by a queer narrative that envisions Madonna as the champion of AIDS-afflicted groups. Since the social history of HIV/AIDS is heavily branded with queer nuances and since the artist is known for having been vocal against the epidemic through her charity work, the performance is inevitably read from a queer perspective. With the lyrics' confessional tone illustrating a secret never to be revealed, a concealed malady, or even a love that dare not speak its name, "Live to Tell" sees Madonna, the gay icon, upon the disco cross, sacrificing herself against the HIV/AIDS signifier, a performance that builds narrative bridges with the 1980s queer community as well as evokes the figurative death of disco, which in part was an aftermath of the epidemic and its paranoia discourse. Madonna's glamorously grotesque crucifixion scene eventually becomes a camp exposition that braids together the frivolous with the serious, as the queer undertones behind AIDS and the disco are hard to miss, and simultaneously designates Madonna's disco goddess status.

The artist's camp indeed emerges as a complex mode of performance that cannot be simply labeled political or apolitical. In fact, she makes sure to occupy both ends, working toward a synthetically immersive effect. The show's Never Mind the Bollocks segment, or simply Glam-Punk, adds more to this point. Drawing her inspiration from the Sex Pistols' seminal one-off album, *Never Mind the Bollocks, Here Come the Sex Pistols*, Madonna camps all notions and axiomatic traditions that come in hand with the history of punk rock. The Glam-Punk segment is in fact a parody of rock's heterosexually policed authenticity, one that broadens even more the gap between disco and rock, frivolity and seriousness. Her performance of "I love New York," in which Madonna worships the city that made her famous, is in stark contrast with the Sex Pistols' "New York," a mockery against the 1970s glam rock group New York Dolls, whose androgynous image destabilized rock's heteronormative core. While disco faced backlash from outsiders, rock started being corroded from within. The 1970s glam rock was the colorful cell inside rock's rigid organism and the culture associated with it. According to Auslander:

[T]he gender-bending of glam challenged both the dominant culture's standard masculinity and the androgyny favored by the hippie counterculture, for glam did not posit androgyny as a "natural" taste. To the contrary: glam rockers specifically foregrounded the constructedness of their effeminate or androgynous performing personae. (*Performing Glam Rock*, 63)

Concerning New York Dolls, Van Cagle notes that the group played on androgyny to a camp effect, generating misconceptions as regards their sexuality and fans (185). Such confusion is evident in the Pistols' "New York" whose lyrics insist on the faux image of the Dolls, poking fun at their "made in Japan" unoriginality, while, taking androgyny-as-gayness for granted, they reduce them to "faggots" and "pile of shit."[10]

Madonna's performance is a camp response to the Pistols' alleged authenticity and blatant sexism. The performer appears dressed in full leather and sings "I Love New York" with the Manhattan skyline as her backdrop. Contrary to the Pistols' political resistance against British authority—consider their *Bollock*'s essential singles "Anarchy in the U.K." and "God Save the Queen"—Madonna's act celebrates and promotes her cultural anchoring in a deliberately plastic way. What is also crucial about this performance is Madonna playing the electric guitar, thereby inhabiting a masculine rock position. Examining the performances of Mick Ronson and David Bowie, Auslander views the position of the lead guitarist as the guitar hero, "a position that is coded as masculine in the rock culture" (*Performing Glam Rock*, 141) or, in Steve Waksman's words, "a ritual that validates masculine prowess" (249). In "I Love New York," Madonna is only accompanied by her band and sings her lyrics firmly in the microphone, transforming her disco dancefloor into a pseudo-rock concert. Toward the end of the song, she engages in a guitar solo and rocks her guitar in the air over her audiences. As a symbol of masculinity, the electric guitar carries the power of the phallus, therefore allowing Madonna to camp up the phallo(go)centric discourses of rock in a mock performance of masculinity.[11] By doing so she reinvokes the camp imagery of the Dolls in order to debunk the power of the guitar-phallus and toy with the rigidity of rock's masculine ideal.

The iconicity of *Confessions*' Glam-Punk segment draws from the tradition of rock: the electric guitar solo, leather clothing, outspoken lyrics, rigid posture, all serving as Madonna's symbolic tools. The artist does not simply draw from it, but in fact camps it up, thereby foregrounding, first of all, rock's differentiation from the frivolity of disco and, furthermore, underlining the latter as the primary artistic source that she aligns with. Prior to releasing *Confessions on a Dance Floor* and embarking on tour, Madonna explained her decision to tap into disco. In an interview with MTV's John Norris, she admitted being politically "agitated" throughout her previous album, *American Life* (2003), and felt the need to take a more "buoyant" turn for her next project (Madonna, "Madonna–COADF Promotion"). She also openly embraced her "inauthenticity" as regards the album's indulgence in intertextuality of, and borrowing from the Pet Shop Boys, ABBA, Depeche Mode, Kylie Minogue, and, most obviously, herself (Madonna, "Madonna– COADF Promotion"). Evidently, her tour showcase was expected to exhibit all these references in a way that are culturally and musically recognizable by the audience and presented effectively so that intertextuality does not eclipse "Madonna," the icon. The epitome of that is the final section of the tour, the Disco segment, which brings the show full circle and revels in a bombardment of clichés by reviving the disco camp with all those well-known conventions that prescribe it as such in the public memory. As Andrew Ross argues about Pop camp: "In reviving a period style, or elements of a period style that were hopelessly, and thus 'safely,' dated, camp acted as a kind of *memento mori*, a reminder of Pop's own future oblivion which [...] Pop cannot help but advertise" (320). For the writer, "Camp was [is and will be] an antidote to Pop's contagion of obsolescence" (321). In this light, the show's camp stands as the antidote for the obsolescence of disco and, for that matter, the Disco segment is not frugal in its purpose of reminiscence to (re)use everything disco-coded. It is a synecdoche of a resurrection, prefiguring Madonna's already forced resurrection as a cult item.

A point worth mentioning here, which has been given little attention in current analyses of the Madonna phenomenon and will be central for the remainder of this chapter, is Madonna's very own body. Since time is important in understanding the performer's camp, it is imperative that we conceptualize Madonna's body, a muscular, actively contributive, dynamic body, parallel to axes of gender, age, and capital production. The artist's longevity in the show industry requires from her to retain all these feats that originally propelled her to fame. Madonna exists in the public mind as a performer who continuously ups the ante with each new project. Apart from controversy and iconicity, durability is also what characterizes her history of performance. Madonna's show-woman status entails singing, dancing, and acting, a triptych that renders her body a site of performing action. Though this seems to be "effortlessly" carried out by, say, a 30-year-old female entertainer, expectations are different for a woman in her sixties. In order to keep up with the high energy of her spectacles, not only does Madonna have to preserve the quality of the abovementioned triptych but also to once again actively assert her status of a professional entertainer. In the past, she would casually expose her body as part of publicity stints. Now, she continues to do so by framing her body as a body of a certain age, partly to promote herself as an ardent show-woman with lasting iconic appeal as well as to challenge cultural notions of aging women in the show industry.[12]

Apart from confronting ageist clichés, though, Madonna's body is a living, performing, and performed memory, indeed a cult item. Her action-packed choreographies and acrobatics on stage attest to her skillfulness as a dancer. The adaptability of her body posture into each setting allows her to smoothly blend with the scene's narrative and augment its physical realness. In the *Confessions Tour*, Madonna's leotard-clad body, well into its 40th decade by then, in concert with her dancers' body and the 1970s attire establish the apparent link with the performing bodies on the disco dancefloor. As part of nightlife entertainment, the disco dancefloor is a site of energy that invites bodies to show off their dancing prowess, to interact with each other, and, most of all, to express themselves freely. Since disco's origins were gay, the dancefloor was an inclusive space that allowed queer bodies to embrace their sexuality and be praised at; in other words, to acquire visibility and generate eroticism. Moreover, considering we are talking about the pre-HIV/AIDS era, the queer body had not yet become pathologized through the paranoia discourse and was unashamedly promoted as muscular, sexual, and vibrant.[13] Here, Madonna's invocation of the dancing disco body attempts to invite the erotic gaze in a way, though, that is tinted with an aura of retro. The audience is encouraged to look at the bodies on stage in a nostalgic-cum-erotic way, as if they were tangible manifestations of a titillating night at the disco. With additional soundtrack support, Madonna's body occupies an epicenter and sets itself as the living proof of the disco past, executing routines of past and present numbers, all meticulously undergirded into a seamless musical performance.

Confessions' Disco segment incrementally unfolds around Madonna's body. The segment begins with a video interlude featuring Madonna's past hits and smoothly shifts to a mash-up of the 2000 single "Music" with The Trammps' "Disco Inferno." There are instances in the video where Madonna makes visual and choreographic references to Tina Turner's *Tommy* performance of "Acid Queen". On top of this retro musical explosion, Madonna's dancers are roller-skating across the stage, and Stuart Price, the show's musical director, shares the spotlight as the dancefloor's DJ. The latter's onstage presence throughout the tour is in fact key in this meticulous simulation of disco. The emergence of the DJ figure and its contribution to the scene has been fundamental since it transfocalized audiences' attention from performer to sound. According to Lawrence, the figure of the DJ was a catalyst for the disco dancefloor "[b]ecause the disembodied recording artist could be heard but not seen, the dancer could also begin to think of her or himself as a contributor to the collectively generated musical assemblage" (236).[14] Here, though, the DJ's mixing does not erase the performer, who is far from disembodied and whose presence is continuously felt even in the form of a video projection. On the contrary, the disco experience is embodied on Madonna in its entirety.

As the interlude transitions into "Music," Madonna emerges on stage to perform the song live with dancing poses and white flared trousers that make the allusion to *Saturday Night Fever* hard to miss. She even distances herself from her dancers and moves to the minor stage where she recreates Travolta's "You Should Be Dancing" solo routine. "Music," of course, makes the perfect soundtrack for Madonna's specific act with its retro catchy line "Hey Mr. DJ, put a record on." What is more, it takes camp to a jittery level as, according to Stan Hawkins, "the pleasure in 'Music' is based around an erotic sensibility that proposes something quite glamorous and technically ambitious" (*Dragging Out Camp*, 7).[15] With an already camped-up original production,[16] and alongside Price's savvy sampling as well as a Travolta-inspired Madonna, the final outcome becomes energetically playful and fluidly gendered. Madonna's performance here stages a multicultural and multigendered synthesis similar to what disco reified on any given night. Backed from "Music's" lyrics—"Music makes the people come together/Music makes the bourgeoisie and the rebel"—the act is driven by a carnivalesque sentiment emphasizing camp's power to regenerate the disco past and immerse its audience in the carefree nostalgia. As with the disco dancefloor, the *Confessions'* stage offers its space for entertainment that is partly derived from sonic contribution and partly from the ostentatious movements of Madonna at the center of it.

This act of display, for which the artist flauntingly proves that she is both the king and queen of disco, is energized by disco's attraction to plasticity, one that is both gendered and eroticized. By the time "Music" is finished, Madonna strips her Travolta apparel on stage and performs "Erotica," which has been vamped to fit the segment's tonality and aesthetic. The song's inclusion in the *Confessions'* setlist might strike one as bizarre, considering the complete absence of other Madonna songs, such as "Express Yourself" or "Vogue," that would seem more appropriate for the disco revival. Its staging and remixing, though, compensate for these omissions. The song is performed on tour for the first time in thirteen years, after *The Girlie Show Tour* in 1993; and although *Confessions* imagines the song's sensibility in terms that are different from *The Girlie Show*'s S&M and burlesque,[17] it manages to maintain the original exhibitionistic eroticism. Madonna now reveals a purple-white jumpsuit copied after Agnetha Fältskog and Anni-Frid Lyngstad's famous outfit during *ABBA: The Tour* (in 1979–80), and the choreography is reminiscent of Jane Fonda's aerobics, thus rendering Madonna's body a veritable 1970s spectacle. Once again, the artist employs her performing body to invoke her own beginning in the entertainment industry as a dancer as well as to reaffirm herself as the dramatic core of a scrupulously choreographed show, ultimately offering it as a fetish for voyeuristic pleasure and at the same time verifying its guaranteed aptitude to entertain as well as carry layered structures of iconicity—that is, ABBA, Fonda, and early 1990s "Madonna."

It is the segment's finale—also the show's finale—that brings everything into a camp apogee. Madonna has donned a neon-glowing cape that reads "Dancing Queen" to perform "Hung Up." The song has appropriately been left for the finale with every creative detail of the Disco segment pointing to this climax. Madonna launched the *Confessions* era with "Hung Up" as the lead single, in 2005, which Price produced by sampling ABBA's "Gimme! Gimme! Gimme! (A Man after Midnight)" and Johan Renck visualized as a tribute to John Travolta and Bob Fosse. The song's worldwide success breathed fresh air into

Madonna's iconicity in a conceptual process that distanced her agenda from the politically agitated *American Life* toward more joyous image and sound. "Hung Up's" popularity disseminated a retro, colorful "Madonna" whose camp value is intense and highly persistent. Her pink leotard, for that matter, which appears both in the video and on the album's art cover, along with the notorious scene of her making love to a boombox, has become a widely recognizable camp instance of Madonna's *Confessions* era. It is this coded reality after all that vitalizes artists' iconic ontology as well as their audiences' perception of their personae at a given time. Once such codes are established as reflections, nuances, or simply reinventions of the performer, they are reenacted in live performances to address the audience's semantic familiarity with them. In this sense, the performance of "Hung Up" here displays cognitive integrity. Price has injected sonic references of the ABBA sample in the song preceding "Hung Up" so as to make known of what is to follow as well as create a seamless long medley. Contrary to other concerts that play with the element of surprise in their encore acts, the *Confessions* show lets known of its trump card: the audience is aware, but the medley's effect of delay prolongs the pleasure. As "Hung Up" finally kicks in, Madonna enters the stage in the infamous leotard and executes the song's original choreography. The reenactment of the boombox scene, of course, is set to be the pinnacle of the performance for which the singer struts down the runway toward the minor stage where a boombox is being surfaced, having already become by then the quintessential *Confessions* prop upon which the artist will simulate masturbation. Madonna reaches her musical climax amidst hundreds of golden balloons that shower her surrounding crowd, an apt double entendre for the show finale.

The particular act demonstrates that, despite all the seemingly distractive practices of sampling and intertextuality, "Madonna" resides at the core of the show. Almost performed in ritualistic devotion, the show's autoerotic act elicits the audience's cheers, who in turn acknowledge and, by extension, approve of Madonna's power to iconicize her stage/persona behavior. Being instances of solipsism, acts like the boombox scene rely on performative skills that have little to do with simply executing a choreographed set. As symbolic derivatives of the catwalk culture, the movements are theatrically composed to resemble posing, which is, more often than not, home to female subjectivity. Posing, of course, does not preclude nonfemale subjects, as we will see with voguing further down. It does, however, prefigure femaleness as synonymous with femininity, and more specifically one that is glamorously standardized. Think about, for example, stage runways and the posture of the performer on them in female-led concert shows in juxtaposition to male-led shows. Even when performances by either queer or heterosexual male artists, including the camp flair of David Bowie, Michael Jackson, Mick Jagger, or Prince, to name just a few, employ posing, it is considered to be at least apparent due to the conspicuous gender play. Yet, posing and the (heterosexual) female performer seem to be naturally consonant not only because of the femaleness/femininity conjunction, but mainly because traditionally women on stage, especially in the spectacle domain, were set to embody femininity.[18] Madonna, here, inhabits the position of the diva on a pedestal; her glamorous femininity appears natural on stage, while her egocentric eroticism is comfortably displayed to attract "look-all-you-want" gazes.

Although such position seems to confine female subjectivity in objectified and passive *loci* of power, it is interesting to see it from the perspective of the show(wo)manship tradition. Robertson has commented that Madonna's camp relies on the performance of femininity as masquerade: "The masquerade mimics a constructed identity in order to conceal that there is nothing behind the mask; it simulates femininity to dissimulate the absence of a real or essential feminine identity" (*Guilty Pleasures*, 12). It has the potential to underline and expose the construct of gender as innately hollow by inflating its surface and corroding its core. In its history of caricaturing gender, the masquerade has been a powerful tool in camp's parodying arsenal. In terms of stage performance, the practice of masquerading exists within a parental theatrical environment that aids in our understanding of gender performance and its exaggerated constructedness. In ways that date back to the pre-twentieth-century burlesque tradition and its exposition of gender roles, the diva concert allows the performer to theatricalize her femininity. For Madonna, the play of acting out femininity, as this is culturally, socially, and dramatically defined, aligns with the performance of her very own icon. She does not simply parody femininity, but rather reenacts her own persona who mockingly dons various iconic femininities, including previous versions of herself.

Best explanatory of that is her performance of the song "She's Not Me" for the *Sticky & Sweet Tour* (in 2008–09), a show that saw Madonna departing from *Confessions*' disco sound and aesthetic. Whereas musically "She's Not Me" is an upbeat song, its live performance unravels in a more dramatic, even painful delivery. Emerging on stage alongside Madonna are four female dancers appearing as mannequins. Their looks are based on past "Madonna" personae, including her "Monroe" from "Material Girl,"[19] the boyish Minnelli-esque persona from "Open Your Heart," the bride from "Like a Virgin," and the cone-bra-clad fashionista from "Vogue." Madonna approaches and disturbs her past selves, stripping off articles of clothing and accessories, unbalancing their fixed positions, and calling them "Bitches" and "Wannabes." She even reaches the point of touching her dancers' body parts and French-kissing one of them. Although this act may invite readings of self-eroticism, since it is Madonna flirting with her own image, it tips the scales toward self-harassment. Deconstructing her past icons is a moment that evidently, albeit briefly allows the audience to take a short glimpse into Madonna's struggle in the industry, mainly as a female artist. The repetition of the lines "she's not me" and "never let you forget" watches Madonna assaulting her doppelgangers, taking off their wigs, strangling her "Vogue" persona with the bride's veil, and finally executing a frenetic dance solo, as the "wannabes" vanish down-stage.

As a woman in the performing world, the artist takes a stand to dramatically expose the constant need to reinvent herself in an effort to continuously rekindle the public's interest. The abovementioned performance, thus, stands critical against the repression imposed by glamorous femininity upon the artist's "real" self. Nevertheless, the fact that such opposition to her former images/roles is voiced within her show reveals the irony behind her position as a show-woman. After "She's Not Me," Madonna hastily returns to her club culture origins, clarifying any obscurities this performance might have created. She gauchely puts on her mannequins' discarded wig and jacket, and crawls on the runway toward the main stage, as the lyrics of Indeep's "Last Night a DJ Saved My Life" are being played. Her crawling is accompanied by acts of entreaty as she reaches out her hands in call for rescue. Upon stepping on the main stage, "Music" explodes. Contrary to its disco-vamped version in *Confessions*, *Sticky & Sweet*'s electro-house rendition of "Music," which samples Fedde Le Grand's "Put Your Hands Up for Detroit," sees Madonna bringing her past into the present by staging her nostalgia for the '80s urban scene. By being antithetical to "She's Not Me" in terms of narrative and performance, the visual presentation of "Music" sees Madonna reembracing her stage self and 1980s musical descent in order to reaffirm her status as the Michigan-born-and-bred, but inevitably New York-influenced Queen of Pop amidst a bombardment of personal references.[20]

These artistic allusions to the past are indeed inseparable from Madonna's stage. While the *Confessions Tour*, a retro-indulging enterprise par excellence, stood out for presenting a time-traveling experience into a specific moment of 1970s entertainment, the rest of the artist's tours, conversely, revive a plethora of past moments of entertainment and playfully fuse them with the present. The *Sticky & Sweet Tour*, the *MDNA Tour*, as well as the *Rebel Heart Tour* derive their inspirations from local and global artists, from mainstream and underground scenes, and, most importantly, from Madonna's own oeuvre, which is constantly being reconfigured to meet each show's aesthetics. What is noteworthy about Madonna's cultural borrowings is the excessive amount of intertextual information incorporated into them. The *Sticky & Sweet Tour* featured an abundance of musical references, making it perhaps Madonna's most intertextual enterprise. *The Guardian* reviewer for the show, Kitty Empire, accurately writes that "[one] do[es] not come to Madonna for dignified austerity, and the *Sticky and Sweet* tour delivers on visuals, pace and sheer physicality," underlining that "the show radically remixes old favorites and showcases the newer songs from her *Hard Candy* album" (Empire, "Mama Don't Preach"). Musical director Kevin Antunes and Madonna's longtime tour director Jamie King composed the specific show to contain as many audiovisual stimuli as possible, thus making it a truly diverse postmodern piece of spectacle whose plurality is both demonstrative of its commercial nature and indicative of its time.

Austerity, as Empire mentions, is not part of Madonna's f(l)air ("Mama Don't Preach"). As with every pop and camp instance, the artist's fetishist approach to spectacle exists within capitalistic grids that do not allow its bombastic drive to be otherwise expressed. Camp's colorful reality, for that matter, has traditionally been symbiotic with affluence. Here too the very essence of Madonna's camp makes manifest a lavish pop universe pulsating around her icon. We will see, though, how Madonna's camp ventures can actually enclose problematic interrelations especially when we take into account her notorious exchanges with queer culture and the way the artist manages to ascribe cultural power to her icon via these exchanges. Margaret Thompson Drewal underlines that "[w]hen corporate capitalism appropriates Camp in its own interests and then poses as its signifier, then the representation bears only the residue of Camp politics" (150). The writer here challenges canonized notions of camp's politics of subversion, especially when this is being viewed from its exchange value perspective. Drewal identifies capitalism as the patriarchal and heterosexist ideology that mitigates the "gay signifier" when camp practices are corporately appropriated. Although this argument is at its most parts valid, we cannot be monolithic when it comes to camp occupying a mainstream diva's stage. It is true that Madonna's incorporation of queer elements into her show could be a magnet to draw in queer audiences. Yet, one cannot dismiss that the artist also sets the stage as a visible space that materializes queer culture's artistic and social history. At the same time, her exposition of camp is vitalized by means of nostalgia and tradition, the power of which lies in addressing queer audiences with a past that has become an identity-bolstering cult item via its iconization. In order to explore this argument further, I will now turn to the practice of vogue and Madonna's appropriation/borrowing of it.

The legacy of "Vogue"

The camp practice of vogue is another shared tradition that is frequently performed on the contemporary music stage. A wide array of divas, including Kylie Minogue and Katy Perry, have incorporated the intricate dance and its accompanied culture in their show routines, thereby acknowledging it as a form of queer spectacle.[21] Madonna's engagement with vogue on stage, in particular, has developed in parallel with the history of her involvement with the vogue scene as this originates in her seminal song and video of "Vogue" (in 1990). Not only has "Vogue" been a *tour de force* in Madonna's worldwide career, but it was also fundamental in widely consolidating her status as a queer icon. Ever since, the artist has included the song in her tours, always approaching it with different creative moods for each show, yet never abandoning its quintessential camp proponents. Nevertheless, her dealing with voguing and its ballroom culture origins and, by extension, her exploitation of its queer potential appears problematic. Most academic criticism sees Madonna's dealing with the vogue scene as cultural appropriation and commodification of a subcultural practice that originally dwelled in a dynamic counter-(hetero)normative space (Harper; hooks, *Black Looks*). Almost 30 years after the song's initial impact, though, Madonna seems to have left her own imprint on the cultural evolution of vogue, presenting it as an inextricable part of her icon and stage. It is worth laying focus on Madonna's specific staged tradition that seems to have partly shaped the performer's affiliation with her queer fandom as well as demonstrates queer culture's acknowledging of pop artists who tap into these queer practices to inform their performances.

Historically, voguing has been a street dance practice established by working-class queer Latinx and African American groups in the 1960s. Its name derives from the eponymous fashion magazine due to the fact that voguers' contortions emulate fashion models as if walking down the runway or posing for a cover shot. Within the context of the ballroom contests, voguers would don a certain role/character, such as the suburban lady or the butch businessman, in what is known as categories, and would come to drag balls to compete with each other on "realness"—the ability to present each character in the ballroom as accurately and realistically as possible. Progressively, these competitions have included an array of categories that in turn have helped separate voguing into three distinct major showcases: Old Way, New Way, and Vogue Femme (Bailey, *Butch Queens*; Prodigy). While each category has its own features—for instance, Old Way entails clean-cut geometrical posturing, whereas New Way relies more on agile and flexible moves—all three center on the performance of gender. Vogue Femme, for that matter, is the category in which the performer has to effectively display a feminine character by acting out the signifiers of femininity as truthfully as possible. Vogue's treatment of gender has piqued the interest of queer theorists due to its ability to underline and present the social percept of gender as performative mainly through drag performance (Butler, *Gender Trouble*; Harper; Senelick). It has indeed served as a political site to investigate the performativity of gender, yet its potential to critically oppose normative structures and effectively challenge the systemic materiality of gender remains rather ambiguous.

Theory-wise, vogue's camp politics of subversion has entered academic discussion from the very moment the scene was brought to the forefront. Gender scholars have underlined its parodic efficacy to imitate and reproduce conditions of gendered expression, while, simultaneously, challenging a somewhat idealistic notion that these performances can effectively overthrow the established gender order, which remains culturally, socially, and historically ingrained. Judith Butler, for instance, performs an analysis of *Paris Is Burning*, Jennie Livingston's documentary on Harlem voguers and the ballroom scene, explicating why drag's alleged subversion in fact reiterates normative gendered structures, despite its seemingly effective exposure of the ideology of gender. In particular, Butler argues that: "'Realness' is not exactly a category in which one competes; it is a standard that is used to judge any given performance within the established categories. And yet what determines the effect of realness is the ability to compel belief, to produce the naturalized effect" (*Bodies that Matter*, 129). In this argument one also has to factor the aspect of performance as spectacle. As part drag showcase, vogue's competence is limited within the contours of the stage/dancefloor where the body is to imitate and thereby reiterate an already existing reservoir of established gendered codes. Both performers and receivers of vogue are exposed to gender-fluid realities on stage, but what happens outside of this always already theatrical environment is more complex. The stage's theatrical representation of reality juxtaposes itself with the actual one, therefore framing gender parody as solely stylistic, stripping it off of its potential to radically destabilize offstage social gender. As Philip Brian Harper argues about the *Paris Is Burning* stars and extends to the ball world in general, "when Realness queens exit the ball milieu, which constitutes a type of imaginary realm, they must—to all appearances, at least—conform to the norms of the larger social context that effectively constitutes the symbolic order" (97). In this sense, the basic premise of subversion serves little if we are to restrict analysis within the argument of performance on the stage/dancefloor and performance in a broader social environment. Thus, its political valence should be sought elsewhere.

If one pays attention to the culture and legacy of gender fluidity that vogue has established through its years of subcultural and mainstream existence, what emerges is a cultural history that operates its own queer reality and has significantly foddered queer culture's understanding of gender performance. In this light, vogue has to be examined as a durable camp tradition that bears instantly recognizable queer signifiers that read gender as performable and imitable. These signifiers reside in camp's extravagant conceptualization of gender, style, and attitude. Precisely because these signifiers rely on an essentialist perception of gender and coded behavior, they can easily be mimicked and showcased. Vogue may in part fail to serve as a radical critique of gender, yet the conspicuousness and effortless decipherability of its signifiers allow its queerness to be visibly manifest. Its power is its queer kinesis. Through its spastic movements—bent wrists, flexible limbs, and ferocious strutting—the voguing body fleshes out the quintessential campness, that is, effeminacy. Andrew Britton explains that "[c]amp always connotes 'effeminacy,' not 'femininity'" (138). The writer adds: "[b]eing essentially a mere play with given conventional signs, camp simply replaces the signs of 'masculinity' with a parody of the signs of 'femininity' and reinforces existing social definitions of both categories" (138). Effeminacy, thus, is the process through which a body of any gender is given dramatically feminine attributes; in short, femininity is the source, the stereotypically fixed tank wherefrom camp draws in order to feminize the body. Vogue's effeminacy is explicit because its camp-fueled choreographic presentation manages to visibly feminize the performing body.

Effeminacy has always been connotative to quondam perceptions of the gay male body. More like anathema in the heteronormative mind, it led toward framing homosexuality as "faggotry," which in turn drove a plethora of gay men to consciously and subconsciously internalize masculinity, usually perceived as White and Western, as the antidote against their sissiness in order to blunt homophobia and smoothly integrate with heteronormative reality. By redressing this precise image of the gay body, vogue invokes effeminacy as a means of outspokenly flaunting the said faggotry, a faggotry that entails ethnic and racial markers as well. It proudly reinstills voice into the exorcized effeminate man in order to both underline queer men's embodiment of machismo as hypocritical and designate "the camp" to a more central place within queer culture. Ironically, it employs the power of a stereotype to reenergize the effeminate body and celebrate sissiness with a sported in-your-face attitude. Being performed by a plural corpus of bodies—bodies that can be male and female, transgender, bisexual, White and non-White, young and old—vogue's camp valence dwells on the ability to revive and channel the signified camp by and through the performance of effeminacy. In fact, its essentialist, albeit queer-forward language bears the inclusive quality that makes it easily understood by, and widely appealing to a global audience, who has taken to venerate vogue as a queer tradition. After all, that is exactly what Livingston's voguers, representing a subcultural caste of marginalized queer groups, claimed to dream of.

Importantly, vogue's language was introduced to a mainstream audience via two key mediums: Livingston's documentary and Madonna's "Vogue." The former presented voguers within the Harlem ballroom milieu and was one of the first media to document the vogue scene and its on- and offstage reality. Livingston helped shed light on the marginal life of Harlem's gender outcasts by providing insights into the drag practices within the contests and the Houses.[22] The documentary was a welcome addition to queer theorists' investigations on gender performance and performativity, yet issues of cultural authorship emerged with regard to Livingston's auteristic and at times sentimentalized approach of the vogue queens. In her review of the film, bell hooks underscores:

> Jennie Livingston approaches her subject matter as an outsider looking in. Since her presence as white woman/lesbian filmmaker is "absent" from *Paris Is Burning* it is easy for viewers to imagine that they are watching an ethnographic film documenting the life of black gay "natives" and not recognize that they are watching a work shaped and formed by a perspective and standpoint specific to Livingston. (*Black Looks*, 151)

On a par with hooks' argument, Butler maintains that Livingston's "white Jewish lesbian from Yale" status is in stark contrast with the voguers' status quo, presenting her documentation of ball culture as the vehicle of desire that promises to rescue voguers from marginal oblivion and lead them to worldwide recognition (*Bodies that Matter*, 133–35).[23] In these readings of *Paris Is Burning*, one comes to realize that inasmuch as the vogue scene came into the cultural forefront, it did so by means of exoticization, being presented as not an ideal, albeit significantly glossed-over culture whose lifestyle celebrated the convergence of sexual, racial, and ethnic Otherness. Livingston's gaze into the spectacular stage presence of the voguers and its further juxtaposition of it with their problematic offstage daily life led to idolizing the glamour of vogue and importantly shaped the reception of queer African American and Latinx communities. Its glorification of balls' life-style and voguers' breakthrough success, not to mention its inability to conceal the performers' wide internalization of the 1980s American materialist ethos and suburban life aspirations, seem to obscure the parameters under which the documentary lays focus on the subversive edge of vogue. Ultimately, *Paris Is Burning* provided clear glimpses of the scene's future engagement with, if deep submerge in, the mainstream pop industry, which, in turn, capitalized on it.

This is the precise axis around which Madonna's "Vogue" revolves as well. Its Old Hollywood-inspired video featured Madonna dancing and striking poses among voguers, while her Gaultier conic bra left its own imprint on her fashion experimentations and has time and again stood synonymous with her icon. Significantly, Jose Gutierez Xtravaganza and Luis Xtravaganza, members of the renowned House of Xtravaganza, choreographed "Vogue" and subsequently assisted Madonna in the creation and staging of her *Blond Ambition World Tour*, as explained in the tour's documentary, *Truth or Dare*. The artist's collaboration with the Xtravaganza duo was a declared proof of Madonna's close liaison with the underground queer scene. Similarly with Livingston's documentary, though, the immense popularity of "Vogue" and its trend-setting choreography bespoke of Madonna's blatant exploitation of a subcultural expression for lucrative goals. Her pre-vogue plundering of Hispanic and Black culture already burdened her with a history of cultural appropriations, which "Vogue" seemed to pile on, despite it being cocreated by actual members of ball culture. The song was brought over into the pop music market conveying an all-inclusive "Strike a pose/ There's nothing to it" message. Although the discourse of the lyrics might appear egalitarian, it carries a subtext that in fact erases the ethnic and racial nuances that gave birth to the practice of voguing in the first place. The lyrics "It makes no difference if you're black or white/ If you're a boy or a girl" along with the overwhelmingly White profile of both Madonna and the Hollywood stars name-dropped throughout the songtext seem to perpetuate the singer's "blond ambition" behind her alleged affiliation with the cultures her project cites from. Nevertheless, in Madonna's contemporary performances of "Vogue," it becomes evident that the artist did not actually strip voguing off its cultural markers, but, rather, managed to fit herself along its evolution, creating thus a legacy that has been mutually preserved by its initial creators and "Madonna," the icon, alike.

Being one of her signature songs, "Vogue" is almost always included in every one of Madonna's tour stage. For each tour, the song is appropriately reinvented to match the show's aesthetics, yet there are certain characteristics that remain stable and manage to preserve its camp philosophy when performed. Flair and pomposity along with the inevitably extravagant wardrobe and the gender-fluid playfulness are integral in every performance. Two more key constituents that camp infuses into vogue are retromania and intertextuality, further proving the point that camp on stage has to address the audience's familiarity as regards the position of the performance and the performer, of course, into the world of pop. The *Sticky & Sweet* rendition of "Vogue," for instance, places the performance of the song in the Pimp segment of the show, which is "a mash-up of 1920s deco and modern gangster style" (H. Brown). The musical production of the song contains elements of the singer's duet with Justin Timberlake, "4 Minutes", and Timbaland's "Give It to Me", two chart-toppers of their respective years that attribute a sonic contemporaneity to "Vogue".[24] As far as wardrobe is concerned, Madonna and her dance troupe are dressed in black leather-and-lace couture, a highly stylized approach of S&M attire. What should not go unnoticed here is that the conceptualization of "Vogue's" wardrobe is an onstage nod to Kylie Minogue. Minogue had previously included "Vogue" in her *Showgirl: The Homecoming Tour* (in 2006–07), in a performance also approached with an Art Deco and S&M aesthetic. By acknowledging Kylie's tribute, Madonna's response to cite *Showgirl's* fashion was not simply an act of borrowing. The intertextuality of the performance highlights the importance of camp to be shared on the diva stage as a means of targeting same audiences: here, queer audiences.

In addition to that, Madonna's body invites queer readings. The execution of a vogue choreography requires sharp movements motioned by swift, flexible hands that are mainly used to frame the performer's face as if posing for a photo shoot. In the beginning of the performance, Madonna follows a ritualistic routine that sees her suggestively putting her hand microphone in her underwear so as to release her hands for her solo voguing act. As was the case with the electric guitar in the *Confessions Tour*, here again the artist plays in double entendres: the microphone is used as a penile substitute, a dildo, and is left protruding through her underwear while she is executing her solo. Unlike the guitar position that allowed Madonna to usurp a masculine position of power, the microphone as dildo here camps up the performance in a rather different way. To flaunt her microphone/penis is to highlight the plasticity of the phallus in a genderfuck effect. June Reich argues that "[g]enderfuck, as a mimetic, subversive performance, simultaneously traverses the phallic economy and exceeds it" (264). The writer adds that "[t]he play of masculine and feminine on the body and/as the text, subverts the possibility of possessing a unified subject position" (264). Leich allocates subversive power to the genderfuck praxis of the dildo as this exists within lesbian sexual performances of butch-femme role-play. Madonna toys with the sexual conventions of queer sex in a rather risqué manner, further binding her vogue performance as well as her own persona with camp poetics. The genderfuck effect foregrounds queer subjectivity through Madonna in the camp union of vogue's effeminacy—as connotative of the effeminate queer—with the dildo signifier—as derivative of lesbian sexual practice.

The artist managed to effectively repeat the exact genderfuck effect in the performance of "Vogue" for the *MDNA Tour*, which brought the reality of the spectacle in collision with the actual reality. "Vogue" was the opening act for the tour's Masculine/Feminine segment and, appropriately, the whole act played on gender. Introducing the segment was a video interlude of Madonna reenacting "Justify My Love." As in the original video of the early 1990s song, Madonna is seen performing a stripping act inside a hotel room. She is playing with the camera lens, at times inviting the voyeuristic gaze, while at others deflecting it from her body back to the viewer, using props such as a magnifying glass, a mirror, and a mask. Having established exhibition and voyeurism as its central themes, the segment transitions into "Vogue," whose gender spectacle is now placed in the already imposed mystique of the section. The way gender is exhibited in the performance alludes to an act of exploring one's curiosity. The set is built on black-and-white visuals with the lighting simulating flashing cameras. Also dressed in black-and-white attire, dancers appear in drag—some of them with their faces covered—and start striking poses in sync with the flashing lights. Madonna emerges carrying the mask that appeared in the preceding video. What is interesting to pay attention to here is her costume: she sports a suit-and-tie ensemble combined with a Gaultier-designed corset with conic bustier that exaggerates an hourglass body figure. Her combed-up hairstyle and makeup in combination with the suit make an apparent allusion to Marlene Dietrich's androgynous style, while the corset is worn over the suit like an exoskeleton.

Reading this act as the ideal host for a gender-bending performance would indeed be an understatement. Madonna draws power both from her fashionista icon via the cone bra and from Dietrich's camp icon, whose heterosexual profile was not only time and again questioned, but her style exemplified the lesbian chic of the 1920s. Here, Madonna underlines femininity as purely stylistic to be worn as an exoskeleton—and all of that firmly positioned within "Vogue's" drag spectacle. The apparent genderfuck effect through dragging and voguing exists here in symbiosis with a tradition of camp manifest through the signifiers of Dietrich and the cone bra as well as the dramatics of drag and vogue per se. It is an extravaganza baptized in camp and an epitomical showcase of ball culture. The performance does not hold back from overplaying the camp factor to such a degree that it eventually manages to traverse the show's reality. As a matter of fact, in February 2016, four years after the *MDNA* showcase, the Sydney Gay and Lesbian Mardi Gras paid a video tribute to Madonna that featured two hundred dancers in a classic "Vogue" routine. According to *Attitude*'s Ben Kelly, "the Mardi Gras organisers say it is 'a heartfelt tribute in recognition and respect of Madonna's support for our LGBTQI communities throughout her career'". For the performance, "the dancers were accompanied by a Madonna impersonator dressed in one of the *MDNA Tour* outfits [...] Also featured in the video are some drag queens performing 'Express Yourself' and a group of children who recreated the 'Material Girl' video" (Kelly). Instances like the aforementioned tribute reveal how Madonna's icon has been contributive in the socio-artistic evolution of queer culture worldwide. Moreover, despite the iconic aura of the original performance of "Vogue," the Mardi Gras dancers recreate a relatively recent reinvention of it, that is, the 2012 tour version, proving Madonna's enduring appeal to and cultural communication with queer audiences.

As has been stated earlier in this work, camp has to be treated contextually. Reception of diva camp—here, Madonna's camp—may vary depending on sociopolitical context. The *MDNA* rendition of "Vogue" was indeed an iconic moment for the Australian LGBTQ+ community and was certainly not out of context. At the time, Madonna's *Rebel Heart Tour* was on the road and was about to visit the Australian territory for the first time in 23 years (the last tour which did so was *The Girlie Show* in 1993). It was the buzz around Madonna's highly promoted and anticipated tour in Australia that gave the Mardi Gras organizers the opportunity to host the specific tribute by celebrating Madonna's tradition of tour performances in light of her arrival. The sharing of Madonna's camp appears to be at home in the Australian community's perception of queer culture. Conversely, the same performance and show received quite the opposite welcome in the tour's stop in Russia in August 2012. Following the political turbulence around the guerilla performances of feminist punk band Pussy Riot, who fervently opposed Vladimir

Putin's anti-LGBTQ+ policy and were due to face the court of law at the time, Madonna voiced her support both for the band's political art and for the Russian LGBTQ+ community. The tour show was met with conservative criticism for being a "gay propaganda" that morally contradicted traditional Russian values.[25] The alleged homosexuality-promoting show was decried by the Russian Orthodox Church, while the US embassy in Russia issued a warning for possible eruption of violence outside the concert (Elder, "Russia Passes Law"). In considering locality here, it becomes clear that reception within both the Australian "Vogue" tribute and the Russian anti-queer atmosphere points to camp's inescapably queer-inflected nature. This brings me back to the argument that vogue and, by extrapolation, camp's gender play is indeed an explicitly queer praxis and language that is recognized for what it is. Madonna's performance, thus, politicizes this specific aspect of "Vogue," which is conspicuous precisely because of its inextricable association with the queering of gender and its assertive poetics of flaunting.

Regarding vogue culture, such instances are apt demonstration of how pop culture has come to shape the history of a marginal art form and its surrounding experiences. Despite being antithetical in their reception of vogue's camp, both incidents have come to filter its queer language through Madonna's icon. Madonna may have initially appropriated vogue from the ballroom culture, but she is currently an inseparable part of its history. As a result, she can (re)generate camp, which is solely based on her own iconic legacy. Most recently, the *Rebel Heart Tour* included two vogue performances fueled by Madonna's camp treatment of Catholicism and Hispanic culture, respectively. The first performance was a mash-up of "Vogue" with the *Rebel Heart* track "Holy Water", for which female dancers dressed as nuns performed a pole-dancing routine with Madonna fondling their bodies; the performance culminated with male dancers joining them to simulate an orgy-like version of Leonardo da Vinci's *Last Supper*. The second performance was not based on "Vogue," but it featured a vogue choreography for the song "Living for Love". The song was remixed to acquire a house-music vibe and its staging was a reenactment of the music video, in which a *traje-de-luces*-clad Madonna appeared as a matador fighting minotaur-resembling dancers. The vogue routine here bears a feminist subtext as well with Madonna inhabiting the traditionally male subject position of the bullfighter and with her symbolic slaughtering of the aggressive minotaurs. Considering the singer's lesbian-esque flirtation with the nuns and her campification of the matador figure, one can argue that, despite the fact that Madonna seems creatively derivative as regards her drawing from an already exhaustive referential pool, vogue serves as a constitutive basis in highlighting her camp(ed) tradition. Voguing offers its camped-up body language to queer Madonna's approach of the Catholic and Hispanic performances, successfully energizing the acts with her theatrics of gender.

In seeing how vogue and, by extension, camp praxes vitalize the diva stage, one has to be constantly aware of the means by which these praxes are materialized. As part of popular culture and spectacle consumption, divas' reproduction of camp is and will inevitably be a mass-mediated commodity. Speaking about Madonna's cultural transactions with African American culture and her seemingly subversive gender politics in the early 1990s, hooks has argued that "Madonna is not breaking with any white supremacist, patriarchal *status quo;* she is endorsing and perpetuating it" (*Black Looks*, 163, original emphasis). The critic has also added that Madonna's "white girl" profile "is that position of outsider that enables her to colonize and appropriate black experience for her own opportunistic ends even as she attempts to mask her acts of racist aggression as affirmation" (159). The artist's relationship with queer culture seems to reiterate patterns of identity colonization and cultural appropriation. As a matter of fact, this argument in part stands valid for other queer icons, such as Kylie Minogue and Lady Gaga, whose cultural relationship with queer culture is one of transaction, as well. However, one has to consider a counterargument to hooks' view: first of all, cultures do not only belong to insiders, especially if we think of today's global sharing of cultures across all forms of media; and, second, the commodification of a culture is a two-way process that equally concerns producers and receivers of culture. Performers like Madonna and Kylie may indeed appropriate or borrow from queer culture as outsiders, but this process is not something that queer consumers do not approve. Had it been otherwise, we would not be talking of celebratory acquiescence, but of unsettling disdain against the said appropriations. Quite the contrary, as the Sydney Mardi Gras tribute indicates, queer audiences sanction this cultural exchange between divas and queer praxes, simply because divas are also an inextricable and revered component of their culture. In fact, divas' pedestal-placed position within queer culture proves that as much as they rummage through its practices for inspiration, they too are being used and consumed, in response, as spectacles.

With reference to vogue and divas' interaction with ball culture, Derek Auguste, also known as Jamel Prodigy, a member of the legendary House of Prodigy, underlines how important the contribution of gay icons has been for the scene. In an interview I conducted with the artist, he explains that

> the exposure that artists, like Lady Gaga and FKA Twigs, have created for the ballroom kids is doing amazing things [...] They can actually think what they've been doing and turn it into dollars; they can turn it into fashion; they can turn it into a career. And those are the things we were told that we couldn't do younger as creative artists. (Prodigy)

THE MUSIC DIVA SPECTACLE

It is not coincidental that the careers of contemporary vogue performers, such as Benjamin Milan, Leiomy Maldonado, or Prodigy, have at some point been propelled through their collaboration with pop music artists, as was the case with prominent scene figures, including Jose Xtravaganza and Willi Ninja, in the 1990s. Prodigy even attests to the fact that not only voguing Houses still retain strong kinship among them, but also that some of them are even strictly developed as production companies—the Haus of Gaga stands exemplary of that. Here is exactly where the line between politics and spectacle is blurred. For, performers may seem to capitalize on subcultural praxes, yet they offer the communities a much-needed visibility by sharing and disseminating their culture. As Dick Hebdige explicates:

> As soon as the original innovations which signify "subculture" are translated into commodities and made generally available, they become "frozen." Once removed from their private contexts by the small entrepreneurs and big fashion interests who produce them on a mass scale, they become codified, made comprehensible, rendered at once public property and profitable merchandise. (357)

The writer accurately describes the lapse of subcultures into fixity, once they become commodities. However, it is the codification and comprehensibility that help in rendering subcultures visible and widely understood. The subcultures' permafrost state certainly drives any counter-dominant force that may derive from the liminal margins into conformism, as part of an assimilative process that diffuses the said force into a broader mainstream site of reference. However, the subcultural residue left becomes a time-resisting mark that is and will be acknowledged for what it is, becoming, thus, an era-traversing signifier, a fixed cultural insignia.

Madonna's case proves that as much as she appropriated/borrowed from the culture of vogue, she did not manage to render the culture frozen. She did place her icon, though, inside its queer history by means of citation and by rules of the pop industry. Nevertheless, vogue's democratic perception of a gender-bent reality is a resilient queer signifier that can never be obliterated in the processes of appropriation or decontextualization. To appropriate a culture after all does not equal its demise *qua* some original authenticity. On the contrary, vogue and ballroom culture currently enjoy a central place within queer culture and appeal to a variety of audiences. Prodigy adds: "We don't have to play victim anymore. Our story has far surpassed *Paris Is Burning*. We're here and we're here to stay". Furthermore, the existence of vogue within the touring spectacles of divas establishes a global network of audiences who approve and celebrate the diva camp legacy on a par with its queer politics and poetics. It is interesting, though, to lay focus on issues of agency in relation to the position of the diva and her power to channel this legacy. As we will see in the next chapter, divas' production and exposition of camp is indeed a multiauthored process that, among other things, has to rely on the audiences' familiarity with a diva's ever-shifting icon.

NOTES

1. For further reading, consider Chasin; Susan Faludi's *Backlash: The Undeclared War Against American Women* and, Stuart Hall's "What Is This 'Black' in Black Popular Culture?".
2. Drake's repulsive response to Madonna's impromptu kiss generated negative comments from social media users, who derided Madonna's inappropriate-for-her-age behavior (Good).
3. The song and its accompanying video have been placed under scrutiny, with academics hailing its content as "truly avant-garde" (Paglia, *Sex*, 4), which manages to highlight Madonna's "autorepresentation" and "polysexual eroticism" (Whiteley, *Women and Popular Music*, 149, 200) and her ability to occupy "multiple sexual subject positions" (Robertson, *Guilty Pleasures*, 131). However, its debut raised many conservative eyebrows because of its porn-tinged content.
4. *OUT's* Christopher Glazek suggests that "Flynn introduced the teenage Madonna to a global culture that reached beyond the suburban narrowness of her Michigan upbringing. 'He would bring me to museums [she admits]. He also brought me to the first gay disco in Detroit, Menjo's'" (Glazek).
5. With regard to Monroe and Marie Antoinette, not to mention *Erotica*'s Mistress Dita, Madonna's personae, just like their archetypes, inhabit sites of sexual ambivalence, being thus a vital performative template for the artist's politics of female sexuality and gender parody.
6. As Frank explains,

    > Disco marked a radical departure from the organization, artistry, and sexuality of rock music. While rock music was a medium with an emphasis on the relationship between performer and fans, disco was organized in terms of dancers and recorded music [...] As well, the musical sign of rock music par excellence, the guitar, was no longer predominant or even present. (291)

7. In her essay "Disco Knights: Hidden Heroes of the New York Dance Music Underground," Carol Cooper makes a reference to female disc jockey Sharon White, a prominent figure of the 1970s cult of DJ, who was discovered by producers at the Sahara, a lesbian club (162).
8. For more, consider the following articles: "Madonna's Rome Concert Outrages Vatican," https://people.com/celebrity/madonnas-rome-concert-outrages-vatican/; and "Madonna's Rome show crosses religious leaders," https://www.cbc.ca/news/entertainment/madonna-s-rome-show-crosses-religious-leaders-1.615273. Accessed July 14, 2021.

THE MUSIC DIVA SPECTACLE

9. In his seminal work "The Culture Industry," Theodor Adorno argues that "[t]he fetish character of music produce its own camouflage through the identification of the listener with the fetish" (40). Taking into consideration that we are not talking here about the "listener" as the individual who solely takes pleasure in music, but a live audience, it is only reasonable that the identification with the fetish is amplified; for, music, icon/performer, and performance, being in close contact with the audience, enhance the fetishistic pleasure.

10. Specifically, some lines highlight the Dolls as "An imitation from New York/You're made in Japan in cheese and chalk"; "You think it's swell playing in Max's Kansas"; "You're just a pile of shit/You're coming to this/Ya poor little faggot" (The Sex Pistols, *New York*). Max's Kansas City, a hip nightclub in 1970s Manhattan notorious for its clientele (Madonna included), cannot escape the Pistols' critique either.

11. In other guitar-led acts, especially in her *Sticky & Sweet Tour*, Madonna uses her guitar as a penile substitute to simulate sex in her rock rendition of "Hung Up," and masturbation in her performance of "Human Nature," to a similar effect.

12. Attending the annual Met Gala in May 2016, Madonna stirred up controversy for choosing to dress in a sheer gown that had her breasts and buttocks exposed. Acknowledging that, Madonna updated her Instagram account, stating:

> We have fought and continue to fight for civil rights and gay rights around the world. When it comes to Women's rights we are still in the dark ages. My dress at the Met Ball was a political statement as well as a fashion statement. The fact that people actually believe a woman is not allowed to express her sexuality and be adventurous past a certain age is proof that we still live in an age-ist and sexist society. I have never thought in a limited way and I'm not going to start. (Harwood)

13. For more information on the homosexual male body and the club life, consider Martin Levine's *Gay Macho: The Life and Death of the Homosexual Clone*.

14. Carol Cooper also accounts that

> gay discos, black mainstream clubs, fashion-trend dens, "new wave" discos, and hip hop parties all squared off against one another during the early eighties. A cult deejay affiliated with a particular club felt constant pressure not only to reinforce his reputation but to protect his steady gig. (161)

> With regard to the roller-skating performance, Cooper suggests that Gail King, a renowned female DJ of the 1970s scene, "had formed a rollerskating performance group that would tour the local rinks for fun and profit," proving, first of all, that women, despite being numerically less than men, were quite influential for the disc jockey cult (163). Cooper adds that, thanks to King, "[r]oller disco was a major trend among dating-age blacks and Hispanics, and it took a particular ear to choose the perfect records for skating routines"

(163). As part of the *Confessions* album promotion, Madonna had released a video for the song "Sorry," in which she had presented her roller dancing skills. Although "Sorry" was performed during the Bedouin segment, it lacked the roller skating choreography. Instead, parts of the video's roller dance routine were appropriately brought over into this final interlude.

15. The writer asserts that

> the technological expertise found in "Music" is responsible for contributing to a style that is camp. Elements of digital editing and computer-based approaches to layering one track over the other are constantly daring and yet cheeky. Often to the point of being over-decorative, it is as if the mix liberates artistic expression from taking itself too seriously. (*Dragging Out Camp*, 10)

16. Not to mention here the already existing camp play in and queer projections of the song's video, with Sasha Baron Cohen's Omega-male "Ali G" juxtaposed to Madonna's "lesbian goddess" glam image.

17. In his review of *The Girlie Show Tour*, Richard Corliss explains that for the show's opening performances of "Erotica" and "Fever,"

> the proscenium stage is fronted with red drapery suitable for a Louisiana bordello; the title promises and delivers burlesque. But burlesque in the older sense of parody, travesty, impudent fun. There is humid sexuality at the start of the two-hour extravaganza (topless acrobat on a phallic pole, Madonna easing a whip past her crouch, dancers gyrating at automassage), but it soon gives way to simpler, sunnier images. (21)

18. The history of women on stage has walked alongside the cult of true womanhood as this can be traced in the nineteenth-century melodrama genre. In his work *Horrible Prettiness: Burlesque and American Culture*, Robert Allen explains that "[t]he melodramatic heroine was, to a large extent, the stage embodiment of the 'true' woman, whose spirit pervaded sentimental novels and sermons alike, and whose image was reproduced in paintings, prints, and magazines" (84). The tradition of melodrama, though, was in juxtaposition with the one upheld in burlesque. Allen argues that burlesque "presents a model for the sexual objectification of women in popular entertainment. Thus, it can also be seen as a progenitor of modern pornography" (27). Burlesque has come to connote "the exotic, displayed female body" (26). Hence, the stage has traditionally been a site where female subjectivity was either portrayed as angelical and stripped off of her political power or as an exoticized object to be looked at. Arguably, both images have made their way deep into popular culture, which celebrates femininity and encourages that women be worshiped as such. For further reading, also consider Laura Mulvey's seminal essay on "Visual Pleasure and Narrative Cinema" and Robertson's *Guilty Pleasures*.

19. This impersonation is based on the image of Marilyn Monroe from the performance of "Diamonds Are a Girl's Best Friend" for *Gentlemen Prefer Blondes*. The scene of Monroe in the iconic pink dress singing an ode to materialism might as well be the campiest moment of her career, offering her up as a camp idol to be consumed, appropriated, and emulated. Madonna, Kylie Minogue, and Christina Aguilera, among others, recreated the particular scene in referential acts that captivate Monroe's glamorous femininity.

20. The sampling of Le Grand's song is a nod to Madonna's home state of Michigan. The house music tinges in "Music" rely on Madonna's affiliation with the respective dance scenes of New York and Detroit, respectively, while alluding to the artist's early career steps in local clubs, hence the pun created with Indeep's lyrics: "Last night a DJ saved my life/And if it wasn't for the music/I don't know what I would do."

21. Kylie Minogue has incorporated vogue in most of her tour shows, while Katy Perry paid homage to Madonna's song itself for her *Prismatic World Tour* (in 2014–15) in a vogue showcase that played a camp twist on the musical *Cats*. Other notable diva vogue showcases, to mention a few, include Lady Gaga's performance of "Black Jesus + Amen Fashion" for the *Born This Way Ball* tour (in 2012–13), Rihanna's dance segment for her *Anti World Tour* (in 2016), as well as FKA Twigs' hosted vogue presentations for her *Congregata* shows (in 2015), including a battle showcase among well-known voguers for her New York gigs.

22. Houses in ballroom culture are the collectives formed by voguers. Their structure has been of great interest primarily because its formation resembles a biological familial home: a House consists of a Mother, a Father, and the Children. The collectives are often named after eponymous fashion houses, such as the House of Prada and the Houses of St. Laurent. For a concise account, consider Marlon Bailey's work *Butch Queens up in Pumps: Gender, Performance, and Ballroom Culture in Detroit*, Livingston's documentary (*Paris Is Burning*), and my article "Strike a Pose, Forever: The Legacy of Vogue and Its Re-contextualization in Contemporary Camp Performances. https://doi.org/10.4000/ejas.11771. Consider also Ryan Murphy's FX series *Pose* (2018–2021) and HBO reality competition web-series *Legendary* (2020–present) which both deal with ball culture and the Houses.

23. Harper's critique corroborates Butler's reading of Livingston's authorship, arguing that

> while the impact of *Paris Is Burning* may depend on how successfully it renders ball culture generally recognizable the intervention thus effected is registered specifically as that of the filmmaker, who is accordingly interpelled as a figure of some social standing, rather than that of the queens in the drag-ball circuit, who clearly are not. (99)

24. Both songs are produced by Timbaland and Timberlake; "Give It to Me" was a collaboration of Timbaland with Timberlake and Nelly Furtado, while Madonna's *Hard Candy*, which the tour promotes, was produced by both men almost in its totality. One could argue

that the Pimp segment pays musical homage to *Hard Candy*'s hip-hop-based musical producers, including productions by Pharrell Williams and Kanye West as well as a noteworthy reference to Britney Spears' R&B sounds of the time.

25. Pussy Riot's activism and Madonna's support for the group were part of the political background connected to Vladimir Putin's policy to regulate LGBTQ+ cultural promotion and maintain traditional Russian family values. The political turmoil culminated a year later, in June 2013, with the Russian government passing the LGBT Propaganda Law according to which any "non-traditional sexual relations" promoted from any source, either media and intermaterial or gay pride rallies, would be federally punishable (Elder, "*Russia Passes Law*").

2

LaLaLas and WowWowWows:
Approaching Kylie Minogue's Extravaganzas

Boy George: "[Kylie] put the amp in camp!"

Kylie Minogue: "I put the amp in camp? Maybe I put the K in kamp."
(GLAAD Media Awards)

I change characters when I do a photo-shoot. I'm like the eight-year old with the dressing-up box. It's kind of avoiding being me—rather than being captured, I become a new character and let that take over.
(Kylie Minogue, cited in Nigel and Stantley-Clarke, *Kylie Naked: A Biography*, 190)

Introducing Kylie Minogue for the GLAAD Media Awards ceremony in 2014, Boy George highlighted the singer's advocacy for the LGBTQ+ community. Kylie then proceeded with a speech that referred to her relationship with the community throughout her 30-year-long career. The Australian performer's music is widely known in the Eurasian territory, while over the past two decades she has crossed over to American audiences mainly as a gay icon. From playing popular gay clubs, such as London's G-A-Y and New York's Splash, to headlining Pride parades, such as the 2012 Sydney Gay and Lesbian Mardi Gras and the 2018 New York Gay Pride, Kylie has made her icon synonymous with contemporary gay culture. In particular, her audience nowadays mostly comprises gay men. Essentialist as this might sound, Kylie's demographic results from and attests to the *modus operandi* of "pink money," and despite claiming that she has denied offers by record companies to market herself toward the "pink" direction (Geen), the economic and cultural core of her icon arguably blooms within and nourishes in return a "pink" market. While Kylie asserts how she has been adopted by the gay community (Geen), this pronounced relationship is certainly more complex.

Revisiting the diva worship pattern, it becomes clear that the "adoption" of Kylie abides by a vast camp tradition that sees gay men glorifying (heterosexual) female celebrities. Upon acknowledging their gay icon status, the latter respond by partially or completely (re)orienting their praxis of spectacle toward their allotted direction.

As a case in point, Kylie's stage presence and persona serve as a fecund ground where gay politics and the subject matter of camp converge. Boy George may have recognized the amp in Kylie's camp, yet Kylie's spontaneous, albeit accurate response that she has put the K in kamp acknowledges a distinct trademark and personal devotion to her production and preservation of it.[1] In terms of artistry, Kylie's sound mostly inhabits a generic dance zone, ranging from Euro-pop and electropop to synth-pop and disco, while her limited balladry consists of dramatic piano-based pieces or trip-hop productions. In what appears to be a surplus of ultra-pop sound, one finds Kylie's cheerful and erotically teasing lyrics that portray themes commonly found in contemporary pop songtexts, such as partying/nightclub life, attraction, love, and sex. Her image, however, is the key constituent in fusing sound and lyrics into a coagulation of pop camp as perceived by her contemporaries, including Madonna, Pet Shop Boys, and Eurythmics. Alternating between roles—perhaps the quintessential camp component—Kylie has moved from the girl-next-door profile, established by her role as Charlene in the Australian TV series *Neighbours* (between 1986–88) and her first singles ("Locomotion," "I Should Be So Lucky"), to the sexy adult ("Better the Devil You know," "Shocked"), to the defining sex symbol ("Spinning Around," "Can't Get You Out of My Head," "Slow"), to the cult diva ("Wow," "All the Lovers," "Dancing"). The longevity of her career has allowed Minogue to play with profiles without, however, deviating subversively from the pop mold of image reinvention. Unlike Madonna, whose initial transformations were promoted via controversial identity politics, Kylie's metamorphoses are rather limited within the flexible marketability of her persona and display an apolitical devotion to reinvention. This is precisely, though, where the (c)amp of Kylie resides.

Prior to exploring this argument further, it is important to posit Kylie's reinvention tactics in juxtaposition with that of Madonna's and the influence the latter exerted upon her. Image reinvention and role-playing have been key concepts in the construction of pop icons, especially after the rise of music television established image as equally important to sound. Madonna's cultural impact in the 1980s helped shape the contemporary music stage not only with regard to reinvention but also in terms of sound and image, performance, sex, and fandom. Her politics of gender and sexuality, as tantamount to her chameleonic and indeed rapid changes of style, rendered her reinventions rather fluid in nature and, by extrapolation, allowed her to glide though fixed identities.[2] Therefore, Minogue's first appearance in the pop scene in the later years of the 1980s would inevitably be filtered through the already established and perhaps leading female performer of her time. Regarding camp, the key constituent that gender and identity are theatrically understood and performed is a core dynamic that permeates both artists' personae. In this sense, Kylie's refashioning of identity contains the same political dynamic that Madonna's camp has in its deconstructive qualities of gender. When I argue though that Kylie's reinventions are apolitical, it is not to adopt Sontag's view on the apolitical character of camp. By juxtaposing Kylie's camp with that of Madonna's, one sees that Madonna's camp accrues from an oppositional stance against an adversary as part of her political stage—as in her mocking inhabitance of the male rocker position (see Chapter 1), whereas Kylie's camp, as we will see shortly, makes no specific political statement against any sort of agency. As Marc Brennan argues,

> Kylie as a performer, like most pop performers, is about spectacle. What possibly makes her unique is the degree to which she is portrayed as having fun in her performances. It is this that in turn signifies a sense of innocence. (182)

Revisiting her own words in this chapter's epigraph, it is understood that Kylie's spectacular transformation is representative of her "innocent" play. Her camp thus stands for entertainment and escapism. It is a camp praxis that views the stage as a playground whereupon identities are part of its carnivalesque. This playground, however, through its allegedly apolitical innocence, can serve as a potent space of cultural critique since it invites layered readings that connect Kylie's diva performance with understandings of gendered mechanisms, queer art, and the erotics of the spectacle.

This aspect of camp that Kylie personifies is to a great degree a result of her collaboration with William Baker. Being her longtime creative director, her "gay husband" as she herself notes in her 2007 *White Diamond* documentary, Baker has played a significant role in Kylie's exportation of camp. It is important therefore to acknowledge Baker's sensibility and artistic taste behind the performer's profile and stage. In my interview with him, the director commented that his work with Kylie is in its base influenced by Madonna: "I think that everything in pop music done by a female [artist] is influenced by Madonna really" (W. Baker). Baker's perception of Kylie's persona is certainly mediated through and perhaps modified by the impact Madonna had had on him as a teenager: "If I hadn't seen *Blond Ambition* when I was at school, I don't think I would do what I do today, because that's what makes me want to do it. And that's what formed my way of looking at a show" (W. Baker). Evidently, Kylie's stage becomes more akin to Madonna's from the mid-1990s onward and, specifically, from the *Intimate and Live Tour* (in 1998) for which Baker is officially credited as the creative director. Baker extends the Madonna influence to the structure of Kylie's shows:

> The modern pop concert experience was created by [Madonna] really and her *Blond Ambition* show. That's what I think has become the template for the theatrical kind of pop show which is split into sections that pretty much everyone copies or everyone is inspired by. (W. Baker)[3]

Apart from the act-led composition of the shows, Baker notes that Kylie's stage fashion is another area that Madonna has influenced. His collaborations with the likes of Jean Paul Gaultier and Dolce & Gabbana have a prerequisite that Kylie's tour costumes bear the iconic flamboyance that Madonna's wardrobe has (W. Baker). To trace this supposed ubiquitousness of a Madonna-esque aesthetics over Kylie's stage is to conceptualize Baker's understanding of what constitutes an iconic spectacle and thus prefigure him as the artistic (gay) authority behind the spectacle of Kylie. In light of this and along the lines of camp production and reception, this chapter also examines the power of the gay male gaze upon the stage and body of the diva.

Drawing largely from the lush pool of burlesque and Classical Hollywood, but also paying homage to a tradition of camp iconicity, the tour shows of Kylie are the par-excellence ground wherein diva camp fully materializes. Kylie herself is a persona who embodies the poetics of diva worship within contemporary queer culture. Her queer and, more specifically, gay male audiences, not very dissimilar in demographic to those of Madonna, reveal a relationship with camp that is importantly different from past forms of diva worship. As Daniel Harris indicates:

> For gay men under the age of 40, the classic film star has become the symbolic icon of an oppressed early stage in gay culture in which homosexuals sat glued to their television sets feasting their eyes on reruns [...] For the contemporary homosexual, who prides himself on his emotional maturity and healthiness, the use of the diva to achieve romantic fulfillment through displacement is the politically repugnant fantasy of the self-loathing pansy whose dependence on the escapism of cinema must be ritually purged from his system. (22)

Although Harris's argument partly holds true considering gay men's pre-Stonewall engagement with Hollywood camp, the writer does not account on how contemporary gay culture has sought means of escapism elsewhere. As has been explicated earlier in this work, music divas have now largely replaced the model of the film star in the diva worship tradition. Contextually different from its predecessor, the music diva camp appeals to a generation of queer consumers who are generally more immersed in an open, ubiquitous, and self-conscious queer culture (at least by Western standards). Kylie's camp, for that matter, exemplifies more of a celebratory turn to diva worshipping, rather than a guilty pleasure of a vicarious identification. Undertaking thus an analysis of Kylie's tour stage from the *Showgirl: The Greatest Hits Tour* (in 2005) and *Showgirl: The Homecoming Tour* (in 2006–07), to the *KylieX2008* tour (in 2008),[4] to the magnum opus of *Aphrodite: Les Folies Tour* (in 2010) to *Kiss Me Once Tour* (between 2014–15), and to the most recent *Golden Tour* (between 2018–19), this chapter examines how Kylie's persona and stage actively materialize camp as a cultural form of entertainment that reflects and simultaneously nourishes contemporary queer culture's ideals, mentalities, and expressions with regard to the queer self and community.

The cult of the showgirl

As a pop phenomenon, Kylie has significantly evaded academic scrutiny and this is evident in the limited literature referring to her persona and stage. Gerardo Rodríguez-Salas and Sara Martín-Alegre ascribe this noninterest to the overemphasis laid on Madonna's body of work (157). The writers argue that Madonna's provocative persona and phallic femininity stand in stark contrast to what Kylie embodies: "[Kylie] has been practically ignored by academia due to the generalised perception that she represents precisely the kind of bland femininity that Madonna challenges" (157). In the same vein, Lee Barron underlines that "[s]ince the arrival of Madonna, and the resultant critical and academic interest, women in pop are often unfairly compared to this post-feminist juggernaut" (178). Essentially, according to the writer,

> Pop princesses, unlike Madonna, do not always attempt to be subversive, they often don't write their own lyrics, they may not challenge the male gaze, and they rarely upset established institutions. In short, pop princesses give cultural critics very little to write about. Easy to denigrate, difficult to celebrate. (178)

What both Rodríguez/Martin's and Barron's arguments imply is that Kylie's ultra-feminine persona fails to be radical in the performative manner that Madonna realizes and, for that reason, she poses a non-threat to systemic gender, thus dealing no analytic merit.

With that being said, theorization of Kylie's camp is apparently limited as well primarily because the artist's camp performance, when viewed in the context of stereotypical gender reiteration and, of course, under the always problematic rubric of the consumerist-bound nature of her pop spectacle, appears devoid of subversive potential. The surprisingly exiguous critical sources on Kylie's camp per se, which mostly argue in favor of camp's deconstructive qualities, limit their analysis to Kylie's postmodern stylizations of gender and those musical references of her that are rooted in disco and its frivolous aesthetics. Janice Miller makes a small reference to Kylie's camp as part of her case subject that is the camp act of Scissor Sisters.[5] Miller remains simplistic in reiterating Sheila Whiteley's generalized view of Minogue's Barbie-doll image and the rather unexamined argument that even Kylie herself "admits that her appeal to gay men is that they love to brush her hair and dress her up" (Whiteley, *Too Much*, 63). Elsewhere, Barron identifies Kylie's camp as an aspect of her disco revival for the *Light Years* album (in 2000) and rushes to define Camp Kylie as simply another coming-and-going phase in the performer's series of transformations (56–58). From a Deleuzian perspective, Sunil Manghani concentrates on the technical visuality of Minogue's tours and remains static in explaining how the post-*Intimate and Live* shows are a reminder of Kylie's camp homage to her gay following (253). The reason why these arguments cannot provide us with a comprehensive view of Kylie's camp appeal is because there is the need to solely attribute deconstructive power to camp as a device of subversion, whereas its function as a communicative discourse and performed tradition remains practically unstated—or, in the case of Manghali, rather vaguely defined as homage.

As has been previously argued (Bergman 13), camp in its clandestine phase was employed as a secret language of "passing" among homosexual men who dared not risk exposure. In this context, camp was more of an intra-communal code of communication that brought gay men closer (through a common identification, for example, with the pleasure derived from sharing knowledge on a Hollywood melodrama or reciting lines from the repertoire of a camp icon like Bette Davis), rather than a radical form of politically queer antithesis against the heteronormative grammar of dominant power. Richard Dyer supports that:

> Culture is not for the main part done in order to say something or make a point, and queer culture is in this no exception. The processes of cultural production in Western society are primarily concerned with pleasure, with making things that are enjoyable and giving vent to the need to speak, to express and communicate. (*Culture of Queers* 9)

To try to read Kylie's camp as a subversive form of gender parody will only take us so far as arguing on her bland masquerade of hyperfemininity, which to a great deal remains compromised. To revisit, however, her exposition of camp as a form of shared pleasure is to, first, highlight her poetics of camp with the resilient quality of a performed cultural tradition, and, second, approach and explain the appeal of camp to her queer audiences less from a strictly polemical position, as expressed by those who usually rush to crown camp's politics with queer subversion, and more from an emotion-based one.

First and foremost, in its exposition of camp, the stage of Kylie has accommodated a variety of queer-associated acts, scenes, and covers from the musical canon of gay culture. As Kylie's showcases demonstrate, disco, the paradigmatic gay musical experience, remains a primary source of artistic citation for the diva stage. Kylie has made her name synonymous with disco not only in her late 1980s beginnings, when the echoes of the era were still audible, but, most significantly, in her millennial comeback with the *Light Years* album and most recently with her album *Disco* (in 2020), a quintessential homage to the scene. The *Light Years* era, specifically, marks Kylie's departure from the indie-based sound of deConstruction Records and her complete turn to dance-pop productions.[6] Importantly, *Lights Years* and its lead single "Spinning Around" revamped and repopularized the disco sound and aesthetic, thus recruiting a new generation of queer audiences into Minogue's fanbase. As a result, each one of her tours reserves at least one section dedicated to Kylie's disco roots. With regard to continually staging disco acts within the tour shows, Baker explains how he understands the sound of disco as a "fundamentally gay music" (W. Baker). Upon acknowledging its origins from the gay clubs and its connection to Kylie, the director feels the need to balance between fitting disco acts within the shows without, however, risking turning Kylie into "a nostalgia artist" (W. Baker). "How many times can you re-do this?" he wonders (W. Baker), even though he is aware he has creatively differentiated every new act from a past one without deviating from the camp essence of disco. As evident in Kylie's tour history, acts incorporating disco are not just a plain homage to the era, but a synthesis of camp spectacle that is mainly based on camp's power of intertextuality.

Examining the artist's tour acts, we see the Beach Party segment of the *KylieX2008* tour attesting to Baker and Minogue's need to revitalize the theatrics of disco with an abundance of camp references. The segment begins with a video interlude featuring Kylie's dancers as semi-naked sailors whose accentuated poses and hypermasculine profile allude to the homoerotic art of Tom of Finland.[7] Kylie appears and starts flirting with the sailors on a deck, a reenactment of Quentin Crisp's scene from camp classic *The Naked Civil Servant*. Dressed in sequined nautical attire, Kylie is then propelled along with her crew via a deck-like prop onto the stage to perform "Loveboat" from *Light Years*. When producing the album in the late 1990s, Kylie described what she wanted it to sound like in four words: "poolside, beach, cocktails, and disco" (Brennan 181). Subsequently, the album was reviewed as "a shiny, sparkly, early noughties disco record" that has acquired a "camptastic" status (N. Levine). This is the precise camp feeling the specific segment cares to bring into the *X Tour*. Following "Loveboat" is a cover of Barry Manilow's "Copacabana" for which Kylie and her dancers recreate the actual narrative of the song.[8] Registered to the segment's tonality, "Copacabana" also draws distinct lines between the song's showgirl and Kylie's showgirl profile. The Beach Party concludes with the signature *Light Years* track, "Spinning Around," the song that preluded Kylie's millennial comeback and return to form. The performance takes place amidst the setting of a cocktail bar and palm trees that previously propped "Copacabana," thus effectively realizing both the theme of the segment and Kylie's joyous feeling of *Light Years*.

As much as Baker would like not to see Kylie becoming a nostalgia artist, the degree to which nostalgia informs her stage is far from dismissible. This is evident more soundly in 2018's *Golden Tour*. Supporting her homonymous album of the same year, which was partly recorded in Nashville and bears a felt country vibe, the tour envisions Kylie in a road trip setting, a staged excursion across landscapes and eras strongly reminiscent of American culture. Despite the fact that for this project Baker was not the creative director, Kylie along with her current director Rob Sinclair followed similar stage formulas that brand *Golden* with the diva's distinct camp flair. The show demonstrates a plethora of acts that simulate the American desert and highway, a dive bar setting as well as a biker rally. With apparent allusions to Dolly Parton, Kylie's performance has a personal tone that is further emphasized by the show's narrative arc of a life journey. Being a typical Kylie show, *Golden* also saves room for a proper disco act which here pays tribute to Studio 54 and is where Kylie's camp icon is at home. For the act, a number of dancers appear in drag, impersonating the club's most famous patrons, including Andy Warhol and Grace Jones, among others, while Kylie enters the stage in a sparkly golden dress, a nod to the promoted album, therefore establishing her own icon alongside those of the disco era. The said act was particularly stimulating for the artist who admitted that it actually inspired 2020's *Disco* (Minogue Apple Music 'DISCO' Interview). Though it is yet to be seen how the diva will approach a *Disco* tour in the future, it is certain that creatively she cannot deviate much from a retro-indulging project—possibly her own *Confessions Tour*—since this is also what her audiences expect from her. The decision to fully immerse herself in the camp of disco presupposes an embracing of a reality of entertainment that is long gone and is only preserved by means of nostalgia, as we already saw in Madonna's case.

Nevertheless, Kylie's showgirl persona is firmly embedded in the world of camp spectacle which means her acts, though nostalgic at times, are grounded with referential context. Camp after all, as a postmodern recycling and recyclable aesthetic, *is* nostalgia. Angela McRobbie argues that "[l]oss of faith in the future has produced a culture which can only look backwards and re-examine key moments of its own recent history with a sentimental gloss and a soft focus lens" (*Postmodernism*,

142). Arguing, however, against this Jamesonian "gloomy prognosis of the post-modern condition in this 'mass flight into nostalgia,'" the writer underlines that nostalgic acts are indeed capable of having depth and their pastiche exists in a rather celebratory character (142). Unlike postmodern pastiche, though, as Pamela Robertson argues, "camp redefines and historicizes [...] cultural products not just nostalgically but with a critical recognition of the temptation to nostalgia" (*Guilty Pleasures* 5).[9] Similarly with Madonna's retro showcases, Kylie's aforemen-tioned multilayered camp acts employ a poetics of nostalgia with semiotic depth without falling into mere pastiche, thus proving to be quite entertaining as well as instructive to her intergenerational queer fanbase. The *X Tour* references to the erotica of Tom of Finland and to Quentin Crisp as well as *Golden*'s simulation of Studio 54, for that matter, are culturally and chronologically relevant in the sense that although their status and history may be known only to specific connoisseurs of queer culture, Kylie revives and (re)popularizes them by fusing them with her stage and persona, thereby preserving their camp legacy. The nostalgia politics of her stage foreground Kylie's disco soundtracks as indispensable from the camp imagination, while her persona serves as the familiar instructor that guides her audiences through the layered iconicity. In order to effectively build on nostalgia, her mediating role requires a firmly established connection with the repository of camp, something that Kylie has achieved by bringing (part of) her own personal narrative into the dramaturgy of her stage.

Taking into consideration that the majority of history's camp icons embodied dramatic narratives of loss, death, and survival is to further approach Kylie's appeal as one. Queer culture entails a long history of pathologization that became inevitably inscribed both into queer subjectivity and into its ensuing social iden-tities. From the nineteenth-century "homosexual species" (Foucault 43) to the epi-demic propaganda of the 1980s (M. Levine), Western queer culture is permeated with discourses of a medicalized and fragile corporeality. Regarding gay men, Eve Kosofsky Sedgwick stresses that "[a] very specific association of gay male sexu-ality with tragic early death is recent, but the structure of its articulation is densely grounded in centuries of homoerotic and homophobic intertextuality" (210). Notions of homosexuality as pathologic and, specifically, the queer body as aber-rant exist within ideological patterns that have largely infiltrated popular culture and, by extension, queer culture, whose absorption of images is deeply socially and psychically associated with a tragic sense of reality and self.[10] As a result, popular culture icons adored by queer culture in part seem to foreground and perpetuate tragic narratives as central parts of their built iconic appeal. A broad history of queer icons attests to the aforementioned narratives that are more often than not cinematized into mythical proportions through the media and tabloid lens.[11]

Kylie's icon appeal has too, in part, relied on her personal tragic narrative of breast cancer. The artist was diagnosed in 2005 while touring *Showgirl* around Europe; as a result, the tour, which was scheduled to move on to Australia, had to be cancelled. Her diagnosis, which was immediately and massively made known to the public, led to an instant increase of broadcasts on breast cancer and health topics as well as mammogram bookings (Chapman et al.). Upon undergoing surgery and chemotherapy, Kylie went on a hiatus and decided to abstain from performing before resuming *Showgirl* in 2006. The revamped show, named *Showgirl: The Homecoming Tour*, mostly maintained elements of the previous show, but was also shaped from Kylie's cancer experience, especially in terms of production. The interludes were slightly extended to allow further rests, while the overall itinerary of the tour included short-term residencies in few Australian and British arenas, contrary to the wider geographical coverage of the 2005 version.[12] Accordingly, her onstage icon acquired a more professional and, perhaps, more nonchalant character regarding performance and kinesis. The fact the she had lost her hair while in treatment gave Baker and Minogue the opportunity to experiment further with her onstage outfits by alternating between wigs and headpieces and thus creating a rapid array of chameleonic images—an approach reminiscent of a Cher-esque aesthetic. The two-hour extravaganza saw Kylie changing into eight different characters, moving from her Vegas-inspired showgirl persona, to a cat-woman, to a torch singer, among others, before doing the encore in casual style with a simple hat that was finally taken off to reveal her post-chemotherapy pixie cut.

The symbolic final act of losing the hat as suggestive of the existence of a human being underneath the glittery costumes signifies Kylie's genuineness in front of her audiences. This is the central topic of *White Diamond*, the documentary that adumbrates the construction and itinerary of the *Homecoming Tour*—"a symbol to her recovery" (W. Baker)—and Kylie's personal post-cancer journey. Being the director, Baker felt that it was time to "rip the surface away" and go beyond the public's perception of her, namely her being "[a] result of *Neighbours*, 'I Should Be So Lucky,' Michael Hutchence,[13] gold hot pants,[14] 'Can't Get You Out of My Head,' cancer" (Minogue, *White Diamond*). *White Diamond* presented post-cancer Kylie as a highly professional, albeit fragile woman who manages to balance between the demands of her showbiz persona and be the ordinary person who runs barefoot on the beach. Despite Baker's attempt to peel off the surface, though, and present this everyday aspect of Kylie, the documentary rather rounds off the edges by sentimentalizing views on the artist through its cinematography and further emphasizing her feminine fragility—for example, through the sharp antithesis of the heavy costumes over her petite and still in-recovery body; or the scene of her being carried in Baker's arms following the interruption of one of her Manchester shows due to a respiratory infection.

Instead of allowing a deeper critical look into Kylie's life, *White Diamond* hardly rips any surface away, when, in reality, it seems to inflate the mythology around the showgirl. According to Rodríguez-Salas and Martín-Alegre, "this peculiar postmodern product produces an illusion of intimacy with the star while at the same time thickening the screen protecting her privacy" (158). Being the account of *Homecoming*, the documentary inevitably lays heavy emphasis on the production of the tour. Kylie's image is mostly positioned within wardrobes and boudoirs, on the stage, as well as amidst musicians and fashion designers. If anything, it is a deeper look into the life of a showgirl, where the backstage ground functions as a mythologized space of glamour. It is a disclosure of the out-of-view territory where the ordinary girl transforms into the showgirl prior to emerging on stage. Despite the fact that Rodríguez-Salas and Martín-Alegre argue against viewing Baker as the man who is "making her into a gay man's fantasy of femininity" (160), they do not account on how, from a camp perspective at least, the ideological discourse of *White Diamond* points to an iconic narrative—it is, after all, a *portrait* of a celebrity—of Kylie as a White Diamond: an epitome of White glamorous femininity so endlessly adored within camp culture. The documentary exudes a strong camp appeal in the sense that, first, it revels in a profusion of glamorous onstage and poststage images. Second, it sets Baker on a hierarchical pedestal to be acknowledged and identified by other queer men as a creative role model, further perpetuating the cliché of an excelling gay man in the performing arts. Third, its attempt to delve deeper into Kylie and present her as an ordinary human presupposes her status as an already mythologized state of stardom. Last but not least, Kylie's diagnosis evokes cultural narratives of the sick person as the "queer," a person who is of no use by standards of (re)productive heteronormativity. Yet, abiding by camp's envisioning of a dramatic mystique surrounding pop icons, the documentary accentuates and transcends Kylie's struggle by proposing her world of glittery costumes as recuperative of the threat of cancer—a breast cancer, for that matter, which, first and foremost, jeopardizes her femininity and, by extension, her career and life.

Kylie's cult of the showgirl is indeed a dense corpus of camp. Her vulnerability simultaneously exists with a poetics of extravagance, both equally informing her hyperfeminine persona. In fact, what is fundamental in the queer appeal of Kylie is her ability to play along the lines of intimacy and spectatorial distance. Her camp can be seductive as well as over-the-top at the same time. Examining closely, one can identify its roots in a performance of femininity that is deeply instructed by the burlesque tradition. Burlesque, for that matter, is a key source for Minogue's onstage perception and performance of glamorous femininity, as is evident in her show acts where burlesque elements are virtually omnipresent. Based on the tradition of the Las Vegas scene and the Parisian Folies Bergère, Kylie's fantasy costumes and erotic performances are a camp testament to her showgirl status. Claire Nally aligns burlesque performance "with camp, with a heavy criticism of hetero-normative genders, and ultimately with the queering of identities" (625). With regard to traditional burlesque, Kylie's is a rather bastardized version of its source in the sense that it does not contain either strip acts or radical nudity. It does, however, contain elements of playfulness and humor that are energized by her sexuality. Committed to the glamorous femininity and the theatrical discourse that surrounds it, Kylie's burlesque can certainly be acknowledged as a careful study on femininity as well as a generic platform that can highlight the tongue-in-cheek character of her textual catalog. *Showgirl* and its revamped version, *Homecoming*, attest to Kylie and Baker's vision of fully embracing the star's embodiment of a burlesque showgirl. Both tours construct Kylie's profile as such by placing her at the center of a diverse stage, which is elaborately structured to convey a lavish quality and is home to a variety of scenes and styles. Built in a retro, Art Deco aesthetic, both shows present Kylie dressed in blue and pink plumage, respectively, and being surrounded by her dancers who sport underwear and oversized plumage on their backs.[15] Every new style adopted for each act carries important signifiers of glamorous femininity: from the *gitana* figure in the flamenco-inspired performance of "Please Stay" in *Showgirl*, to the *Barbarella*-esque space queen in *Homecoming*, Kylie inhabits roles that are stereotypically erotic and overplayed through hyperfeminine body language.

Largely informed by burlesque, these femininities are more often than not home to exoticized ethnic representations as well, which is another overlapping area between burlesque and camp.[16] From *Showgirl* onward, Kylie has included performances of ethnic femininities in her various manifestations of her showgirl persona. Most of these are approached from a rather playful-cum-sensual perspective and in an exoticized manner, which departs from the sexualized, if pornified, acts of classical burlesque and moves toward a female-to-female drag perspective indicative of a neo-burlesque approach.[17] Imbued with high glamour and a risqué appreciation of gendered reality, the artist's exposition of exotic femininities indeed tilts to a drag aesthetic. The *X Tour*'s Naughty Manga Girl segment is demonstrative of the showgirl's poetics of exotic femininity. Overviews of the tour underlined Kylie's stage as "a whole lot of fun, veering between sexy, sophisticated, futuristic pop and the cheesy Saturday night talent show aesthetic" (Pollock). The performer herself is described as "relaxed and particularly playful," while the "camp element is kept to a minimum" (Adams). Although hardly can it be argued that the *X Tour* keeps camp to a minimum, the array of adjectives referring to Kylie's performances by both reviews point to a sexy, cheesy, and playful show. The Manga segment, which fuses elements of Japanese popular art in its citations of the genres of kabuki and manga, merges high drama with whimsicality to produce a stylized performance of femininity that is simultaneously flirtatious and cartoonish. The segment's opening act of "Come into My World" sees the artist emerging in a kabuki mask-veil only to reveal, shortly after, her manga-based outfit. Kylie welcomes the audience to her Japanese-themed world whose propped *washitsu*[18] visual setting and *hanami*-inspired[19] petal blizzard establish a transcendental atmosphere for the song's electronic sounds. This ambient, almost trance-imbuing act of "Come into My World" is juxtaposed with the ensuing performance of "Nu-Di-Ty", a self-consciously noisy act wherein the Naughty Manga Girl materializes. Regarding its production, "Nu-Di-Ty" was deemed as "a grating, baffling mess" (Ewing), "the bitter aftermath of a sugar rush" (Hughes), and "presumably intended to sound coy and sexy, but it makes you think of Adrian Mole getting his ruler out" (Petridis, "Kylie Minogue"). For its live performance, Kylie does not even try to eschew her critics' derision; instead, she deliberately embraces its failing status. Voicing her titillating lyrics in staccatos and squeaks, Kylie teeters nervously through her stripped male and female dancers and occasionally covers her eyes with her palm embarrassingly. In brilliantly camp manner, she concludes the performance by addressing a "Douitashimashite" ("You are welcome" in Japanese) to the public and letting off a mischievous giggle.

As a fusion of its source genre with drag and burlesque, Kylie's Manga Girl generates a queer effect that is central in the artist's camp. The image of the Manga Girl has its roots in the Japanese *shojo* manga genre, which means young girl and, according to Maana Sasaki, "further implies a character that 'personifies desirable feminine virtues,' embodying elements of *kawaii* (cuteness), naiveté, and sexual immaturity" (5). Drawing also from kabuki's androgynous *onnagata* performances,[20] Kylie's act is powered by female-to-female impersonation and cites from a cross-cultural history of performed femininities. The convergence of manga, kabuki, and burlesque instills an almost child-like sexual naiveté in Kylie's persona who takes guilty pleasure in watching her semi-naked dancers engage in erotic poses during "Nu-Di-Ty." Kylie inhabits a position of sexual limitation—also signified by her elaborately elegant couture that leaves only small parts of her body exposed—and becomes a voyeur in this act, turning for once the power of the gaze away from her own body and onto the dancers'. In fact, this position that veers between sheer elegance and a self-undermining sense of femininity is fundamental in delivering the camp effect. According to June Reich, "[c]amp is the celebration of passionate failures. The triumph of theatricality over substance, it is cynical, ironic, sentimental, pleasure-seeking, naively innocent, and corrupting" (263). The Manga Girl's trickster-like disposition creates a camp act that does not only inflate traditional femininity (as dictated by the manga and burlesque tradition) by turning into a cartoon bubble, but, importantly, allocates pleasure upon this playful moment of inflation. The performance is this exact moment when the Manga Girl realizes her non-alpha position within her world and her inability to cope with the imposed standards, thus embracing her failing status and turning it into play.

When asked how Kylie manages to preserve her relationship with queer audiences through the years, Baker replied that "she has a very gay sensibility" (W. Baker). As the director explains:

> When she was starting out as a performer, all her songs were about being second best: "I Should Be so Lucky," "Got to Be Certain," "Hand on Your Heart" [...] It's all about not being the super-strong [...] it's definitely a kind of vulnerability to Kylie that gay people are attracted to. (W. Baker)

The gay sensibility that Baker attributes to Kylie is to acknowledge her persona as more than adequate for him as a gay man to identify with. It can be argued that her sensibility sufficiently addresses the queer subjectivity through the emotional basis that constitutes the state of being queer in today's culture. One has to be cautious, though, with the plural nature of queer subjectivity. Being queer entails more than gendered and sexual categories since it is a psychic state crossed with a spectrum of sociocultural signifiers, such as race, ethnicity, and class. It is thus expressed variably across the widely applicable model that audience reception is. Kylie's camp cannot possibly exert its sentimental appeal equally to all queer groups. Historically, queer groups have evolved rather diversely and, as a result, have each developed a unique understanding as to what pertains to their embodied living of queerness. For instance, British gay men's queer experiences and lifestyle may come as tellingly different to those of queer women of color in America. Yet, what practically binds the cross-cultural state of being queer into a more coherent category are those characteristics that define the very basis of it, one of them being the imposed failure to realize heteronormative standards and values of being. Therefore, to be "second best," as Baker underlines, or to perceive queerness as a state of vulnerability are notions deeply ingrained in the ideological configuration of queer subjectivity as the polar and indeed defective end of a "normal" heterosexuality.

To take pleasure in Kylie's camp is to turn the imposed failure, be it sexual or gendered, into a celebration. For queer men, who comprise much of Kylie's fanbase and whose socially expected role in terms of gender expression and sex stands in stark contrast with what camp culture offers, it means to be at war with those imposed standards of (Western) masculinity that equates male subjectivity with masculine power. It is, thus, to derive power from a seemingly disempowered position, that of camp's effeminacy. Such power, however, resides rather regulated within the contemporary politics of gay identity. According to David Halperin,

> [the] basic problem with the political functioning of gay identity nowadays is that in the course of claiming public recognition and acceptance of the fact of homosexual *desire* (sometimes at the expense of gay sex, to be sure), the official gay and lesbian movement has effectively foreclosed inquiry into queer sensibility, style, emotion, or any specific, non-sexual form of queer *subjectivity* or *affect* or *pleasure*. (77, original emphasis)

The writer's premise that social visibility and acceptance as promoted by the modern gay and lesbian movement comes at the expense of queer subjectivity, along with its desires, emotions, and pleasures, is indeed legitimate as regards contemporary gay male culture. The need to reconcile two purportedly contradictive qualities—the gendered conformity leading the way of a contained image of socially visible homosexuality versus the queer colorations of gay culture that are still met with discomfort and cringe-making attitudes by inter- and intra-communal politics—results in confusion. This confusion makes itself manifest in the antitheses permeating contemporary gay male culture and its struggle to make polar ends meet. Consider the binaries of muscle culture versus camp culture; urban versus peripheral communities; institutional approval of gay marriage versus the sociospatial concealment of gay flirting and sex. This is, of course, not to overlook the sociopolitical progress being achieved through the politics of the movement, but to highlight, perhaps emphatically through the either/or nature of these dualities, the ambiguities and imprisoning ideologies that pervade gay culture.

To celebrate camp and its performed tradition involves sentimental devotion to a practice that is still rooted in shame both within and out of queer culture. With regard to Kylie's camp, Baker explains how it has always been a part of her and how her relationship with it appeared problematic for her record label:

> [A] constant battle that we had with Parlophone[21] is that camp is like a bad thing. People think it's a bad thing. Parlophone were famously unsupportive of [*Light Years's*] "Your Disco Needs You" and really didn't want to put the Kylie and Dannii duet on the Christmas album.[22] Just because they hate camp. (W. Baker)

Baker does not elaborate further on Parlophone's disapproval of camp, yet he points out that "they would argue, in their defense, that she's better than that" (W. Baker). Although, ironically, Baker has overlooked the fact that Kylie's production of camp, especially in her live shows, remains vivid, he makes quite an important remark on the label's attitude toward it. If we extrapolate the physiognomy of Parlophone to an institutional source of (artistic) control, we come across the unsettling paradox that permeates the nature of corporate power to openly criticize camp as a degraded artistic form and simultaneously invest in and capitalize on it. Camp's embracing of its low, lite, and shame-ridden nature, though, underscores its liberating effect to be entertaining and exert appeal. Baker stresses that he loves camp glamour because it is fun and acknowledges it as part of gay culture's legacy (W. Baker). After all, it is with camp poetics that the director has been energizing Kylie's performances for years. With that in mind, let us now lay focus on Baker's contribution to Kylie's camp and see how his personal sensibility has come to shape the performer's stage.

Spectacular Athletica, or the queer gaze on masculinity

Baker initially started working as Minogue's stylist prior to becoming the creative director behind her persona and stage. Although the two share different opinions with regard to Kylie's performances, they manage to braid together their personal tastes when it comes to a final outcome. Baker, for one, admits that he would rather invest in the theatrical aspects of a show, such as choreography, props, or costumes, while Minogue tilts the scales in favor of a more band-oriented production (W. Baker). This is an important statement when thought within the context of agency in camp production. As part of Kylie's production team, Baker, following Minogue, holds perhaps the second most important position as the creative director—alongside Steve Anderson, Minogue's long-time musical director—in the sense that literally every aspect of a show, performance, or album-based artwork is filtered through him. It is his sensibility that pours through the stage and posture of Kylie and his creative moods that are engaged in the conceptual process of turning an aural project into an audiovisual one. This is not, of course, to downgrade Kylie's investment in her own persona. She is in charge of selecting, writing, and producing her music, a process over which Baker has limited say, and, in fact, she is the one to finalize decisions about her shows. Theatricality, though, is not always a domain that Kylie prioritizes since, according to Baker, she really enjoys those segments of her shows where she interacts directly with the audience and the band (W. Baker). As a case in point, following the lush *Aphrodite Tour*, Kylie decided to celebrate her silver jubilee in the music industry with the *Anti Tour* (in 2012), a minimalist production that included only her band and back-up singers and was played for a total of seven dates in small British and Australian venues.[23] The typical extravaganza that Kylie's persona has been associated with is undoubtedly connected to Baker, who relies largely on his personal sensibility for the structural process of a show.

In this light, the camp of Kylie takes shape under the productive aegis of a gay male authority. Regarding the deliberate production of camp and the intentions of its "author," Cleto queries whether the camp icon of stars, such as Mae West, Tallulah Bankhead, or Marlene Dietrich, to name just a few, was a result of a self-aware cognition of camp production instructed either by themselves or by a directorial figure or, rather, is a result of the viewer's perception (27). The complexity of this conundrum, which has its roots in the deliberate vs. naïve debate that Sontag posited, cannot be addressed monolithically. Realizing the complex nature of the authorial intent, Cleto argues that:

> [W]e can't really settle whether each of [these icons] made a conscious deployment of the camp fascination strategy [...] or if they were articulating that strategy in spite of themselves, be that through an exercise in camp decoding (either retrospectively or contemporary), or through the assignment of "stage directions" that promote the star as camp icon, without her/his being conscious of that. (27)

Indeed, it is rather reductive to allocate authorial power either to the camp icon or to the directorial figure who remains a vital component in the structural "script" of the stage. On the other hand, it is impossible to solely place emphasis on the outcome itself as disengaged from its source, following the Barthean logic that overlooks the contribution of the author's sensibilities and their projection upon the text/performance.[24] As Cleto maintains, "the director's 'choices' should be inscribed within the cultural horizon in which his/her subjectivity, and the personality of the star, is produced along with the artifact" (27). Thus, camp can be a cultural exponent of its director's personal taste and perception which, in our dealing with Baker's authorship, are socially, historically, and sexually marked as "gay," bearing both the qualities inherent in the queer/gay subjectivity and those dwelling in the identity forged by the sociopolitical discourse of the LGBTQ+ movement in the Western world.

With that being said, one could posit that Baker applies a gay gaze when approaching the spectacle. Arguably, to talk about an intrinsic quality of queer viewing might sound essentialist and anachronistic in its evocation of queer sensibility as a unique asset that every gay man carries. However, as Brett Farmer postulates, "[h]omosexuality *is* a central determining paradigm in modern, Western cultures, and many subjects articulate their desires, make their meanings, and live their lives, whether in part or whole, whether centrally or peripherally, through it" (10, original emphasis). In this light, being gay and having a queer viewing of the world should not be solely understood in their stereotypical sense of having a keenness for fashion, musicals, and interior architecture, but rather in the sense that gayness materializes through an established network of desires and meaning-making processes that eschew from heteronormative standards and foreground homoerotic attraction. Baker's approach of the Kylie spectacle balances between those qualities since the queer gaze is informed, among other things, by a camp appreciation of reality as well as homoeroticism. Itself an ideological construct, attraction in gay male culture is greatly instructed by the sociocultural standards of heteronormative masculinity, which requires from men to be and behave in specific ways.[25] On the opposite end, camp denotes effeminacy and is largely detached from the gravity assigned to erotic attraction and sexual arousal. Halperin illustrates this polarity in his schema of beauty and the camp, arguing that "[t]he traditional split between camp and beauty, or between humor and glamour, coincides specifically, with the old sexual division between queens and trade: that is, between effeminate and virile styles of performing male sex and gender roles" (205). Despite the seeming incompatibility of the split, the two ends are not simply antithetical. Halperin explains that: "[t]he polarity between camp and beauty, though strict, is not absolute [...] Drag queens and muscle boys always perform together; each of them requires the presence of the other" (210). Therefore, albeit oppositional, the relation between camp and homoeroticism also arises as complementary.

Bringing this complementarity into the diva spectacle not only results in an accentuation of the camp quality of the show but also legitimizes typical masculinity as the exemplary source of gay eroticism. In Kylie's stage, one sees how Baker's camp treatment of it is based on this mutually foddered relation between masculinity and camp. For Kylie, the epitome of (hyper)femininity and camp glamour, what functions as the complementary force are the male dancers surrounding her on stage. The muscular and, more often than not, exposed bodies of the dancers stand in stark contrast to the elaborate costumes adorning Kylie's body. Conversely, her female dancers in most shows usually intermingle with the male ones, but there are times when they either occupy the position of a supportive chorus for Kylie or are completely absent from the stage. The artist's shows, in fact, display a noticeable presence of male dancers with segments that feature Kylie interacting solely with them outnumbering those where she performs only with her female crew.[26] Most importantly, male dancers frequently reenact roles that are based on the performance of masculinity and appear on acts that reinforce their position as objects of the erotic gaze. In other words, men in Kylie's world employ their masculine profiles as part of a spectatorial fantasy. Though, here is precisely where the staging of machismo, as inscribed on the dancers' muscular posture and juxtaposed with Kylie's glamorous femininity, allows us to read it as a stylized performance of gender. One can always assume that Baker creates a sexualized image of men on stage by projecting personal desires and views upon the male body; spectacles after all are built upon and amplify the erotics of the body as a means of appealing to the audience. Yet, with camp at work at the same time, onstage masculinity is to a large degree underlined as theatrical.

In *Homecoming*'s Athletica segment, for instance, the image of the macho male becomes blatantly eroticized by being posited as an object to be looked at. Athletica is introduced with the "Butterfly" interlude in which a male dancer acts out a solo demonstration of gymnastic skills, performing backflips and somer-saults. He eventually strips into his speedos and exits, only to join moments later a quartet of men showering in a gym locker room set. This simulation draws from the prominent locker room trope of gay male erotica that exists as a homosocial space and has time and again been home to queer interactions. The dancers stand with their backs against the audience, establishing a scene where the audience occu-pies a voyeuristic position. When they finish showering, they turn suggestively to invite erotic gazes. Interactions between them are limited and carefully remain on a homosocial level, being expressed through "manly" handshakes after the shower. The scene effectively stages social interactions among men in sports that strictly prohibit the expression of any homoerotic sentiment. As Roger Horrocks argues:

> [H]omoeroticism [...] links with the intense homophobia and misogyny which has existed in male sport. These attitudes express an unconscious ambivalence: as well as asserting the true "manliness" of sportsmen, they also seek to bury the homo-erotic and "feminine" desires of men with each other. (152)

As in the arena of male sports, the simulated shower scene on Kylie's stage ensures that the fragility of the exposed male body in what appears to be a sensitive moment repels any associations with homosexuality. The movements of the dan-cers are dynamic, nonchalant, and sturdy, carefully foregrounding a stereotypic-ally manly posture.

Juxtaposed to that is Kylie, who emerges on stage delicately positioned on a pommel horse. More interestingly, her ensemble consists of a leopard-print catsuit paired with high heels and red boxing gloves that feature her initials, proposing thus a highly stylized concept of sportswear. "Red Blooded Woman" is performed (with a brief intermission of "Where the Wild Roses Grow")[27] followed by the performance of "Slow." Both being singles from the *Body Language* album, the songs illustrate Kylie's lustfulness for her male partner, while their mid-tempo composition allow the act to unravel rather leisurely. The dancers surrounding Kylie exhibit their toned bodies in physical tasks, lifting weights and performing push-ups. The performer erotically interacts with them, waving her hand to her face as if to ease off the heat and casually grinding on their bodies while they are exercising. Both acts envision the contrast between Kylie's slinky femininity and the dancers' muscular physicality as a terrain of animalistic, albeit simulated power play, which is invigorated by Kylie's feline persona and the exaggerated body-builder physique of the dancers. In this blatant juxtaposition, the queer/gay gaze reads both power corpuses as stylized performances, but is encouraged to identify with the camp diva and thus revel in the sight of the performed machismo, further acknowledging the masculine male body, whose authentic—read heterosexual—masculinity has already been verified as a generative site of sexual desire.

In Kylie's theatrical worlds masculinity does not maintain its close-ended, rigid qualities. Baker at times endorses the ideals of masculinity in order to inflate and thus hollow their already magnified proportions from within. Not very much unlike *Homecoming*'s Athletica, the *Aphrodite: Les Folies Tour* has dealt with the exhibition of the masculine male, albeit from a classical perspective. Drawing inspiration from Greek mythology, the Parisian Folies Bergère as well as the "aquamusicals" of Esther Williams (Empire, "Kylie–Review"), the *Aphrodite Tour*, whose cost reached approximately £20 million, combines Greco-Roman aesthetics and Busby Berkeley-esque concepts in a lavish "theatrical spectacular" that sees Kylie as the "supreme authority" of "arena kitsch" (Collinson; Power). With regard to *Aphrodite*'s display of camp and the male form, the concert critics' verbose descriptions were not modest in seeing Kylie's muscular dancers as the eye-popping feature of the show. *The Guardian*'s Kitty Empire, in fact, states that the tour embodies "the ancient Greece of widespread man-love, one in which male dancers, barely clad in Dolce & Gabbana, are frequently entwined, dangling on rope swings or playing bongos on each other's bottoms" (Empire, "Kylie–Review"), while *The Telegraph*'s Ed Power sarcastically states that throughout the show Kylie "perched atop a gold Pegasus and rode a chariot pulled by hunky centurions whose six-packs glistened so fiercely it was a wonder Dublin's entire supply of baby oil hadn't been exhausted". What these reviews indicate is that there was no purpose whatsoever on Kylie and Baker's behalf to restrict the show from pompously exhibiting the male physique.

As a matter of fact, the dancers' muscular bodies were further stylized to mirror and simultaneously camp up the mythological qualities of the classical male body. From togas to gold lamé speedos and skin-tight underwear, the dancers' attire is fashioned on ancient Greco-Roman clothing style and is importantly kept to a minimum so as to highlight their toned muscles. More importantly, they are a consciously kitsch configuration of body adornment that effectively undermines the authentic, simple, and minimal character of classical masculinity. In multiple acts, such as the opening number of "Aphrodite" and the performance of "I Believe in You," as well as in most of the show's visual backdrops, the male body is presented as statuesque and bulky. As Dyer explains, the popular masculinist perception of the male body derives from the tradition of bodybuilding that, in its fundamental basis, relied on the ideal of the classical Greek body (*White* 148–50).

The writer argues that "[t]he built body presents itself not as typical but as ideal. It suggests our vague notions of the Greek gods and the Übermensch" (*White* 151). The heroic muscular body has infiltrated and influenced Western popular culture to a great degree via mythologizations of the male form that were largely derived from the repository of classical Greek and Roman representations of deities and heroes. Significantly, Dyer argues that classicism is a "specific, strongly white representational tradition" and "[e]qually, many of the formal properties of the built body carry connotations of whiteness: it is ideal, hard, achieved, wealthy, hairless and tanned" (*White* 150). The discourse of this ideal has permeated gay culture in its adoption of the social codes surrounding the muscular male body as best exemplified by the post-Stonewall clone image of the 1970s and its subsequent influential role in the rise of modern muscle culture. According to Martin Levine:

> This image heralded the masculinization of gay culture. Gay men now regarded themselves as masculine. They adopted manly attire and demeanor as a means of expressing their new sense of self. They also adopted this look to enhance their physical attractiveness and express improved self-esteem. (28)

Instead of simply residing on the passive site of gazing at the male ideal as dictated by popular culture and Hollywood standards, the urban gay man decided to become the ideal male by structuring his lifestyle upon the mentality of an unapologetically sexual body that instantly affected his social reality—the gym, for instance, quickly emerged as a space of queer interaction and socialization. With regard to race, Levine stresses that the clone was mainly middleclass and White, whereas gay men of color, such as Black and Latino, were the minority groups that abode by the model only because of their rough and authentic working-class masculinity (M. Levine 10–11, 82). As a representational model, therefore, the muscled male body expresses White masculinity as the Western cultural ideal.

As demonstrated in the *Aphrodite Tour*, classical masculinity provides the basis for the eroticization of the dancers' muscular bodies. However, Baker does not choose to simply set the male body up for the sexual gratification of the queer/ gay gaze. Instead, similarly with *X Tour's* Manga Girl, Kylie is once again placed as the mischievous camp character—this time through the amorous nature of Aphrodite—to disturb the static posture of the male dancers. In the performance of "Wow," Kylie and her priestess-resembling vocalists watch the male dancers, who appear as Spartan gladiators performing war-training routines. Kylie then moves through the gladiators and caresses their bodies. In response, some of them slowly raise the shields held in front of their crouch as if to simulate erection, working a comic effect. Eventually, Kylie enchants the dancers with her melodic performance and sends them dancing and hopping around. The imagery of the Greek warriors and, by extension, the heroic war discourses abundant in classical antiquity have forged masculinity with impenetrable seriousness and carefully constructed ideals of discipline and self-restraint—consider, for instance, Odysseus' encounter with the Sirens in the Homeric narrative. The performance of "Wow" here debunks the seriousness of these heroic discourses by employing Aphrodite as a camp vamp to upset and thus undermine the seemingly adamant qualities of classical masculinity. Discussing the shame-ridden treatment of camp and its juxtaposition to muscle culture, Baker expressed his frustration:

> I think it's all bollocks! I think the muscle culture is just like another clone, another ideal of the mustache and leather jacket from the seventies [...] I'm a really big fan of the art and the kind of legacy of underground gay culture [...] I love all that and I think it's all really important. (W. Baker)

To therefore address masculinity with camp fun offers a valuable critique with regard to gay culture's internalization of masculinist behavioral patterns, which, at times, become intolerant and phobic toward nonmasculine gender expressions.

On the other hand, Baker's endorsement of masculinity might just as well reflect a corporate need to attract more audiences by offering stripped muscled male bodies as mere eye candies for voyeuristic pleasure. It is quite complex, though, to simply overturn the discourse of ingrained masculinity, especially when it remains bound by/with the commercial rubrics of the spectacle, without first endorsing it. Baker seems to be aware of that complexity when he utters his disidentification with the muscle culture. Classical machismo in the *Aphrodite Tour* is simultaneously an upheld ideal and a parodied notion. Kylie's male dancers, as the bearers of masculinity, are not simply to be looked at, but they are on stage to be toyed with. Baker manages to gaze at masculinity from a more flexible position by utilizing the playfulness of camp. This becomes more evident in the *Aphrodite* follow-up show, *Kiss Me Once Tour*, and, more specifically, its Dollhouse act, which again places machismo alongside camp. This time, however, their interplay relies on an already plasticized version of gender. A medley of Kylie's late 1980s songs, the Dollhouse opens with female dancers dressed as Barbie dolls, sporting pink attire and plastic blond wigs, and playfully interacting with each other. Dressed in a pink frilly frock, Kylie emerges on stage next to two motionless male dancers who resemble Ken doll mannequins. While performing, Kylie rearranges their postures, gracefully touching their buttocks and faces before passing them over to her female crew. The transition between songs, here from "Hand on Your Heart" to "Never Too Late," sees Kylie gradually stripping down to reveal pink garters and crinoline, while her female dancers simulate housework with retro vacuum cleaners and ironing boards. For the next transition to "I Got to Be Certain," the

Barbie dancers strip the Ken dolls to their underwear, performing sexual acts on them and taking pictures of their naked bodies, while the latter run embarrassed backstage. In the final act of "I Should Be so Lucky," the male dancers return with pink bath towels wrapped around their waist to assist Kylie on taking a bath in a tub filled with feathery froth, as a visual reference to the song's original video.

In its simulation of household life, the Dollhouse segment is Baker's radical camp parody of the cult of domesticity and his queer viewing of gender. As the female dolls, Kylie and her dancers perform from and thereby upset the position of the suburban housewife—the foundational rock of reproductive heterosexuality and the traditionally aspiring model of the ideal of the postwar Western middle-class home. Camp praxis is further invigorated by the glamorization of those housework aspects, such as cleaning and ironing, which are conventionally perceived as trivial. The Dollhouse is set as the quintessential space of femininity wherein Kylie and the Barbie dolls, literally and metaphorically, are made to be at home. On the other hand, the Ken dolls are placed within this female-run space as mere objects of utility; their passive status is highlighted by their being used as sexually subservient to Kylie and the female dancers. The sexual objectification of the male image, though, is not by any means executed in the penetrative sense that scholars of sexuality ascribe to the male and the queer gaze respectively.[28] With the parodic aegis of camp, Baker here decompresses the alleged seriousness of objectification cast by the queer gaze and transforms the macho dancers into boy-toys. In addition, doll-playing, a children's game to be practiced by preadolescent girls, envisions Baker as the directorial puppeteer that occupies a position traditionally dwelled by young females, who, through the practice of playing, are encouraged to reenact stereotypical femininities and thereby aspire to a heteronormatively ordered social role. By doing precisely what males are not supposed to do, Baker could be seen as disturbing social stereotypes by giving himself, an adult gay male, the social space of the stage to enact doll-playing. Authorial intent thus allows him to employ camp in order to manipulate and thus destabilize gender norms imposed by the simulated reality of the doll game.

Despite this effective camp treatment of genders, the subject matter of the creative director's authorship must always be approached cautiously. Acknowledging that the Dollhouse was "camp as tits," Baker was candidly positive when I asked him whether he has to convince Kylie to do things, such as be part of a concept, and he replied that the performer initially expressed her disapproval of the Dollhouse medley: "In [the] *Kiss Me Once [Tour]*, she really wasn't into the Dollhouse [...] I think in the end she got it. You know, she takes time to process things. But that was one she really wasn't into" (W. Baker). As previously stressed in this chapter, Baker and Minogue may take different approaches on the visual content of the performer's stage. Baker maintains: "I always think she works better when things are kind of more theatrical and darker and that's a constant battle I have" (W. Baker). Kylie's musical extravaganzas indeed work better for her due to the fact that a theatrical(ized) environment, contrary to the minimalist template of the classic rock gig, is more apt for the staging and accentuation of her camp icon. It is impossible or, to be precise, it is thought impossible to imagine Kylie outside of the camp glamour that has for years nurtured her stage persona. Although Baker's instrumental role in her production of camp might raise concerns over an authorial instrumentation of what appears to be a gay fantasy world, what must be taken into consideration is that Baker in collaboration with Minogue is rather meticulous in gauging the components of the audience, who, according to him, "is predominantly gay" (W. Baker). The gay audiences' lasting investment in the cultural icon of Minogue attests to the fact that Baker's creativity, which derives from his own tastes and desires as these accrue from his personal experience from, and engagement with contemporary queer culture, seems to resonate with them.

Being a Western gay man, Baker can be regarded as an insider of queer culture who manages to draw from the large repository of camp. This statement, however, appears problematic when one factors in issues of race and ethnicity in camp production as juxtaposed with the multiethnic nature of Kylie's spectatorship. What we have seen so far in the production of Kylie's stage, whether this is the camp tradition of burlesque or the performances of Western masculinity or, even, Kylie's blond bombshell profile per se, is an inevitable foregrounding of camp as a default-White, urban queer practice. Of course, one cannot simply accuse Kylie of blatantly promoting Whiteness. Rather, issues of race largely go under the radar in the sense that Kylie's White persona seems to eclipse any racially nuanced camp traditions, such as disco, whereas Baker's sensibilities might reflect a cultural input of the British and American camp paradigm, as is evidenced by the shows' intertextual references. It is important thus to move beyond the seemingly White legacy of camp and the prefiguring of White urban gay culture as dominant. In light of this, it is vital that gay icons dealing with the praxis of camp and being engaged in the diva worship tradition from a non-White perspective are equally acknowledged as contributors to the cultural formation of contemporary global queer culture. With that said, I would like now to turn to the next diva case that is Beyoncé Knowles.

NOTES

1. Cleto underlines that *kamp*, as a stylistic variation of camp, is a word that circulates gay slang in Australia and New Zealand, although carrying the exact same meaning and connotations (10). Considering that Kylie is from Melbourne, Australia, her mentioning of

kamp is a noteworthy pun that plays both the Australian version of the slang term as well as her signature "K" behind it.

2. Madonna does not stand out because she was the first one to infuse her style with sexual and gender politics, and thereby occupy multiple identity grounds. Before her, Annie Lennox, David Bowie, Michael Jackson, and especially Cher had successfully adopted a postmodernist understanding of the multiplicity of identity. Madonna was rather the one to up the ante in terms of velocity and popularization of her reinvention tactics by employing a radical politics of pornography against what was a conservative mainstream media environment.

3. Inspired by the theater stage, David Bowie's *Glass Spider Tour* (in 1987) is actually credited to have innovatively functioned as the act-divided template upon which subsequent concert shows were based (Youngs).

4. When the tour moved to North America, it was renamed *KylieUSA2009*, alternatively known as *For You, For Me*, due to being Kylie's first ever headlining tour in the region. Because of that, the show was rather a retrospective enterprise of previous tours, fusing elements from the *X Tour* and *Homecoming*, as a recapitulation of her oeuvre to be showcased for the American audience. *For You, For Me* does not deviate significantly in content from the previous tours. Some noteworthy exceptions include Kylie's new costumes, the revamping of some acts, and the cinematic and musical references to Hollywood camp classics, such as *The Wizard of Oz* and *The Sound of Music*. Segments or acts of this specific tour are not discussed here mainly because most of them are addressed within their original productions.

5. Scissor Sisters are renowned for their flamboyant performances and titillating lyrics. Minogue has been associated with the American band, particularly, with frontman, Jake Shears, who has produced songs for various Kylie albums, including "I Believe in You" (in 2004), "White Diamond" (in 2006), and "Too Much" (in 2010).

6. Following the lukewarm commercial and critical success of her *Impossible Princess* album (in 1997), Kylie left Deconstruction and signed with Parlophone, a move that saw her immediately reaping the benefits of her new deal as *Light Years* brought her again atop the British and European charts and, thus, back into the public eye.

7. Tom of Finland serves as the pseudonym for mid-twentieth-century Finnish artist Touko Valio Laaksonen, known for his highly eroticized gay male graphic art. His art now stands synonymous with the pornographic hypermasculinity exemplified by his characters.

8. Manilow's song talks about the tragic love story of a showgirl named Lola who was performing at the nightclub Copacabana and fell in love with the bartender, Tony. One night, a mobster-like character, named Rico, tries to seduce Lola and ends up fighting and killing Tony. Thirty years later, Copacabana became a disco and Lola, as the tragic heroine, sits there devastated by her lover's death and still wearing her showgirl costume.

9. Contrary to Fredric Jameson's perception of pastiche as "blank parody" (*Postmodernism; or, the Cultural Logic of Late Capitalism*), Robertson supports that "if we understand camp

to have been always mere 'blank parody,' we simply dehistoricize and 'postmodernize' camp's parodic and critical impulse" (*Guilty Pleasures*, 5, original emphasis).

10. As by-products of this ideological construct, consider the trope of the "sad young man" in mid-twentieth-century popular culture as illustrated in Dyer's essay "Coming Out as Going In: The Image of the Homosexual as a Sad Young Man" (*The Culture of Queers*). Also, consider the disempowering effect of the epidemic rhetoric in the 1980s upon the "empowered" model of the 1970s macho clone as described in Martin Levine's essay "Fearing Fear Itself" (*Gay Macho: The Life and Death of the Homosexual Clone*).

11. Consider, for instance, the tragic/ironic end of Marilyn Monroe, the epitome of an extremely dramatic femininity proved deeply fragile, or James Dean, the archetype of American virility brought to death by what was a very "masculine" sport; and likewise, the somatic decadence and grotesqueness that usually accompany rehabilitation narratives, as the likes of Elizabeth Taylor or Amy Winehouse indicate.

12. For a more explanatory analysis on the differences between *Showgirl* and *Homecoming* consider Rodríguez-Salas and Martín-Alegre's article ("Forget Madonna").

13. The frontman of Australian rock group INXS and former love affair of Minogue in the early 1990s. Hutchence's rock profile has been acknowledged as a significant influence on Kylie's creative turn toward a more sexually confident persona in her *Rhythm of Love* album (Barron 52). Hutchence's death in 1997 impacted Minogue on a personal level, while, on stage, she has paid homage to his icon by incorporating a cover of *INXS*'s "Need You Tonight" in her *Kiss Me Once Tour*.

14. The notorious gold pants in "Spinning Around" that were partly responsible for Minogue's millennial comeback and establishment as a sex icon.

15. The pink-colored plumage in *Homecoming* may as well be a nod to her cancer survivor status.

16. With regard to film, Jack Babuscio's essay on "Camp and the Gay Sensibility" supports that certain films' camp aesthetics is being instructed by the "realms of the exotic or subjective fantasies" and places emphasis on Carmen Miranda's performance of "The Lady in the Tutti-Frutti Hat" (choreographed by Busby Berkeley) in *The Gang's All Here*. Similarly, Robertson's essay on "Mae West's Maids: Race, 'Authenticity,' and the Discourse of Camp" discusses how Mae West's burlesque and blues songstress profile are sustained by an appropriation and performance of Black femininity (cited in Cleto).

17. In her book *Burlesque and the New Bump-n-Grind*, Michelle Baldwin argues that

> [b]y the late 1920s, burlesque was synonymous with striptease, explaining why, despite its rich history in comedy and satire, most anyone today equates the word *burlesque* with stripping. Strippers were the main feature in burlesque, and the rest of the program—the comics, the variety acts—was there to fill out the show. (9, original emphasis)

The rise of the neo-burlesque movement in the 1990s barely made any impact because, as Baldwin explains, "[it] simply was, to most people, synonymous with modern pole and small-stage stripping" (24), while "[p]erformers, audiences and the press [...] referred to it as performance art, or female-to-female drag, or just creative striptease" (27). Progressively, though, it acquired a more egalitarian attitude toward the female body and sexuality by embracing a multitude of gendered, ethnic, racial, and corporeal subjectivities.

18. Traditional Japanese interior decoration.

19. The traditional Japanese custom according to which people gather outdoors to watch the blooming of the cherry blossom in springtime.

20. As indexed in Samuel Leiter's *Historical Dictionary of Japanese Traditional Theatre*,

> *onnagata*, also *oyama*, [are] the "female person" actors who play girls and women in *kabuki*. Women were banned from *kabuki* in 1629, so young men who occasionally had played women before, now took over their roles exclusively [...] The *onnagata* represents an idealization of femininity and even influenced women's behavior and styles during the Edo period. (296–97)

21. The British record label accommodating Kylie from 1999 onward.

22. The allegedly ultra-camp song "100 Degrees" that Kylie recorded with her sister Dannii for the *Kylie Christmas* album (in 2015).

23. The *Anti Tour* completely omitted hit numbers that made Kylie famous, such as "I Should Be so Lucky" or "Can't Get You Out of My Head" and, instead, incorporated songs that had never been performed live before or were only known to Kylie's hardcore fanbase.

24. In his seminal poststructuralist piece on "The Death of the Author", Barthes pointed out that "it is language that speaks, not the author; to write is, through a prerequisite impersonality (not at all to be confused with the castrating objectivity of the realist novelist), to reach that where only language acts, 'performs', and not 'me'" (144). Barthes wished to release the literary discourse from the allegedly hegemonic nature of its (modernist) author arguing in favor of a more liberated textual production whose exploration from the reader will not necessarily include "the important task of discovering the Author beneath the work" (147). However, as upheld by critics of Barthes and the postfeminist thought on the private as political—see Camille Paglia's *Sexual Personae: Art and Decadence in from Nefertiti to Emily Dickinson*—a literary text and, in our case, a performative/audiovisual text, is rather unimaginable without the subjectivity of its author.

25. Nurtured by a variety of popular media, be they online dating platforms, the gay porn industry, or films and TV series, cultural input regarding the sexual relations between queer men in contemporary culture is growing upon a perpetuation and idealization of masculinity, one that promotes macho behavior and muscular looks. From the clone image of the 1970s to the post-HIV/AIDS rise of the gym culture onward, a discernible majority of the aforementioned media portrays the modern gay man taking pride in his masculine profile

and eroticism. The macho gay male, specifically, functions as an aspiring subject position as well as an object of desire to be conquered—in plain terms, gay men are instructed to *be* and to *have* masculine males.

26. There are, however, exceptions here where Kylie is solely surrounded by her female dancers on stage, as in the *Les Folies* version of "Slow" for the *Aphrodite Tour*. There is also one instance where the performer shares the lead role of the showgirl with a female dancer, as was the case in the performance of "Copacabana" for the *X Tour*, in which Kylie was inhabiting the position of the singer-narrator, whereas her showgirl dancer was the protagonist of the enacted narrative.

27. Kylie's duet with Nick Cave and the Bad Seeds that appears in the band's album *Murder Ballads* (1996). The lyrics and video of the song imagine Cave as a criminal character that has murdered his lover, Kylie, who appears as an apparitional figure. Kylie's gothic fragility here creates vibrant contrasts when mixed with the lustful femme fatale from "Red Blooded Woman", pointing to her rapid interplay between female/feminine characters.

28. Laura Mulvey's and Steve Farmer's approach on the male and gay gaze, respectively, highlight the transgressive qualities of it. Yet, one has to be conscious of the mechanics of objectification since both men and women have occasionally set themselves up for eroticization, willfully reflecting the traditional attributes ascribed to their gender. Regarding the objectification of men, Farmer insightfully extends Mulvey's position that "[a]ccording to the principles of the ruling ideology and the physical structures that back it up, the male figure cannot bear the burden of sexual objectification. Man is reluctant to gaze at his exhibitionist self" (Mulvey 12). The writer argues that [b]ecause the male gaze is largely defined as active, powerful, and penetrative, the homosexual look of desire at the male body in the classic "feminine" role of passive object—a reversal that "traditional heterosexual [masculinity] cannot survive" (213). This is why the gay male look of desire is so troubling to a phallic male economy (213).

> [b]ecause the male gaze is largely defined as active, powerful, and penetrative, the homosexual look of desire at the male body in the classic "feminine" role of passive object—a reversal that "traditional heterosexual [masculinity] cannot survive." This is why the gay male look of desire is so troubling to a phallic male economy. (213)

3

We Flawless:
Beyoncé's Politics of Black Camp

Diva is the female version of a hustler.

(Beyoncé, "Diva")

Is glamour a sense of power?

(bell hooks, "Moving Beyond Pain")

Over the past decade, African American performer Beyoncé Knowles has progressively become the center of analysis. Critics usually focus on topics of feminism, race, celebrity, and media semiotics to approach Beyoncé and her work. Her performances can indeed be a fecund ground for readings on identity politics, gender, and sexuality since they provide an interesting as well as complex look into the relationship Beyoncé's audiences have developed with her. Addressing the artist's body of work, though, has time and again posed challenges for contemporary scholars who seem divided when it comes to discussing power relations and politics. Specifically, Beyoncé is either being dismissed for colluding with "imperialist white supremacist capitalist patriarchy," to quote bell hooks ("Moving Beyond Pain"), or being haloed as a Black woman who is the agent of her own image and potentially serves as a model of empowerment. Another critical debate on the artist more often than not entails her pop treatment of feminism; namely, the way she promotes herself as an advocate of feminist politics while simultaneously presenting a sexualized image of the Black female body. What permeates current Beyoncé readings is the surfacing and compromising need, if trend, to approach her as the modern intersectional advocate of feminist discourse. This is exactly the point where other conundrums sprout: can an affluent heterosexual married Black woman speak from a critically feminist position for women who occupy less privileged statuses? Can her feminist advocacy coexist with patriarchal understandings of gender and sexuality? Are there effective ways to approach the artist's work without overlooking the issues of class and celebrity status? Finally, as the epigraph states, is her glamour a sense of power? If Madonna has come to signify an ambiguous face of postfeminist politics of the late 1980s and 1990s, then Beyoncé definitely represents the updated version in terms of intersectional identity politics, digital media marketing, and gender performance.

Although this chapter, as was the case with the previous ones, focuses on the camp icon and live performances of Beyoncé, the nature of the abovementioned questions is key to understand both the artist's oeuvre and the subject matter of diva camp per se. Beyoncé's stage is not what one would typically characterize as camp—at least not conspicuously. Contrary to Madonna, let alone Kylie, Beyoncé's shows keep the camp element to a minimum; her stage rather underperforms in terms of flamboyance, being minimal in props in order to allow space for choreographic routines, whereas her wardrobe ranges from risqué leotards to glittery bodysuits and evening gowns that are not necessarily pompous in the sense that, say, Lady Gaga's are. Technically, her spectacles involve typical structural devices, such as visual backdrops, pyrotechnics, and even a water stage (*Formation Tour*), but they rarely make use of the camp factor, as is the case with Kylie's or Madonna's over-the-top extravaganzas. Therefore, apart from specific visual corpora in her career that explicitly played up the camp factor, as was the collaboration with Gaga on the pulp-esque video of "Telephone" (in 2010),[1] or the introduction of the pinup persona of "B.B. Homemaker" for the video of "Why Don't You Love Me",[2] one would argue that most of her performances can hardly be related to the subject of camp at all. The reasons why Beyoncé's camp remains clandestine may vary. As of now, the artist has not overtly connected her persona with queer culture the way the rest of the divas explored here have. Queer audiences, though, comprise considerable parts of the artist's fandom and her icon seems to have largely been embraced by queer culture itself. Beyoncé currently enjoys somewhat of a regal status in celebrity culture—even her latest public appearances tone up her queenly divine character[3]—a status that is forged with diva qualities and is where the camp pleasure of her icon lies. The artist's diva camp exists in the ways she stages her body politics as well as in the coded praxes these politics carry, revealing a great pool of referential connections with Black queer and camp culture.

Beyoncé emerged in the music world as a member of R&B group Destiny's Child in the mid-1990s. Ever since, a distinct feminist discourse has run through her songtexts and performances. From the group's empowering hits "Independent Woman, Pt. 1" and "Survivor" (in 2001) to the solo anthems "Single Ladies (Put a Ring on It)", "If I Were a Boy" (both in 2008), and "Run the World (Girls)" (in

2011), the artist has engaged in a performative dialogue with her female audiences by being vocal about the gendered challenges today's women face. In the course of her career, Beyoncé has increasingly identified herself as a modern-day feminist and arduous supporter of the economic equality of the sexes. In fact, she is best known for employing an all-female band on stage, named the Suga Mamas, when the majority of concert crew bands are male oriented. Inextricably linked with her feminist advocacy within her work is race, since the artist performs from the organic position of Black female subjectivity. In particular, the release of her sixth studio album, *Lemonade* (in 2016), saw her making a political and aesthetic statement by placing urban and peripheral Black culture center stage. In doing so, the artist materialized this movement with particular emphasis on Black womanhood and sexuality juxtaposed with narratives of Southern tradition and storytelling. What is important to underline, though, is that as much as her performances openly address a (Black) female audience, they also appeal greatly to a considerable portion of queer male consumers. What I will argue is that the artist's corpus of feminist discourse and racial politics often coexists with a camp sensibility, enticing thus a queer audience. This intersection of camp, race, and feminism will help in gaining a better understanding of the cultural affiliations of the diva with queer culture by laying focus on the camp expositions of her stage. The scope of this chapter is to examine the performances of Beyoncé from a camp lens in an effort to trace queer poetics behind her body politics as well as investigate camp's relation to Black queer culture.

Queer audiences do populate Beyoncé's arenas and her fans pride themselves on their relationship with the diva. As best captivated in the documentary *Waiting for B*, queer and trans fans of color are ardent fans of the artist's work because they can relate to and express themselves through her music and persona (Kehrer 85). Though minimal, the artist too has hinted on her relationship with her queer fanbase: "I've always had a connection. Most of my audience is actually women and my gay fans, and I've seen a lot of the younger boys kind of grow up to my music" (Azzopardi). The elements that form her affiliation with the community, however, point to a network of codes and practices that appear to be long established within the cultural exchange of queer men with pop divas. As has already been made apparent with Madonna and Kylie, Beyoncé too reiterates a familiar diva portrait since her life and icon have been promoted by the media and herself as a typical celebrity narrative that is glossed with the aura of the spectacle and, simultaneously, with a controlled approach of her private life as an everyday story of a young woman. As a case in point, her HBO autobiographical film *Life Is but a Dream* is a narrative of success that presents a glamorous and independent entertainer who, through hard work and with an assertive personality, has now been able to seize her own female American Dream. Interspersed with footage from her professional endeavors are instances where the artist shows her diva/bossy moments and plenty of others where she carefully allows herself to be fragile in front of the camera, especially when discussing issues of depression and motherhood. The film is representative of how the rest of the showbiz media illustrate her icon. Her fans are usually bombarded with images of her onstage persona, whereas their accessibility into her offstage life depends on how she manages her public/private affairs and to what extent she allows their exposure. From music to video to performance, all mediums surrounding the construct that is Beyoncé rely on a mythologization of her that mostly derives from her play on sexuality, femininity, and instantly catchy songtexts. These features are ultimately the elemental basis that has cemented her diva status.

From the beginning of her career with Destiny's Child, Beyoncé was often promoted to stand out from the group, thus creating early enough a self-dependent persona who is in the lead. According to Simone Drake, Beyoncé's father and manager Matthew Knowles was responsible for the public image of the group and, by extension, his daughter's distinctive position within it: "Matthew Knowles arguably decided early on that Destiny's Child would be a crossover group. And just as Diana Ross eventually pulled away from the Supremes to take center stage, Beyoncé was also destined to be a solo pop icon" (84). Years after the group's disbandment, the artist made a savvy marketing of her thoroughly discussed separation from Destiny's Child by reenacting the role of Deena Jones for the film adaptation of *Dreamgirls*. Greatly inspired by Ross's departure from The Supremes, the musical narrates the story of Deena who succeeded in establishing herself in the music industry as a solo act upon her separation from the Dreamgirls group. Beyoncé's leading role in the film not only played on the media obsession surrounding her relationship with her Destiny's Child peers in the late 1990s and early 2000s, but strategically managed to equate her with disco diva Ross, also known as the Boss, thus prefiguring her persona's iconic status. Significantly, after two highly successful solo albums, *Dangerously in Love* (in 2003) and *B'Day* (in 2006), the final Destiny's Child album, *Destiny Fulfilled*, in the years between, and various cinematic endeavors, *Dreamgirls*—itself rich in camp—functioned as a milestone in Beyoncé's transition from the young R&B star to the now mature, dramatic Black diva.

Rather incremental in character, this transition saw Beyoncé's career being significantly influenced by her personal life and her taking steps toward building an independent brand name. Among those noteworthy moments in her life that redefined the public perception of the "Beyoncé" icon was her marriage to hip-hop mogul Jay Z (Shawn Carter) in 2008. In the same year, she managed to found her own production company, Parkwood Entertainment, placing herself as the creative director in every final outcome of her projects (Lieb 77). Explaining how tense her family life had become having her father for manager and how this affected her on a career level, she also decided to part ways with Matthew Knowles in 2011 (Beyoncé, *I am… World Tour*). Finally, she gave birth to her daughter, Blue-Ivy Carter, in 2012 and thus embraced her new social role as a mother, a fact made evident in the postbirth projects of *Beyoncé (The Visual Album)* (in 2013) and *Lemonade*, and further enforced with her second pregnancy in 2017. While keeping her persona's thematic core intact, namely, a racy-cum-trendsetter R&B sound and image, she gradually reduced the number of media interviews given and TV appearances made, relying almost exclusively on the online reproduction of her promotional campaigns via her personal social media platforms.[4] With some widely broadcast performances, including the 2011 Glastonbury Festival (head-lined by an African American woman for the very first time), two Super Bowl Finals (in 2013 and 2016), two fifteen-minute-long performances for MTV (in 2014 and 2016), an extensive Grammy performance in 2017, and, of course, two appear-ances in Barack Obama's inaugural ceremonies (in 2009 and 2013), Beyoncé has succeeded in placing her icon almost out of reach, a truly unsurpassable contem-porary Black diva. It is precisely this unattainable character of the Beyoncé fantasy that nurtures her diva politics and makes her brand not only highly marketable but also considerably influential.

For one thing, Beyoncé's appeal is a result of her performative language. She constantly manages to visualize her songs in ways that make them easily imitable to her audience. Coupled with tongue-in-cheek lyrics, her performances highlight a choreographed and expressive body language that makes use of mannerisms and movements found in Black female and queer culture. As this chapter further explicates, her onstage presentation of Black femininity is instrumental for her exposition of camp. Cultural references to queer icons and other aspects of queer culture are also an essential part of her stage. Examining Beyoncé's tour acts will allow for a closer look into Beyoncé's camp praxes and how these are energized by camp culture as well as endorsed by queer audiences. Moreover, by under-lining those elements drawn from queer culture, this chapter attempts to establish a historicized connection between Black female culture and queer culture, which wrongly comes across as White oriented, in order to better understand the latter as a deeply nuanced and colorful one.

Staging "Queen Bey"

Observing Beyoncé's kinesis and behavior on stage, one soon notices how her body posture and facial expressions instill a swaggering attitude in her performances. In most of her tours, her entrance into the stage is executed in a rather similar way.

As with every opening act of a show, the entrance of the performer relies either on the element of surprise—for instance, Kylie's *Kiss Me Once Tour* introduced a showgirl-costumed female dancer as a Kylie decoy prior to the emergence of the actual Kylie—or on a climactic and pompous introduction—consider Madonna's landing on stage inside the giant disco ball for the *Confessions Tour*. Based on the latter, Beyoncé has developed her own trademark entrance by gradually building on the anticipation of the audience and then allowing herself some time on stage before bursting into the opening number. Either strutting in or emerging onto the stage, the performer always makes use of the dramatic fog effect and slowly materializes before the audience. This atmospheric trick is utilized not only to accentuate Beyoncé's curved silhouette but also to signify and, through its consistent employment, solidify her icon's ethereality by establishing a necessary distance with the audience. After making her way to the stage, she will lock into a mannequin position and there is usually no music heard in the background in order to further intensify anticipation.[5] As a technique popularized by Michael Jackson with his iconic slow removal of the sunglasses, the long pause and pose theatrically underline Beyoncé as a performer who acts leisurely and wants to impose an air of dominance on her surroundings by affirmatively drawing all attention to her stage presence.

Throughout her tour history, the artist has employed the abovementioned technique as the spectacular device that best introduces her audience to her stage world. Renowned for being a perfectionist when it comes to show production,[6] the performer has played on her professionalism and bossy behavior as an acknowledgment of the media hailing her as "Queen Bey" and her fanbase as "The Beyhive." *The Mrs. Carter Show* is the best exemplar of the artist internalizing and performing her queenly status. Foregrounding the image of Queen Elizabeth I, a promotional video for the tour featured Beyoncé as a queen surrounded by her subjects and entertaining court. In slow motion, the visual narrative starts with the help assisting Beyoncé don her regalia and then depicts the performer and her followers entering a court hall striking poses in front of the camera. The video coincided with the online appearance of a song titled "Bow Down/I Been On", which framed Beyoncé as a skilled, independent businesswoman. With lyrics such as "I'm so crown" and "Respect that/ Bow down, bitches," the song affirmed the artist's success in a rather aggressive way and, alongside the show trailer, contributed to a successful marketing of the upcoming tour.[7] A similar version of the video later served as the visual accompaniment of the opening segment of the show. The backdrop video illustrated a coronation scene during which Beyoncé is seen walking with her followers into the throne hall. After being crowned, she stares directly into the camera/audience as her subjects are taking a bow. As soon as the video concludes, the dancers featured in the visual appear with similar attire on the live stage. The artist, having traded her regalia for a sequined athletic outfit now, makes her dramatic entrance and pose before commencing with her performance of "Run the World."

What is important here is that in the tour video Beyoncé appears with her skin painted white, evocative of Queen Elizabeth's "mask of youth." The concept to fully immerse herself in the persona of Gloriana not only renders Beyoncé's approach excessively theatrical but, most importantly, marks it with political valence as she has chosen to toy with Elizabethan standards of beauty, which significantly valued the Whiteness of women's skin as a symbol of chastity. In addition, her leisure in the preparation scene, perhaps a reference to Elizabeth's progressively painstaking process of beautification and dressing, makes Beyoncé's performance consciously camp in the sense that she revels in the plasticity and aloofness of her title.[8] Juxtaposed with the follow-up performance of "Run the World," a song ridden by African beats emphasizing percussion, and Beyoncé's glam sport style, the act creates a camp response not only with regard to the Elizabethan aesthetic and etiquette but also to her performance of race. Camp's everlasting adoration for regality and its conflation with high-brow art is what initially directed camp critics toward following Isherwood's conceptualization of camp as High versus Low. The aristocracy and the elite expressed their cultural superiority through the conspicuous exhibition of affluence, which was often coded in their cultural discourse of taste. In fact, upper-class status was regularly displayed with an aesthetic commitment to camp decorativism.[9] As Sontag argues, "[a]ristocracy is a position vis-à-vis culture (as well as vis-à-vis power), and the history of Camp taste is part of the history of snob taste" (64). A result of class distinction and a sense of superiority, snobbery as attitude has been imprinted upon camp, revealing a need to distinguish oneself from what is thought to be common or low brow, for that matter.

With camp's popularization and relocation in postmodern pop significantly challenging the gap between high and low art, the attitudes of snobbery and superiority as well as camp's fad with regal/aristocratic taste also entered the audiovisual discourses of pop. Honorific names in pop music, for example, partly express a camp aesthetics of royalty and have always been called upon to imagine the icon of a performer atop a social hierarchy. Performance-wise, royalty has time and again been employed as an artistic theme, borrowing all the elements of camp in terms of pompousness, affluence, and superiority.[10] As a derivative of European high culture, however, camp royalty largely conflates its characteristics and, by extension, the sociopolitical space of upper class with Whiteness. Camp after all has been a cultural mode that became widely popular through White, middle-class homosexual men who, aspiring to social ascendance, adopted upper-class mannerisms.

Juxtaposed to this White elitist root, though, is another branch of the trope of royalty that stems from Black culture. David Evans identifies a performance of royalty nominalization from African American blues singers, typically of poor or working-class background. King and prince were titles attributed to male singers (e.g., King Solomon), whereas queen and empress were accordingly reserved for female singers (e.g., Bessie Smith as the Empress of the Blues; Evans 200). Taking into account that most African American performers at the time rose to fame amid harsh socioeconomic conditions and within racist milieus, one can imagine that honorifics were probably attributed by them or by their audience as an acknowledgment of their talent and popularity, but could possibly serve as a subversive (self)proclamation against the notions and practices of White high culture. It is interesting, thus, to see how the White European aspect of the trope correlates with the Black and working-class aesthetic.

Drawing from both traditions, Beyoncé's camp performance of royalty delivers a playful twist on the idea of high White culture by mixing it with her performance of race. Being excessively stylized and mainly static to signify the posh Elizabethan attitude, Beyoncé's performance in Whiteface—a reversal of Blackface—comes in stark contrast with "Run the World's" energetic and aggressive movements. As a reenactment of the choreography executed in the song's original video, *The Mrs. Carter* routine draws from dance styles found in jazz, urban/street genres, and South African culture (Vena, "Beyoncé"). Beyoncé's solo act of the iconic shoulder moves alludes to dance poses popularized by voguers, thus always retaining her performative symbiosis of race with gender. Her onstage performance is a highly inflected one that draws signification from the grassroots "realness" of Black culture. In this light, it can be argued that her employment of camp becomes racialized and is then channeled to parody White elitism. Beyoncé's regal swag accrues specifically from this intersectional point that her performance of camp proposes, resulting in a distinct Black camp style. "Run the World's" lyrics also add to the artist's swagger by aggressively stressing Beyoncé's narrative of success and verifying her status as the Texan girl who worked hard to succeed in the showbiz industry.

The literal staging of Beyoncé as a queen here and, by extension, her camp treatment of it would be referentially irrelevant had it not been for the image of the Queen Bee to cite from, as well. The Queen Bee stands for the self-assertive and usually aggressive Black woman and has indeed been an enduring stereotype within the post-slavery imagery of African American culture. Exploring the social underpinnings of the stereotype in mythic and vernacular discourses, L. H. Stallings argues that the myth of the Queen Bee is based on the actual insect and its mating behavior (172). The writer explains that "[t]he Queen Bee figure surfaces in early twentieth-century Black Harlem Renaissance social life and folk culture" (171).

Often presented as an emasculating matriarch and hypersexualized female, being the equivalent of the threatening Black man, the disposition of the Queen Bee exemplifies deviance, for, as Stalling notes, "[i]n its most denigrating critique and evolution, the [image] becomes the depiction of two stereotypes: the lascivious Black woman and the welfare mother who has children by different male partners, although she never marries one" (174). Her aggressive nature, both in sexual and political terms, cannot be contained by her social surroundings and is, in fact, perceived as a threat. Her non-normative characteristics, namely her being unable to ascribe to her social role as a woman, that is, as socioeconomically inferior to her male partner by early twentieth-century standards, and precisely because her f(l)ailing womanhood undercuts any notion of powerful masculinity, can foreground feminist aspects in Queen Bee's image, who is alternatively presented in certain discourses as "economically and sexually independent and free" (Stallings 175). In this framework, Beyoncé's title and performance of "Queen Bey" is historically grounded since it becomes culturally signified with the marginal poetics of Black womanhood, as this has been shaped by the dominant culture. However, this is done so in a strictly performative sense since Beyoncé's socioeconomic status is by far distanced from the conditions that gave birth to the original Queen Bee image.

As is the case with her archetype, though, the body of "Queen Bey" becomes a focal point and indeed a dense site of discourses. Beyoncé's body has been instrumental in promoting her icon ever since her debut. Destiny's Child offered a successfully packaged and highly sexualized image of the Black female body in songs and music videos, while as a solo performer, Beyoncé continued this consumer-friendly marketing, simultaneously and gradually instilling into her persona a socially aware discourse via the rubrics of feminist advocacy—seeds of which had already been planted with Destiny's Child "Independent Women" and "Survivor". It is still rather ambiguous whether the artist's feminist body politics is radically subversive or whether feminist readings of it have become more inclusive and adaptable in approving Beyoncé's sexualizing tactics as a demonstration of Black female agency. Noel Siqi Duan notes that: "Black women in American history, through slavery and servitude, have not been in ownership of their own bodies or capital. They are either undesirable or hypersexualized" (58). On this basis, the writer is correct when arguing that "Beyoncé's body, consequently, is undeniably linked to her success as a capitalist, as a woman who has succeeded within the current structures of patriarchy and who herself espouses an ableist, neoliberal view of self-determination" (59). Undeniably, it is a positive view when Beyoncé is celebrated as a Black woman who owns her body and inculcates it with political potential. However, this politicization is not by any means unsettling any ideological grids that have for centuries operated to police and commercialize the

Black female body. Is it therefore effective to critically consider Beyoncé's authorship in spite of her endorsement of feminism's primary adversary—namely, patriarchy and its ever-present monitoring of female sexuality?

For what is worth, Beyoncé's body politics have invigorated dialogue among feminists and gender theorists. Although continuous theorization of the Black female body has only perpetuated its ontology as an object of scrutiny, it has helped underline its political nature. What appears to be rather unfruitful an argument, however, are those postfeminist readings of Beyoncé that mistakenly crown the artist's control over her own sexual body as an act of subversion against patriarchal structures. For instance, Marla Kohlman supports that "[r]ather than bemoaning the fate of the 'black female body' as a commodified entity, Beyoncé, and other performers like her have found a way to become an integral part of this process of commodification and reproduction" (37). Reflective of the predominant feminist critiques within Beyoncé studies, Kohlman's view rushes to defend and promote Beyoncé's authorship as a Black woman by comfortingly downgrading the importance behind the process of commodification. Audre Lorde was once adamant when arguing that *"the master's tools will never dismantle the master's house"* (112, original emphasis). Reappropriating patriarchal-friendly images as a tool against patriarchy itself is a conveniently nonexhaustive way to apply a feminist reading over Beyoncé, a fact that problematizes contemporary mainstream feminist rhetoric per se and its neoliberal rationalization of the notion of authorship. Capitalist positions of Beyoncé's cultural production remain camouflaged under the seemingly positive image of feminism that the artist upholds. Nevertheless, since contemporary feminist and gender theory only provides us with a specific political lexicon that can help us critique the ever-adapting power structures, one might indeed have to at least acknowledge Beyoncé's power to promote Black womanhood and imagine it in positions previously inaccessible.

To perceive Beyoncé's body politics not as radically subversive against patriarchal and commodifying practices, but instead as a vehicle that carries the minoritarian Black female subjectivity to an epicenter aligns with the deconstructive potency that camp carries. As previously explicated elsewhere in this project, camp seizes images already found in dominant culture in a playful, albeit always questionable way. Its parasitical relationship with consumerist pop is not an act of subversion against pop's ideological patterns but rather a process that highlights queerness within a hetero-dominantly gendered environment. It is a process that has progressively and significantly added to perceiving contemporary pop as a colorful canvas full of queer colorations. As Helene Shugart and Catherine Waggoner put it, "the mere fact that camp has been commodified as a sensibility does not *necessarily* entail a qualification of its critical rhetorical potential" (42, original emphasis). Through its witty appropriation of images, tropes, and practices, camp's praxis of critical potential—Shugart and Waggoner would opt for "resistive readings" (48)—lies in its power to release tension from highly sensitive and oppressive corpora. As a subcultural strategy, the performance of camp can effectively be employed by its subject to elasticize and self-parody its seemingly oppressed position and thereby recuperate part of the agency it has been stripped off by the dominant culture.

If we were to establish a common ground between camp and Beyoncé's exposition of pop feminism, what is revealed is that both aim at this specific recuperation of a never-granted agency through tension release. As evidenced in most of her performances, Beyoncé's sexuality is the core agent behind her feminist politics, a point elaborately explicated within Beyoncé readership (Drake; Trier-Bieniek). By focusing on camp, though, I want to argue that her performances often shift emphasis on a playful and parodic side of it. While acts such as "Partition" present sexuality in a self-consciously pornographic and serious way,[11] there are acts such as the introductory video for *The Mrs. Carter Show* discussed previously here that employ sexuality through camp relief. A case similar to *Mrs. Carter*'s staging of "Queen Bey," albeit a more definite demonstration of Beyoncé's camp fun, is the performance of "Get Me Bodied" for *The Beyoncé Experience* tour (in 2007). The specific act is introduced with a video depicting a bumblebee and a Beyoncé voiceover that states: "One who is too curious in observing the labor of bees will often be stung for his curiosity. So stand back, 'cause the 'Queen Bey' is about to sting" (Beyoncé, *The Beyoncé Experience*). The performer then emerges in a black-and-yellow robotic armor and helmet, a costume carrying the colorations of the bumblebee. The body-enclosing cast slowly unfolds to reveal the singer in a similarly colored fringe outfit.[12] She then descends to the main stage and is joined by her dance crew to perform the song.

A rhythmically upbeat song, "Get Me Bodied" offers its bounce and R&B sounds for a high-octane performance. What is noteworthy, however, is how the song and, by extension, the performance in *The Beyoncé Experience* places attention upon the body—the Black female body—by trading a corporeality scrutinized by the scopophilic gaze for one that is contagiously choreographic. As is evident by the song's title, the artist establishes a playful mood by breaking the rules of grammar: "body" as a noun becomes a participial adjective and has the ability to receive discursive energy; to "get somebody bodied" would roughly translate as "to get somebody moving/shaking." In addition to that, there is a vital camp substructure at work that effectively decompresses the semiotic burden the Black female body usually carries. Part of the dance routine of "Get Me Bodied" is a reenactment of "The Rich Man's Frug" as it appears in Bob Fosse's 1969 film adaptation of *Sweet Charity*. For the song's music video, Beyoncé fused her own persona with the musical's jovial character, Charity Valentine, appearing in similar

1960s attire while always maintaining a Black feminine aesthetic and cheerfully performing the Frug with her dance crew. The music video was used as a backdrop throughout the live performance, thus placing Beyoncé's emulation of Charity alongside the already introduced and essentially racialized "Queen Bey." As part of the choreography, Beyoncé encourages her audience to act out specific dance moves that she calls out throughout the song. Most of these moves rely on a performance of gender that originates in the praxes of African American tradition and Black womanhood. For instance, Beyoncé imagines her audience as female and invites them to "pat [their] weaves," "pose for the camera," "do the Naomi Campbell walk," and "snap for the kids." All the said dance moves foreground a glamorous performance of Black femininity and are marked with a camp flair: patting one's weaves,[13] Campbell's iconic strut, and the practice of snapping are highly popular practices among African American queer communities and are commonly found in Vogue Femme performances.[14]

Camp indeed brings forth the queer roots within Beyoncé's oeuvre and one can definitely trace elements that establish vertical and horizontal connections between queer and African American culture. Black expressivities in conjunction with Black vernacular are conjured up in the performances of Beyoncé to celebrate the notions of Blackness and femininity. Although one would argue that the artist's work mainly focuses on Black culture, which is not false in its entirety, performances like "Get Me Bodied" attest to the fact that there is also a large pool of references derived from White (gay) culture: *Sweet Charity*, as a generic Broadway product, is only one out of many. Upon referencing such cultural works within her own brand, Beyoncé creates a potent corpus of Black camp by projecting onto it both her icon as well as practices and traditions drawn from her racial background. She then goes on to resell these intertextual performances in a highly Black-inflected way, which can create nuances in the usually default terrain of White culture. As the audiovisual canvas of "Get Me Bodied" illustrates, Beyoncé's camp simultaneously celebrates Black women and Black queer men by placing their culture center stage. In fact, the abovementioned performance has produced a catalog of acts where Beyoncé repeats similar upbeat patterns accompanied by well-known referential motifs that are both entertaining and affirmative in character. The queer undertones and camp vitality resonant within the performance of "Get Me Bodied" indeed became the creative harbinger of the artist's most popular and culturally impactful hit to date: "Single Ladies (Put a Ring on It)".

In order to delve deeper into the discursive and performative legacy that "Single Ladies" has set in motion both within Beyoncé's oeuvre as well as across her audiences, it is of prior importance to contextualize this body of work in relation to the artist's diva camp poetics of her alter ego, Sasha Fierce. The artist's 2008 album, titled *I Am... Sasha Fierce*, demonstrates her decisive turn to a camp-infused aesthetics as first expressed in "Get Me Bodied" and *The Beyoncé Experience* tour. The album features two contrastive sides: the softer *I Am...*, embellished with fragile ballads, and the more aggressive *Sasha Fierce*, which introduced the artist's sexually audacious alter ego under rough R&B and club sounds. Its creative concept relies on black-and-white themes, offering sharp antitheses of Beyoncé's persona that can be traced in the history of the female melodrama genre, as is evident from the multiple, albeit analogous thematic binaries: madonna/whore, passive/aggressive, White/Black, marriage/singlehood, girl/diva.[15] The alter ego has been structured to signify a deviant sexuality, projecting stereotypical representations of Black female promiscuity and brassiness, albeit coupled with an impeccable sense of style. Importantly, the corpus of Sasha Fierce, as its drag-inspired moniker indicates, is permeated by potent camp/queer undertones. Sporting haute couture leotards, pulled and swept-back hairdo, and dramatic makeup, the persona embodies an ostentatious version of Black femininity inextricably linked with an aesthetics of drag and its perception of gender as masquerade. David Hajdu suggests that "[t]he persona that Beyoncé has constructed for Sasha Fierce—a slithery dolled-up parody of a club girl—would certainly make a true drag act if it had a glimmer of self-awareness or irony. It has none" (132). Sasha Fierce may not carry a drag queen's devoted investment in self-parody, her dead seriousness, though, does not prevent her from becoming a source of camp pleasure. As Sontag underlined; "Camp is the glorification of character [...] What the Camp eye appreciates is the unity, the force of the person" (61). The gravity and authority Beyoncé has exerted over her theatricalization of Sasha, veering from the soft-girl-next-door profile to the assertive diva and managing to uphold both roles with equal rigor, prove that Sasha is an enhancement of Beyoncé's icon who simply takes over the stage where the artist already feels at home.

Beyoncé's professionalism here is further supported with performative gimmicks that have been instantly embraced by her audiences. By instilling in Sasha elements of hypersexual femininity and swaggering wittiness, the artist made her body politics a language to be learnt. This is nowhere better apparent than in the audiovisual text of "Single Ladies," which officially introduced Sasha to the public through its instantly attractive lyrics and choreography. Music critics were quick to highlight the song's catchy rhythm and compare it with female empowerment anthems such as the likes of Aretha Franklin's "Respect" and Gloria Gaynor's "I Will Survive" (Crawford). Its viral and cultural impact, though, including YouTube parodies, celebrity cover versions, and perhaps the campiest moment in postmillennial gay culture, namely Liza Minnelli's rendition of it in *Sex and the City 2* (in 2010), relied on the seeming simplicity that Beyoncé adopted for its execution. According to choreographers Frank Gatson and JaQuel Knight, Beyoncé was again inspired by Fosse's *Sweet Charity*: this time the "Mexican Breakfast" number served as the performative template, with Beyoncé and her two dancers recreating Shirley MacLaine's light-hearted routine in an extremely minimal setting. As was the case with "Get Me Bodied," Beyoncé once again infused the allegedly White camp tradition of musical with African American tradition: elements of J-Setting, a Southern dance style developed by female students in Mississippi and popular among Black gay men, are traceable in the choreography (Herndon). The notorious routine is mostly based on simple and easily imitable movements with emphasis laid on the twirl of the hand and the sassy facial expression that accompanies the songtext's call to "put a ring on it" ("it" being the finger). In the music video and throughout the *I Am... World Tour*, Beyoncé would wear a metallic glove—perhaps a symbolic act of Sasha's iron defense against the matrimonial ring—that further underlined the flamboyant twirl of the hand. "Single Ladies" is a multilayered audiovisual text with its vital camp basis found almost in every layer: the bent wrists, the nod to the musical's generic gaiety, the J-Setting poses, the fierce attitude, the iconic outfit, and, on top of these, the tongue-in-cheek language.

As a cultural artifact, "Single Ladies" has lent its performative language for the creation of strong female/feminine communities. Though the songtext is open to interpretation of a pseudo-feminist discourse, since one might argue that as much as it celebrates female singlehood, at the same time it promotes availability for the next man of interest, its impact has been considerable precisely because of its theatrical and cheeky nature. The ability the song has to instantly signify an ostentatious femininity when performed will certainly grant it the status of camp classic over the course of years (if not yet). Its power to overtly feminize the body through its movements partly rests in Beyoncé's performance of femme poetics through the persona of Sasha. Being ultrafeminine and self-aware, the character of Sasha deploys femme-ness fused with abrasive style and Black urban slang. Despite the fact that Beyoncé's celebrity status seems to be quite dissonant with the urban and working-class milieus, Sasha's performance draws from their cultural pool both the aggressive attitude and the street-smart lexicon in order to authenticate her narrative of success, following the discourse of street "realness" that abounds in the works of both male and female hip-hop artists such as Tupac Shakur, Jay Z, 50 Cent, Missy Elliott, and Lil' Kim. Beyoncé's "urban queen realness" is ambiguous, to say the least, yet her attempt comes across as deliberately plastic. Sasha is a self-proclaimed diva and remains a conscious stage act, a camp artifice whose sole purpose is to entertain. It could be argued that her purpose is rather apolitical and perhaps unable to effectively emulate a feminist model. Much like a drag act, though, Sasha's critical power lies at the said self-proclamation of her diva status, the role-playing of which offers an assertive camp mask that serves both a defensive and an offensive purpose.

The performance of "Diva" for the *I Am...World Tour* is indicative of such self-proclamation. Contrary to the camp fun of "Single Ladies" and "Get Me Bodied," "Diva's" camp plays on the idea of seriousness and swagger. Introducing the act is a video vignette where Beyoncé is seen wearing a mechanical suit with leopard-print details. She is robotically walking on a snowed plateau and when the camera focuses on her, she takes off her protective visor to reveal her face, which momentarily transforms into an aggressive leopard's head. The vignette concludes with her shedding tears, as the performer emerges on the live stage. Surrounded by dancers posing as mannequins, Beyoncé/Sasha is clad in a metallic leotard that emits flickering lights from her loins. In the song's riffs, she declares her diva status with technologically altered voice, while in the chorus she composedly utters her own definition: "Diva is the female version of a hustler."[16] With the poetic aid of African American slang, the songtext of "Diva" indeed aligns Sasha with hustlers, the quintessential figures of illegal and shady activity, while presenting her bragging about her achievements. In terms of performance, the choreography, emulating the one originally executed in the music video, entails expressive hand movements as well as catwalk strutting and posing with hands on waist, head kept upward to indicate superiority, and rigid facial expressions to signify seriousness.

Beyoncé's conceptualization of a mechanically feminine body here invites posthumanist readings of corporeality that imagine an artificially constructed body—that is, a female body—that incorporates and simultaneously transgresses cultural standards of femininity. Based on Donna Haraway's seminal concept of the cyborg,[17] Susana Loza explicates the term fembot (femme and robot) that, at this point, applies rather aptly on the praxis of Black diva. Loza defines the disco/house diva as fembot due to her femininely erotic disposition and technologically propped sound: "the fembot is the feminised machine that rearticulates and encapsulates the worst in sexual stereotypes. Her anatomically exaggerated attributes reassure the liberal humanist subject that not all dualities need give way," unlike Haraway's cyborg that epitomizes a bodily fusion of dualities (351). In this light, Beyoncé's performance embodies stereotypical representations that accrue from the strictness of the male/female duality, with the artist's persona sticking fervently to the artificial presentation of the latter. In fact, this may also evoke cultural misconceptions of a constructed female body attaining the status of the desirable by means of adornment and beautification, as opposed to the natural, raw male body. Yet, the fembot Sasha toys with the idea of artificial femininity to a camp effect, presenting her realization of it in an exaggerated manner that underlines its ironic twist.

More importantly, the plastic performance of "Diva" is a mold that binds together cultural elements of Black womanhood under the rubrics of camp. Being a Black female and feminine body, the body of Beyoncé stands as a discursive corpus that bears manifold corporeal histories of racialized female subjectivity. Her invocation of animalistic sexuality signified by Sasha's metamorphosis into the leopard as well as the allusion of the desolate plateau to a *terra incognita* marks her body with cross-temporal references of Black female corporeality from the African past to the years of chattel slavery. The Black female body has for centuries fascinated the Western world, which would often view it as exotic, earthly, and highly sexual; consider the early nineteenth-century case of Saartjie Baartman[18] or, later on, the twentieth-century performances of Josephine Baker.[19] Fascination, however, has always coexisted with a history of racial oppression wherein the Black female body has time and again been subjected to narratives of trauma, torture, and sexual degradation, and has been cooped up in images of lecherousness and deviance. The American popular imagery, as a matter of fact, abounds with figures of jezebels, sapphires, and welfare queens.[20] From the position of camp, though, Beyoncé's Sasha act glamorizes the Black body in a way that not only stresses feminine iconicity as a pure ideological as well as bodily construct but also assertively plays on images and histories of Black womanhood. The clean-cut robotic posing of the "Diva" fembot adds more to the artificiality of femininity and, perhaps, serves as an allegory of a defense/defiant mechanism that highlights the right of a survived body to claim its ontology and celebrate it now, even in an overtly swaggering and superficial way.

Ultimately, Beyoncé's performance and, by extension, her icon itself manage to braid intergenerational Black female corporeal experiences under one: the celebratory corporeality of the Black diva. Born out of the disco era and later transferred to the house music scene, the figure of the Black diva has always been a spectral figure, a fierce mother embodying gendered, racial, and sexual narratives. Investigating the queer house scene, Brian Currid identifies the image and sound of the Black diva as central for its development:

> The voice of the black diva is essential to any generic definition of House music. The pleasures around her disembodied voice on the dancefloor can be described as identificatory—a channeling if you will of the fierceness and soulfulness of her gospel-inflected singing style. (186–87)

Although rarely has Beyoncé's live sound incorporated elements from the house scene, her posture and attitude, as already pointed out, draw from Black disco divas, such as Diana Ross and Donna Summer.[21] In addition, the mechanized performance in "Diva" as well as the distorting effect in her voice and choreography, which foreground her diva body as a hybrid entity, manage to reflect a necessary narrative multiplicity that allows for layered readings. It is this artificially constructed femininity, though, that has for years nurtured the tradition of camp and has succeeded, through its celebration within queer subcultures, in becoming a victorious and sexually assertive site/sight of expression. The image of the Black diva, who stands as a survivor of a sexually and racially oppressed body, provides Beyoncé's icon with essential communal power.

Undoubtedly, it is under the camp-baptized ontology of a diva, be she a glamorous Hollywood icon or a fierce drag queen, that gay communities in part have come and are still coming together. As a Black diva, Beyoncé inhabits the intermediate space between Black/female culture and queer culture. Her being a source of camp pleasure derives from this position and her ability to enrich her stage with praxes enclosed within both. Her icon retains its camp qualities not only due to its theatricalized environment, namely, the terrain of performance, but especially due to the effect this environment exerts upon the subject matters of race and gender, which can expose their ideological fabrication. Therefore, to approach the artist's performance as camp is to read her treatment of gender and race as performable through and through. On this very basis, Beyoncé herself can be viewed as an agent of camp. Albeit promising, this fact alone may be insufficient to let us draw a solid argument regarding Beyoncé's camp appreciation by queer audiences, let alone lead to safe conclusions as to her camp's potentiality to serve an effective cultural critique. Camp per se, after all, has been a subject of ambiguous nature, mainly because of its superficial and at times apolitical nature. In order to delve deeper, one has to look into the joints of Beyoncé's camp where African American (female) culture interacts with queer culture. What accrues from this interaction, as we shall see shortly, is camp's power to ritualize practices of queer culture as a means of forming communal bonds.

Slay trick: Black women and queer men in formation

What characterizes Beyoncé as a leading figure in the contemporary pop music scene is her power to popularize her products through trendsetting. Her songtexts abound in catchy lines that allow her audiences to instantly identify with and often internalize their vocabulary. Beyoncé's lyrics have always pointed to a direct memorable status, a fact that has only been amplified in the social media era and the culture of memes.[22] One might remember how *B'Day*'s "Irreplaceable" (in 2006) popularized the catchphrase "to the left, to the left" and made it synonymous with breakup. Years later, *Beyoncé*'s "Drunk in Love" (in 2013) was taking over the internet with the word "surfboard,"[23] while the same album's "Flawless"— discussed further down—popularized a pop politics of gender equality with its wide usage of the title word (hashtagged as #flawless in media platforms like Twitter and Instagram) and the self-assertive line "I woke up like this." *Lemonade*'s impact was also felt through the seeming ubiquitousness of the word "slay" from "Formation", and the sassy phrases "Boy, bye" and "Becky with the good hair" from "Sorry". Taking advantage of the power of meme culture to rapidly disseminate trends, Beyoncé and her production team knowingly capitalize on the popularity of each catchphrase. The tour merchandise from *The Mrs. Carter Show* and *Formation Tour*, for that matter, featured all kinds of memorabilia such as hats and T-shirts with imprints of already popular lines, including "Surfboard," "I woke up like this," and "Slay all day."

What is important, though, is that each catchphrase is also expressed with a body movement, pointing thus to a performative language. For instance, "Irreplaceable's" "to the left" is performed with both finger indexes pointing to the left side of the body in the way Beyoncé did in the song's music video and repeatedly in every tour performance of it, while "Sorry's" "Boy, bye" is again performed with a hand movement as if to order someone away. The gestures that Beyoncé reenacts for each phrase underline a performance of femininity found in Black female and queer culture. As has been made evident throughout this work, a camp understanding of femininity has for years nourished queer subcultures and underground performing communities. Inasmuch as femininity is permeated by additional markers of, say, race or ethnicity, its camp performance will also adapt accordingly. Historically speaking, E. Patrick Johnson argues that

> black gay men adopt more tropes of black femininity than black masculinity. One reason might be a general connection to black women as another oppressed minority [...] Origins of particular vernacular terms, phrases, and gestures, for example, are often disputed between the two groups because they are performed within both. (*Appropriating Blackness* 89–90)[24]

In incorporating these gestures in her performances, Beyoncé draws from both cultures and brings their minoritarian practices alongside her (hyper)visible icon. At the same time, as we will see, she commodifies these practices by making them available within the economy of her spectacle.

Two pieces of Beyoncé's work that outline this conjunction of Black female and queer cultures are "Flawless" and "Formation." First, "Flawless" is a self-branded feminist manifesto that quickly gained popularity via the social media. The song consists of two parts, "Bow Down" and "Flawless," while a quote from Nigerian writer Chimamanda Ngozi Adichie's TED speech on "We Should All Be Feminists" serves as its interlude. Similar to "Single Ladies" and "Diva," "Flawless" features a memorable and easy-to-copy choreography, whereas its swaggering lyrics point to a readymade self-assertive anthem. Beyoncé invites her audience to shout "I woke up like this"—stylistically pronounced as a vernacular "dis"— twirling her hands in front of her face. Feminism-wise, music and cultural critics have questioned Beyoncé's pop treatment of the movement and the song's overall political effectiveness. Michelle Carroll noted that despite the fact that through "Flawless" the artist has brought mainstream attention to feminism, the song presents an oversimplified version of the movement's message and even fails to fully incorporate Adichie's call to collective action. Furthermore, it can be argued that aside from Adichie's quote, "Flawless's" songtext appears to offer an ambiguous approach of gendered reality, especially when we consider lines such as "Bow down, bitches" and "Momma taught me good home training," which only seem to perpetuate a heterosexist and patriarchal evaluation of female subjectivity. What I would like to argue, though, is that by revisiting "Flawless" through the discourse of camp, the subject of feminism finds an alternative and indeed queer route to successfully emerge.

Beyoncé's take on feminism with "Flawless" has invigorated academic dialogue, which in fact witnesses a dichotomy concerning the core values of the movement. This dichotomy derives from the artist's contradictory stance of occupying spaces of feminist advocacy and, simultaneously, performing under the surveillance of the scopophilic gaze. While there are critics who argue against her effective incorporation of feminist discourse in her work—most notably hooks and her critique of the artist as an "anti-feminist" and a "terrorist" of gender (Trier-Bieniek 1)—there are those who have acknowledged the artist's ability to present her stereotypical framing of Black womanhood as a performative device that wishes to hollow the said framing from within. An intersectional model of feminism sees multivocality and agency in seemingly confining positions and images that are controlled by patriarchal power grids. According to Kohlman, "[i]intersectionality highlights the ways in which categories of identity and structures of inequality are mutually constituted and defy separation into concrete categories of analysis" (34). The writer underlines that

> [b]y noting the ways in which men and women occupy variant positions of power and privilege across race, space, and time, intersectionality has refashioned several of the basic premises that have guided feminist theory as it evolved following the 1950s. (34)

Beyoncé performs from various questionable positions, such as the female hustler, the aggressive Black woman, or the vamp, which, when viewed through the lens of intersectionality, appear to instill agency in the artist's conscious choice to inhabit them. However, one has to be very cautious as to how conscious choices are formed, especially in a culture that has for centuries promoted particular images of femininity, sexiness, beauty, and deviance as well. An intersectional approach of Beyoncé's diva camp, which deliberately utilizes well-known and at times formulaic expressions of character-femininity, may as well enclose a flexible political valence, but this does not make them any more immune to patriarchal ideologies from which they stem. Rather, the intersectional power of Beyoncé's camp should be sought for in the conjunction of queer, Black, and female culture that fuel her performances.

Despite dealing with themes of confidence and perfect imperfections, "Flawless" as an audiovisual corpus is highly stylized, both aesthetically and discursively. In the music video, Beyoncé appears in a black-and-white urban setting, surrounded by female and male dancers whose street style draws influences from punk and rockabilly aesthetics. The artist herself sports denim shorts with plaid shirt and the hip-hop-accustomed bling, thus positing her persona in a street-smart working-class position, as she casually did with Sasha, and perhaps saluting a lesbian sensibility—via the stereotypical image of the plaid-shirted dyke. Her doing so points to a need to authenticate both her affiliation with street subcultures and her radical-ish invocation of feminism. As far as lyrics go, the song is a display of material accumulation, a theme Beyoncé has frequently explored in her oeuvre. Performing from a privileged status wherein her diamonds are flawless and her husband's record company is flawless too, the artist deliberately embraces the incongruity resulting from the collision of her capitalist-haloed position with the "realness" of the working class. She flaunts her street fabulousness and places a siren call to her audience to follow her steps. "Flawless" is concerned with the adoration of sleek surfaces and donning of masks; its discourse is ultimately all about embracing pure artifice. Examining the song as potent feminist critique, Parul Sehgal draws the necessary connection between the word "flawless" and the subculture of drag: "[t]he idea of beauty as performance—and as successful gender performance—is not what's new [...] '[F]lawless' has been part of drag argot for years" (Sehgal). Featured in Sehgal's article is historian of drag culture Joe E. Jeffreys who argues that the word dates back to the underground culture of the 1960s and is probably associated with drag mother Flawless Sabrina, an iconic performer who was in close liaison with William Burroughs and Andy Warhol (Sehgal). By evoking a history of camp, "Flawless" is an exclamation that perfectly resonates with a performance of plastic, yet accomplished femininity. Its camp appeal relies on witty responses and theatrics of self-parody against the imposed gender construct, therefore becoming an ironic feminist invocation crowned with queer poetics. Deliberate or not, the song and, by extension, Beyoncé's usage of camp slang enclose a queer dynamic in the sense that it utilizes a discursive mechanism against gendered evaluations of beauty and is simultaneously linked with a culture, that is, that of drag, which has so fervently challenged the very notion of gender.

From a racial perspective, "Flawless" establishes communication with Black culture in a way that camp's dealing with race becomes culturally grounded. Upon releasing the song as a single in 2014, Beyoncé wrote additional lyrics and had rapper Nicki Minaj featured in it. During its final stop in Paris, Beyoncé's joined tour with Jay-Z, named *On the Run Tour*, saw the two divas joining forces on stage. Minaj is a performer whose public persona has been connected with an oversexualized representation of the female body, yet her approach usually tilts to camp parody. Her frequent experimentations with her icon include a Barbie doll character fashioned out of anime characters, and an alter ego, named Roman Zolanski, a frenetic British gay man living inside her (Vena, "Minaj's Alter Ego"). Minaj brings her own aesthetics into the song, a *Nicki-aesthetics* as Uri McMillan specifies, which "pointedly aligns blackness with camp as interlocutors, rather than antinomies" and "importantly reconfigures camp as a female-centered practice" (82). Also, Beyoncé's street authenticity is further amplified, this time relying on Minaj's hip-hop background. The remixed version toys with the singers' celebrity lifestyle and indulges in explicit sexual references, themes of materialism, and, yet again, regality. In its display of camp, "Flawless" here once more foregrounds Beyoncé's image of the Queen Bee. Revisiting Stalling's argument, it becomes clear that

> [i]n any Queen Bee myth, sexuality becomes power to be wielded for protection, a door to independence and pleasure, and a marker of criminality and outlaw status. The potency of her sexual desire, perceived as abnormal by mainstream society, makes her murderous seductress. (173)

Queen Bee's outcast social status and thereby her developed sense of antagonism in a hostile patriarchal environment are the cross-sectional point of her performance of aggressive sexuality with camp's performance of gender as a counter-hegemonic strategy. Beyoncé and Minaj's "Flawless" is simultaneously energized from both power positions, providing ironic narratives that are nonetheless spaces of empowerment for sexually non-normative subjects to occupy. An intersection of camp poetics, race, and feminism here proposes an elastic understanding of identity that appeals similarly to a spectrum of racial, sexual, and gendered spectators.

Not very much unlike "Flawless," *Lemonade*'s "Formation" addresses Beyoncé's fierceness in consonance with her cultural background, notions of Black womanhood, and queer discourses. Lyrically, the song proves to be repetitive of cliché themes such as materialism, already found in the artist's songwriting catalogue. Nevertheless, by tracing her heritage in the Deep South and highlighting her Creole roots through post-Katrina images of the city of New Orleans, the artist produced "Formation" both as an intergenerational homage to Black female power and an indictment against police brutality over African American individuals. Importantly, the music video lays emphasis on the city's queer culture by incorporating footage from *That B.E.A.T.*, a 2012 documentary on the dancing culture of bounce and its affiliation with the city's queer community. The featured vocal presence of native New Orleans bounce acts, here late rapper and comedian Messy Mya and bounce queen Big Freedia, in the song's lyrics further consolidates the visibility of the city's queer culture.[25] In addition, "Formation's" reiteration of the exclamation "Slay" wishes to place Beyoncé at the heart of contemporary queer culture by employing yet again a slang term (closely related to and sometimes interchangeable with "fierce") that oozes swagger. As Kehrer explains:

> The very language and concept of "slaying" is directly derived from Ballroom culture, and Beyoncé's use of this language outside of its Ballroom context evokes both the competitive nature of balls and [...] the kinship networks that "slaying" constructs and sustains. (89)

The song thus is forged with queer poetics drawn from underground queer scenes and in fact manages to render the queer minoritarian subject visible in a rather celebratory and inviting way.

Forged with camp expressivity, the performance of "Formation" for the homonymous world tour exemplifies a communal call to bring together racial and gendered group. More specifically, the tour's stop in New Orleans in September 2016 gave the city's queer culture the opportunity to emerge central within the Beyoncé spectacle. Being the introductory and perhaps the *tour de force* act of the show, "Formation" here opened with local celebrity Big Freedia. The artist's queer/drag profile and her association with the bounce scene of New Orleans undergirded the performance with a vital local camp flair. By emulating Beyoncé's antebellum-inspired fashion, Freedia appeared on stage to perform her spoken vocals as featured in the song. Her lines are call-outs derived from the bounce scene; in particular, she announces: "I didn't come to play with you, hoes/ I came to slay, bitch/ I like cornbread and collard greens, bitch/ Oh yas, you besta believe it." The wide usage of Black queer vernacular here indicated by slang terms such as "hoes" and "yas," as well as the allusions to Southern cuisine ascertain Freedia's regional authenticity and further bind Beyoncé's icon with a grassroots sensibility. With regard to bounce, Matt Miller explains how "[l]ocal music critics dismissed bounce as apolitical 'rap-lite' with crude 'sex and violence'–based lyrics meant to entertain an underclass in pursuit of pleasure and escape," yet he stresses how it has served "as a forum for the critique of prevailing attitudes and practices within and outside of poor and working class black communities" (7). Freedia's profile, in particular, is representative of how bounce, notwithstanding its crass lyricism and stereotypically gendered narratives, upholds a queer aesthetics and critique in her explicit foregrounding of queerness.

Being part of the allegedly masculinist and homophobic rap culture, the figure of the "sissy rapper" has managed to become a respected and visible figure. As Miller argues:

> The character of the "sissy" has a long and rich history within African American vernacular culture, and the participation of gay performers in New Orleans rap builds on similar efforts in the city's popular music scene dating back to the early twentieth century, if not earlier. (156)

With their sexually explicit lyrics and a distinctive call-and-response performing style that originates in the convention of rap battles, the performances of "sissy rappers" usually entail an antagonistic relationship with performers who fervently disavow homosexuality, including closeted individuals wishing to pass as heterosexuals (Miller 156). Arguably, the image of the "sissy rapper"—here, Big Freedia—attests to a performed Black camp tradition that has developed in a significantly different way to the dominant—read White—camp culture. Sissy rap/bounce evokes a history of homosexuality and effeminacy that deviates from the elitist canon of Broadway musicals and Hollywood diva worship, and remains bonded to the working-class art-making of the African American community. Miller, in fact, notes that just as sexual orientation influenced the artistic personae of "sissy rappers," so did their attachment to New Orleans' grassroots insularity (170). Beyoncé's decision to feature Freedia and the subculture of bounce in her *pièce de résistance* can be viewed as part of the wider recognition Black queer culture has attained over the years. Simultaneously, though, this localized performance of camp is a manifestation of how the diva centralizes Black cultural praxes around her icon in order to authenticate her own performance of Black camp.

"Formation" indeed stands as a visual amalgam created from numerous aspects of African American culture: from the revival of the plantation mansion to the contemporary ghettoized/policed cityscape, to the performance of bounce and the vernacular. Alongside the authenticity and communal call they sought to bolster, these images become highly stylized through the icon of Beyoncé. Expectedly, the artist cannot fit the image of an ordinary Black woman. Quite the contrary, as the music video demonstrates, she is the world-famous diva who fuses her signature leotards with antebellum fashion, repeats almost *ad infinitum* that she slays, and is a force of nature who sinks a police car, the representation of institutionalized state power. Her making manifest her superiority is accompanied with a glamorized exhibition of Black culture. The visual and discursive characteristics of it are thus promoted as authentic, real, and always with a swagger. "Formation" embodies Blackness in a solely performative way, by marking it as attractive, imit- able, and, most of all, marketable. Despite the fact that Blackness per se cannot be fully comprehended and expressed through means of performance—as Johnson suggests, only the "living of blackness" can become "a material way of knowing [it]"[26]—popular culture products like "Formation" arguably offer a glossed-over racial reality.

Because of the wide impact of "Formation" and, later on, its parent album, criticism was directed to the conundrum of cultural appropriation. Specific- ally, critics focused on the appropriation of Black female culture by White gay men. Although clearly not something that can be deemed an emerging phenom- enon, the cultural debate seems to have remained unresolved because of its com- plexity: namely, the socially, politically, and historically different power networks pervading both cultures. In July 2014, an Op-Ed article on *Time*, titled "Dear White Gays: Stop Stealing Female Culture" written by Black female graduate student Sierra Mannie, triggered a barrage of responses with regard to the topic. Mannie opened her article by stating: "You are not a black woman, and you do not get to claim either blackness or womanhood. There is a clear line between appreciation and appropriation". Following Mannie's piece, the 2015 National Union of Students Women's Conference in the UK requested that White gay men stopped appropriating Black female culture and underlined White gay males as a privileged group within LGBTQ+ communities (Apple). Counter-argumentative pieces were also written on various online platforms, including a direct response to Mannie's article (again featured on *Time*), titled "Dear Black Women: White Gays Are Your Allies, So Don't Push Us Away", penned by Steve Friess, a White gay man from Detroit, whose allegedly patronizing tone was met with backlash.[27]

Although both sides of the debate made valid points regarding White gay men internalizing elements of Black culture and the actual extent that this is hap- pening, the issue of appropriation per se largely remained phantasmal. In order to understand how appropriation works one has to investigate both the direct interactions between the communities and, more importantly, the indirect mech- anisms that allow the sharing of culture, namely the commercialization of it via mainstream pop and social media. In the long tradition of camp, there have been instances when indeed cultural appropriation and cultural borrowing, or even appreciation, as Mannie underscores, were hardly indistinguishable; a case in point is Madonna's infamous engagement with vogue culture in the early 1990s (see Chapter 1). As a queer praxis, camp is a performance of gender, a theatricalization of its surrounding environments, and, ultimately, a mimetic strategy employed to parody ideological constructs. For that matter, White suburban womanhood and White glamorous femininity have frequently been targets of camp parody, whose treatment of them walks a thin line of sexism and misogyny, but, usually, their performative discourse is called upon in camp culture to reveal fissures on heteronormative social structures as well as to make manifest queer understandings and livings of gender. Similarly, Black womanhood has been part of camp's arsenal, used both by (White and Black) gay men and (Black and White) women as a means of generating irony or in order to evoke narratives of empowerment against patriarchal ideology.[28] Apart from the contemporary scenes of vogue and bounce, a tradition of Black camp can in fact be traced in the early twentieth-century Black female stand-up comedy of the chitlin' circuit, a descendant of vaudeville and burlesque, as well as in the period of Harlem Renaissance wherein one finds the origins of drag ball culture.[29] As a matter of fact, Black female and gay male communities have been in cultural exchange and communication for over a century now.

To return to Beyoncé, her icon has been fundamental in the projection of Black female and queer culture to the wider gay male culture worldwide. The way, however, this projection comes across points to its inevitable glamorization as is the case with every pop culture icon and narrative. As a result, elements comprising Beyoncé's work, such as African American camp slang or the aesthetics of Black femininity, are mediated through her persona and, of course, are marketed accordingly. Maciej Widawski identifies stylization among the important features of the slang and its popularization, an argument that, besides linguistics, also applies to the audiovisual work of Beyoncé. According to Widawski, "[p]eople imitate someone else's way of speaking for various reasons such as to identify with a style or an attitude" (112). By popularizing elements of Black culture, both female and queer, Beyoncé renders them commercially available. hooks accurately underscores in her review of *Lemonade* that "[v]iewers who like to suggest [the album] was created solely or primarily for black female audiences are missing the point. Commodities, irrespective of their subject matter, are made, produced, and marketed to entice any and all consumers" ("Moving Beyond Pain"). The idolization of Black womanhood through a camp poetics becomes a stylized corpus that Beyoncé requires from her audience to acknowledge and imitate. Through this practice of imitation, namely the sharing of culture as disseminated and absorbed via Beyoncé's mediator-icon, the Black camp experience, much like its White counterpart, is offered up for consumption.

Notwithstanding its consumerist-driven character, this process of imitation can serve both as a feminist and conspicuously non-White device against patriarchal structures, which may usually be White by default. According to Stallings, "[b]oth Black women and gay men have historically been oppressed within the United States, and they have produced cultures from this particular position. Each group forced Western societies to reconsider their axiological categorization of gender" and their community and identity formation are always juxtaposed to, even haunted by, the "rigid fabrication of white masculinity" (119). With that being said, Beyoncé's performed intersection of camp, race, and feminism functions as a model of empowerment for both groups. To pat one's weave and to twirl one's hands as an indication of a flawless femininity, or to identify with a history of social fierceness by exclaiming "Slay" can practically and effectively fortify a position against heteronormative rigidity itself. Considering how gendered standards impose a system of behavioral codes and expressive lexicons, the highly theatrical language and posture that Beyoncé's performances enclose allow her audiences to challenge, even transgress the said imposed system; one can think how the artist's queer male fandom, by employing the camp praxes of twirling and posing, challenges the very notion of masculinity, according to which men across most cultural and racial maps are supposed to behave or move in a very specific manner: that is, to be sturdy and grave in expression and by no means signify effeminate body posture. Beyoncé's camp praxis provides her queer audience with the performative tools necessary for the expression and vocalization of their queerness, thus highlighting her icon with interactive and instructive qualities.

Furthermore, in terms of race, the artist drawing from African American praxes and fusing Black cultural elements with White heterosexual or gay culture creates an amalgam that, despite being mixed with White-inflected corpora, bears marked racial components that can effectively bring forth a Black aesthetics of performance. Her inclusion of Black queer culture in her work, in particular, helps lay emphasis on the praxis and social character of a doubly oppressed culture that still remains vulnerable to phobic attitudes both inter- and intra-communally. In fact, Beyoncé allowing for the visibility and celebration of a distinct Black camp creates racial porousness on the more often than not White surfaces of dominant gay culture, while simultaneously laying emphasis on the queer legacy of Black culture. Even camp's canon of typically White cultural production gains a nuanced perspective and allows for a more inclusive performance that cultivates queer communal bonding. The work of Beyoncé demonstrates that in spite of the imposing social reality of gender and race, the tools required for its construction can also be utilized, not to overthrow it, but, at least, make it more flexible. The artist's camp is audacious enough to revel in its own plasticity and market economy, but, simultaneously, this audacity accrues from the fierceness developed to combat its very own narratives of oppression.

To conclude, Beyoncé's icon is that of an artist who has taken a turn toward bridging communities across gender and racial generations—perhaps unintentionally so. While her performances tilt to a more frugal display of visual camp, they are historically informed since they remain rooted in queer African American practices. With a steadily increasing appeal in the social media world, Beyoncé manages to offer a spectacle that speaks the language of post-millennial culture without severing any ties with traditions and scenes of the past, thus managing to balance between audiences of varying ages and backgrounds. Although her feminist politics remain nebulous and will certainly prompt academic interest for as long as her icon retains influential cultural power and relevance, the way in which audiences identify with her and incorporate her performative vocabulary into their own expressive lexicon is certainly noteworthy. Her "Beyhive" is a diverse and deeply expressive community of fans who remain loyal to their "Queen Bey." Interesting as it is to see how camp permeates the relationship of the diva with her fanbase, I would like now to turn to the artist that has married her identity politics with her performance of camp. For, when it comes to strong queer audiences other than Beyoncé's, Lady Gaga and her Little Monsters stand synonymous with the current model of creating community through pop.

NOTES

1. In her essay "Follow the Glitter Way: Lady Gaga and Camp," Katrin Horn performs a camp reading of "Telephone" whose video draws elements from 1950s lesploitation films and makes references to Quentin Tarantino's *Kill Bill: Vol. 1* (95–99).
2. In her essay "Beyoncé as Aggressive Black Femme and Informed Black Female Subject," Anne Mitchell argues that Beyoncé's High Femme performance of the Betty Page-inspired "B. B. Homemaker" is an ironic twist of the 1950s heteropatriarchal suburban femininity (45–46).
3. Images of Beyoncé reaching the media often portray her as a queen, a goddess, or a priestess. Consider her photoshoot announcing her second pregnancy in 2017, her 2017 Grammy Award performance, and her dramatic entrance for her 2018 Coachella showcase.
4. As a case in point, consider the unexpected release of the *Beyoncé* album in 2013. Beyoncé secretly engaged in recording sessions and video productions throughout the year without making any public comments on the forthcoming project. The unannounced album was launched midnight on iTunes on December 13, 2013, with Beyoncé simply posting a video of the album cover on her Instagram account and a caption that read "Surprise" (Cupid and Files-Thomson 95). *Beyoncé*'s overwhelming sales within the first two days of its release proved that the artist and her management team had not only strategically made use of the shock value but had heavily relied on the concrete public image and fanbase the artist had built over the past few years. The artist followed the same marketing tactic for the follow-up *Lemonade* as well as her studio collaboration with Jay-Z, *Everything Is Love* (in 2018).
5. Alternative options may sometimes include the use of percussion and marching drumbeat or sound effects of alarm.

6. Backstage accounts have often portrayed the artist as a strict business person. In her MTV documentary *Beyoncé: Year of 4*, she is presented as a workaholic who confesses that "I'm a workaholic and I don't believe in 'No.' If I'm not sleeping, nobody's sleeping" (Beyoncé, *Year of 4*). Likewise, the post-production scenes in the documentation of the *I Am... World Tour* show her punning on the idea of being robotic about her work: "When I work, I don't eat, I don't use the restroom. I'm like a machine. I forget that other people have to eat and other people have to use the restroom" (Beyoncé, *I Am...World Tour*).

7. Released in April 2013 online, the song had also sparked rumors about Beyonc's upcoming album. It wasn't until the following December though that *Beyoncé* was officially released. However, the "I Been On" part of the song did not make the final cut, while the "Bow Down" part was incorporated into "Flawless".

8. Queen Elizabeth I was renowned to have taken more and more time to prepare every day as years went by. With regard to the notorious "mask of youth," the heavy lead-based cosmetics used are said to have had poisonous effects on her skin, adding to the ever-grotesque mythology around narratives of beauty. For more on the Queen's court life, see Anna Whitelock's *Elizabeth's Bedfellows: An Intimate History of the Queen's Court*.

9. From the Baroque and Rococo epoch to Louis XIV and the architectural art of the Chateau de Versailles, even to Victorian dandyism, camp culture exemplifies a self-consciously ultra-decorative culture. As a matter of fact, Beau Brummell and Oscar Wilde were key figures in popularizing dandyism and its devotion to style and etiquette (Booth 72). As far as the French monarch and his Palace go, Booth states that

> Louis XIV's well-known policy of diverting the nobility from politics by means of fêtes and other such Versailles entertainments (Walpole called Versailles "a toy" and "a garden for the great child")—in effect, the policy of maneuvering the nobles into the margins of French life made Versailles a paradigm of high camp society. (76)

10. From her 1990 MTV "Vogue" performance as Marie Antoinette to her emulation of Cleopatra for the 2012 Super Bowl performance, Madonna is the most popular case in point. Other cases include Michael Jackson's art cover for his *Dangerous* album, Christina Aguilera's promotional photography for her fragrance "Royal Desire," and Rihanna's Basquiat-inspired crowning as part of the promotion of her *ANTI* album.

11. "Partition" is a song usually performed in a strip club theme act, referencing influences from Parisian bordello and Las Vegas burlesque acts. The song's bridge is a feminist nod to Julianne Moore's character in *The Big Lebowski* (Hobson 19).

12. The robotic ensemble may have partly been inspired by Minogue's opening act for her *KylieFever2002* tour, where she introduced her futuristic Kyborg persona in a similar metallic armor, which was slowly being removed to accentuate the performer's revealing outfit.

13. According to the *Urban Dictionary*, to pat one's weave, an expression derived from African American slang, is used to signify that a woman who sports an extravagant hairdo has to be careful when fixing her hair; instead of scratching, she relies on patting her hair in order to avoid messing up her appearance.

14. The literal snapping of the fingers is performed by Black queens/divas and signifies a camped-up performance of Black femininity (Johnson, *Appropriating Blackness* 180).

15. For more information on the conventions and themes of female melodrama consider Peter Brooks's "The Melodramatic Imagination" and Pam Cook's "Melodrama and the Women's Pictures," both appearing in Murcia Landy's *Imitations of Life: A Reader on Film and Television Melodrama*, as well as Christine Gledhill's *Home Is Where the Heart Is: Studies on Melodrama and the Woman's Film*.

16. According to Patricia Hill Collins, "the female hustler, a materialistic woman who is willing to sell, rent, or use her sexuality to get whatever she wants constitutes this sexualized variation of the 'bitch'" (128). The fact that one has to specify a "female hustler" presupposes that, connotatively, the word indicates a male subjectivity. A hustler relies on typically masculine attributes of aggressiveness and street-smartness, whereas a "female hustler" is obliged to make transactions in sexual terms. Interestingly, Beyoncé's "Diva" draws both from the masculine and feminine discursive strands of the image of the hustler.

17. As defined in her manifesto, Haraway argues that "[t]he cyborg is a kind of disassembled and reassembled, postmodern collective and personal self" that manages to challenge "[t]he dichotomies between mind and body, animal and human, public and private, nature and culture, men and women, primitive and civilized" (163). Although it does melt some of the above dichotomies, Beyoncé's diva icon is arguably not the androgynous form that Haraway conceptualizes. It retains its feminine traits as this is vital for a femme performance.

18. Also known as Hottentot Venus, Baartman was brought in Europe as an African specimen to be exhibited in freak shows for her large buttocks and genitalia in front of a usually inquisitive Western eye (Wallace-Sanders 18). Subsequently, she became a case subject for anthropological studies, thus epitomizing the ontology of the Black female body as deeply and inevitably violated.

19. Playing on the idea of the already exoticized Black female body, Baker, an African American performer residing in France, was a standard act at the Parisian Folies Bergère. She became famous for her "danse banana" for which she would wear a skirt made out of bananas so as to signify an exoticism. Beyoncé has acknowledged Baker as an influential icon for her stage persona and paid homage to the banana dance in her performance of "Déjà Vu" for the 2006 *Fashion Rocks!* fundraising gala (A. Mitchell 47–48).

20. For more on the history of these stereotypes, consider Collins (56); Jennifer Baily Woodard and Teresa Mastin's "Black Womanhood: 'Essence' and Its Treatment of Stereotypical Images of Black Women;" J. Celeste Walley-Jean's "Debunking the Myth of the 'Angry

Black Woman': An Exploration of Anger in Young African American Women;" and Kimberly Springer's "Third Wave Black Feminism?"

21. In fact, she has established performative connections with both: apart from her Ross-inspired role as Deena Jones discussed in the beginning of the chapter, the artist has sampled Summer's "Love to Love You Baby" in her own song "Naughty Girl" instilling into the latter the sensual eroticism and disco sounds of the former.

22. *Merriam-Webster* defines meme as "an idea, behavior, style, or usage that spread from person to person within a culture." In the social media era context, of course, the idea of the broadness of culture is tandem with instant global sharing.

23. A duet with Jay Z, "Drunk in Love," expresses Beyoncé's physical desire for her man of interest. Specifically, in the second verse, the lyrics state: "Boy, I'm drinking, I'm singing on the mic 'til my voice hoarse/ Then I fill the tub up halfway then ride it with my surfboard/ Surfboard, surfboard/ Graining on that wood" (Beyoncé, "Drunk in Love"). Surfboard probably indicates having intercourse in a shower setting, with the "graining on that wood" pun aligning the regular use of the word "wood" as the actual material of a surfboard with "wood" as a slang term for male erection.

24. The other possible explanation that Johnson indicates, "may stem from black gay male misogyny" (*Appropriating Blackness*, 90), which is prevalent in the camp culture in general. The writer adds that "[t]he fact that black gay men choose tropes of black femininity to perform may suggest that black masculinity or masculinity in general is a more stable, fixed construct and therefore is not susceptible to appropriation" (*Appropriating Blackness*, 90). Consider, here, how popular the figure of the drag queen is in comparison with that of the drag king, a fact that points to the always alluring and playful theatricality of femininity as opposed to the serious and minimal discursive nature of masculinity.

25. According to Kehrer, Antony Barr, also known as Messy Mya, rose to popularity with LGBTQ+-themed YouTube videos and was murdered in 2010 (90). Beyoncé's inclusion of the artist in her song may as well be an acknowledgment of genderqueer people and a reminder of brutality against trans individuals.

26. In *Appropriating Blackness*, E. Patrick Johnson argues that

> blackness does not only reside in the theatrical fantasy of the white imaginary that is then projected onto black bodies, nor is it always consciously acted out; rather, it is also the inexpressible yet undeniable racial experience of black people—the ways in which the "living of blackness" becomes a material way of knowing. (8)

27. *Time* magazine issued a third article titled "A White Man and a Black Woman Hug It Out" featuring Friess and Courtney Jones-Stevens in a dialogue over Mannie's and Friess's pieces. The article in question can be found at the following link: http://time.com/3148567/white-gay-man-black-woman/.

28. Consider the performance of Black womanhood by Mae West as explicated in Robertson's "Mae West's Maids: Race, 'Authenticity,' and the Discourse of Camp" (Cleto), and in Shugart and Waggoner's "Macy Gray: Venus in Drag" an analysis of Gray's performance of Blackness and gender parody (*Making Camp*).

29. For further reading, consider the works of Stallings (*Mutha' Is Half a Word*) and Chauncey (*Gay New York*).

4

Highway Unicorns: Camp Aesthet(h)ics and Utopias in Lady Gaga's Tours

And thus began the beginning of a new race. A race within the race of humanity. A race which bears no prejudice, no judgment, but boundless freedom.

(Lady Gaga, "The Manifesto of Mother Monster," "Born This Way")

And so Dada was born of a need for independence, of a disturb toward unity. Those who are with us preserve their freedom. We recognize no theory.

(Tristan Tzara, "Dada Manifesto")

In the now long history of camp, no other contemporary artist with a wide appeal has so fervently baptized their persona with the queer aesthetic as Lady Gaga has. Her decade-long oeuvre includes a variety of performances, acts, and publicity stunts that, more often than not, have challenged established pop(ular) conventions and thus made Gaga's name synonymous with over-the-top theatrics. Obtaining her moniker from Queen's song "Radio Ga Ga", the persona that is Lady Gaga (her birth name being Stefani Joanne Germanotta) has been welcomed by critics and audiences alike as a harbinger of an alternative—read futuristic—approach to pop that successfully combines dance music with sexual politics undergirded by an outlandish sense of fashion. Simultaneously supported by the music and fashion industry, each promotional move of the artist becomes viral news. Coinciding with her late 2000s debut has been the rise of the social media era, which, not surprisingly, has equally contributed in augmenting her appeal and circulating her art globally. Although her experimental approach to performance and the sociopolitical valence inherent in her work finds artistic lineage in performers such as David Bowie, Grace Jones, Björk, even Madonna, it is important to argue that Gaga has been the new-age artist that has reinvigorated the art of making pop sociopolitically meaningful and managed to spark intergenerational interest, with an apparent focus on youth culture, across music genres, gender expressions, and racial and ethnic backgrounds.

The performer first emerged in the music limelight in 2008. A born-and-bred New Yorker, Germanotta received classical piano and ballet lessons at an early age, while she briefly attended NYU's Tisch School of the Arts before deciding to drop out. She would later intermingle with the underground New York scenes where she would play the piano and regularly perform strip acts as a surprise gimmick to attract her audiences. Her subsequent body of work, in fact, attests to an array of cross-temporal artistic influences from the New York scenes and actively involves the shock value as a means of promoting her persona. Evidently, Gaga's understanding of performance is deeply informed by striptease and drag as well as retains close proximity with sexual cultures, such as those of leather and S&M. Since the beginning of her career, her performance art has been in consonance with the promotion of LGBTQ+ rights and feminist advocacy. In turn, queer communities have positively responded to the persona by establishing a loyal fanbase with vivid expressivity and a distinct camp flair, as we will see further on. In terms of marketing, in multiple occasions Gaga directly addressed her queer following, most of the times presenting herself as an integral part of the community, both through an LGBTQ+-focused agenda as well as by paying homage to the vibrancy of queer culture per se.

The cultural phenomenon that is Lady Gaga has in fact added to the visibility of queer culture. Taking advantage of her influential status as an international act, the artist has engaged in queer activism, participating in rallies, campaigns, and Pride parades—most famously, advocating for the repeal of the "Don't Ask, Don't Tell" policy of the US military through her infamous meat dress shtick at the 2010 MTV awards ceremony. Performance-wise, Gaga constantly draws from the pool of queer art and praxis. Her creative team, the Haus of Gaga, is an assemblage of visual artists, producers, choreographers, designers, and stylists, modeled on Andy Warhol's Factory. The conceptualization of Gaga's tours as Balls in combination with the nomenclature of the Haus and the familial structure of Gaga's fandom (i.e., she is Mother Monster followed by her Little Monsters) attest to a cultural affiliation with the ballroom scene. Furthermore, her work and persona have time and again convoluted the nature of gender and sexuality, vacillating between personae additional to her always-already constructed one, and thus proving how flexible sociocultural identity categories can be. At a time when rumors ignited about her intersex or transsexual status, Gaga would fuel them by appearing in drag as Jo Calderone, her male alter ego (Halberstam, *Gaga Feminism*, xi).

Due to the wide impact the poetics and politics of the artist have made over a relatively short period of time, cultural criticism on Gaga has been extensive, though not exhaustive. Scholars and music critics have undertaken analyses of the artist, dissecting her persona(e) and performances from the perspectives of identity politics (Gray, *The Performance Identities*), queer theory (Hawkins, *Queerness in Pop*; Humann), gender and sexuality (Geller; O'Brien), fandom (Bennett; Torrusio), postmodern art (Lush; Moore, "Postmodernism Killed"), consumerism, and digital age production (Auslander, "Barbie"). In relation to camp, critical interest has been profound, most of the times focusing on Gaga's music video history (Hawkins, "I'll Bring"; Horn) or fashion peculiarities (Gray and Rutnam). However, her stage performances and, specifically, her tour extravaganzas have received, at best, moderate interest as far as a thorough examination of camp is concerned—with the exception of Katrin Horn's camp reading of the revamped *Monster Ball Tour* (in 2010–11). In concert reviews, the camp of Gaga is either addressed in terms of style or not at all, precisely due to its conspicuousness. As with the case of Madonna and Kylie, though, this chapter seeks to examine and problematize this conspicuousness of Lady Gaga's camp in an attempt to, first, deal with her rather underexplored tour history; second, update the emergent gap of academic criticism in the post-Monster era; and, last but not least, place her production of camp along the lines of a performed tradition and queer temporality within a global context.

The artist's stage is renowned for its extravagance and cutting-edge technology. Structurally, a Gaga concert derives its conceptual form directly from the genres of opera and musical theater, though references may also allude to eastern theater genres such as noh and butoh, and also builds its acts upon performance art, all meticulously adapted for the arena environment. While most arena shows following the act-led format present specific narratives for each separate act under a dominant theme or aesthetic, Gaga's shows (with few exceptions) are driven by an overarching aesthetic *and* narrative, which unfolds gradually with each new act. This means that, similarly with a conventional piece of musical theater or drama, acts are well-integrated into one another. Indeed, her show acts are not necessarily limiting in fitting multiple songs within them, but can range from a quick medley to a one-song act, usually accompanied with a costume change. However, if an outfit change signals the beginning of a new act, judging by the rapidity of Gaga's transitions to each new look within the two-hour span—an average number of costumes worn in a Gaga show often ranges from seven to nine—it is well understood that dividing her shows into clear-cut sections is a rather challenging task. It is precisely due to this velocity and fluidity, however, that her shows can support an almost seamless narrative, as in the integrated musical format.[1]

In concert with the postmodern sensibility of her music videos, the narratives of Gaga's shows are self-referential and intertextual in nature. As Iddon and Marshall argue, "Lady Gaga's output is firmly embedded in an intellectual pop culture tradition. Her music videos are intertextually linked to icons of pop culture intelligentsia like Alfred Hitchcock [...] and they are open to multiple interpretations" (2). The way she brings an overload of pop trivia into her work not only requires her audience to be familiar with the breadth and depth of popular culture but, most importantly, to acknowledge the constructed relevance of her persona as inextricably linked with pop itself. For instance, the music video of "Born This Way" incorporates an array of pop culture references: from Hitchcock's *Vertigo* prelude to the futuristic surrealism of Fritz Lang's *Metropolis*, and from the visual homage to Michael Jackson's "The Way You Make Me Feel" (1987 video) to the rhythmic similarities with Madonna's "Express Yourself". Likewise, her shows are a pop panorama of texts that smoothly blend with and provide edge to the flow of the performed narrative. Due to the bombardment of meta-textual information, acts within her shows may end up being incongruous to an unfamiliar viewer. Nevertheless, despite the frequent superfluity of certain acts, the coherence of the overarching narrative, which is time and again signposted throughout a show, remains undisturbed.

What is interesting about these narratives is their coupling of the storytelling rubric with the format of musical theater. David Annandale explains that "[s]torytelling is an important part of Gaga's work, whether in the form of monster battles in concert, the stories in the videos, or the mythology of Gaga's life" (149). Each of the artist's extravaganzas presents its narrative in the form of a musical fairytale wherein Gaga is the first-person narrator. Elements of fantasy are also omnipresent in the shows, adding extra flair to an already lavish spectacle. From unicorns to fairies to female deities, Gaga makes sure her stories are always camp-inflected. In fact, the interplay of Gaga's camp with the genre of fairytale/fantasy deserves analytic focus, since her stage successfully highlights queer nuances within the latter through its creative revisions. Most significantly, not only does camp inject a carnivalesque aesthetic into each fantasy narrative, but it also inflates the dramaturgy of the stories toward a moralistic end. As is the case with the genre of melodrama in stage, film, or television, which makes use of excess to present and preserve, perhaps sensationally, the moral high ground, camp here stylizes and magnifies ironies inherent in Gaga's narratives in order to challenge socially constructed truths around issues of gender and sexuality. It is here that a camp aesthet(h)ics emerges.

By romanticizing narratives of Otherness, the camp aesthet(h)ics of Gaga glamorizes a culture of misfits, underdogs, and "monsters." Keeping in mind that her multilayered shows exhibit a generic connection with avant-garde theater, especially the Theatres of Cruelty and the Absurd as well as the latter's camp manifestation of the Theatre of the Ridiculous, Gaga utilizes the parodic praxis of the aforementioned theatrical traditions to shed light on outcast lifestyles. The fact that her performance indulges in the aesthetics of camp bespeaks of a nostalgic attraction to the dynamic past of queer culture and the political potential intrinsic in its subcultural praxis as expressed through pop culture artifacts and urban communities. The camp politics of Lady Gaga, closely related to the expressive mantra of the Dada movement, imagine an illogical world, "the beginning of a new race," where boxed identities and labeling are treated as nonsensical. At the same time, much like other divas' camp, Gaga's act materializes through her own pop brand. It might as well be argued that since Gaga is a pop culture brand, it is only profitably reasonable that her camp icon can rightly serve as a means of queer-baiting gay audiences. She nonetheless actively embodies a queer ethos through her fervent support and stage treatment of non-normative gender, proving to be an ardent promoter of queer expression and self-acceptance, as most of her tour shows demonstrate.[2]

The fantastic stage and the gendered self

After the international success of her breakthrough album *The Fame* (in 2008), Lady Gaga started gaining cultural momentum and forming a solid fanbase. Whereas *The Fame* intended to introduce the persona of Gaga and pique the public interest—the theme of fame was an end in itself after all—its follow-up, *The Fame Monster* (in 2009), a rebranding of the 2008 album, sought to establish Gaga as a culturally and politically aware performance artist by repackaging her persona from the vain blond starlet to the dark eccentric genius. The signature songs of the album, including "Bad Romance," "Telephone" (featuring Beyoncé), and "Alejandro," saw Gaga immersed in her stylized profile of the "mad artist," which actively contested traditional perceptions of gender and sexuality. The audiovisual canvas of the *Monster* hits epitomized surrealist narratives of Otherness, embellished with a potent gothic aesthetic. Gaga's embrace of the notion of the monstrous Other incorporated identity politics that bespoke of non-normative romances, a failing sexuality, and gendered insecurities. A milestone in the artist's career, *The Fame Monster* proclaimed Gaga as Mother Monster and her fans as her Little Monsters. While it is interesting to see how Gaga inhabits and, by extension, campifies the image of the "mad artist," a masculine position as illustrated in the genres of horror and science fiction,[3] it is of equal interest to see how her stage adapts to the said campification by utilizing elements of the fantastic.

137

Upon the first showcase of the album in *The Monster Ball Tour*, the performer followed the typical act-divided concert format. Two LED screens on each side of the stage and a smaller one in the middle provided a sense of perspective while a runway set across the stage presented some of the acts in a linear movement as though they were televised events, with the cubicle-like structure of the stage alluding to a television box. The *New York Times* review of the performance at Radio City Music Hall stated:

> The staging layered more complications onto the songs, placing Lady Gaga in otherworldly realms. She first appeared behind a scrim showing a computerized grid, with a lighted costume that made her more of a collection of white dots than a body: a figure in an electronic universe, like a digitized pop star. (Pareles)

Gaga herself described the show as "an avant-garde-performance-art-fashion installation, put in a blender and vomited on a pop show," with the basic concept being that the box-like stage functions as a garage where Gaga and her friends experiment with music (Montgomery, "Lady Gaga Reveals"). In the entirety of the show, Gaga alternates between looks, yet there is no specific narrative that binds the show together. The abstractedness of the interwoven acts might as well serve as a symbolic representation of digital reality as this is constructed from and, by extension, saturated with images from electronic/social media. Gaga feeds her onstage reality with those core themes that permeate and formulate contemporary consumer culture; namely, sex, violence, and vice. The conceptualization of these themes relies on metaphors of monstrosity, an apt motif that can perfectly underline the consuming nature of the aforementioned instincts.

Most importantly, the dramatization of this metaphor is perhaps inevitably expressed through a gothic aesthetic that is simultaneously linked with camp. Gaga here embodies a monstrous femininity, the performativity of which remains a thematic arc throughout the history of camp.[4] For instance, the performance of "LoveGame" explores the theme of sex and sees Gaga transmogrifying into a skeletal creature. The song is a synthpop club number that, illustrating the artist's physical desire, quickly garnered criticism for its sexually ambiguous lyrics and catchphrase: "Let's have some fun/ This beat is sick/ I wanna take a ride on your disco stick" (Lady Gaga, "LoveGame") As in the song's video, Gaga on stage holds an actual stick with an illuminated crystal with which she repels her sexually voracious dancers. The performance turns out to be a grotesque camp praxis wherein Gaga in her glittery exoskeleton costume wields the phallic disco stick as a weapon against sexual consumption. Inspired by the 1980s disco scene and with its video citing references from Michael Jackson's "Bad", "LoveGame" includes strong queer undertones. In the history of queer culture and, specifically, gay male culture, penile intrusion constituting a sodomitical act has always been demonized by heterosexist discourse. In relation to the 1980s underground scene and the pathology of HIV/AIDS that wrought both psychological and physical havoc upon queer communities and in part signaled the end of disco (M. Levine), anal sex became a source of anxiety for queer men who viewed sexual abstinence as the best means of precaution against the virus. The performance of "LoveGame" here possibly evokes a queer memory, albeit in a rather eroticized and certainly abstract way. Ironically, toward the end of the performance, Gaga loses her disco stick and abandons her skeletal body in the arms of her dancers to highlight the utterly consuming nature of sexual indulgence.

Although much of what is described above may only be part of a moral narrative viewed from the perspective of Western/American history of queer culture, one cannot dismiss the fact that Gaga's performed stories make manifest their moral in a highly graphic way. The spectacle of the grotesque here, always a vital force for Gaga's stage, provides the poetic aid in making a story luridly dramatized. Grotesqueness, especially in *Monster Ball* and later on in *Born This Way Ball*, serves to glamorize Gaga's eccentricities by presenting familiar tropes to the audience. Gaga's alleged artistic insanity and identity politics of marginality are here aligned with a history of outcast personae that became iconic within popular culture. Kelly Nestruck draws the connection between Gaga's extravaganza with book musicals, highlighting influences, among others, from *Sweeny Todd: The Demon Barber of Fleet Street* and *The Phantom of the Opera* (Nestruck). Both Sweeny Todd and the Phantom are unstable personalities driven by obsession; the artistry of both, namely barbering and composing, is expressed through human pain and death in a traditional gothic manner.

Likewise, Gaga in *Monster Ball* presents herself as the tortured artist who stages her battles with obsession in grotesque acts. Similarly with the gothic musicals, here too the moral outcome of each story has to be made manifest through a cause-and-effect principle. As dictated in the dramatic conventions of melodrama, punishment is reserved for acts transgressing the socially imposed boundaries and, of course, in the patriarchy-ordered melodramatic imaginary, these acts are most of the times gendered (Landy 196). In a rather stylized manner, Gaga's moral stories enclose the principle of (self-)punishment, thus prefiguring her acts as inherently transgressive and, by extension, foregrounding her mad-artist profile. Consider the performance of "Paparazzi" wherein a latex-clad Gaga is suspended from her hair that remains tangled in large rings attached to an iron bar. Two dancers control the movement of the bar, hence Gaga herself, across the runway.[5] By involving bodily pain in the performance, the artist here explores the theme of fame, thereby signaling the extent to which fame torturously invades the privacy of corporeal reality. Drawing (post)dramatic technicalities from the Theatre of Cruelty as well as the body art of Marina Abramović and Yoko Ono, Gaga presents the world of celebrity lifestyle as a surrealist gothic inferno that culminates in her screaming for rescue amidst frenetic camera lights. One should keep in mind that although her narrative acts are guided by the principles of transgression and punishment, it is ensured there is some sort of redemption following—as we shall see in both narratives of *Monster Ball* and *Born This Way Ball* further down—a cathartic end to her dramatic journey that throws her acts of violence into relief.

Gothicism, as the dominant trope here, appropriately accommodates Gaga's monstrous treatment of fame but, importantly and through stylization, manages to underscore the impact of showbiz politics upon the female body by means of camp irony. Similarly with Madonna's frantic assault on her past images in *Sticky & Sweet Tour*'s "She's Not Me" (see Chapter 1), Gaga's performance here takes on the construct of glamorous femininity. It could be argued that, as fame impinges upon Gaga, she revives a gothic tradition of mad women in which female subjectivity dwells on a sane/insane border. Exploring the history of mad women in the genre of gothic, Karen Stein underlines that "[i]n their Gothic narratives women reveal deep-seated conflicts between a socially acceptable passive, congenial, 'feminine' self and a suppressed, monstrous hidden self" (123). Yet, according to the writer, some gothic heroines take their socially branded condition of madness to be an opportunity for exploration of their inner self, "a stage on the journey toward self-knowledge" (124). In deliberately promoting her persona as borderline mad, Gaga wishes to render her performance art a socially aware project. Although it remains nebulous as to whether and how the real self behind the Gaga persona treats mental instability as self-exploration, it is true that her onstage self glamorizes madness in order to expose the irony behind the themes she acts out as well as effectively promote her art by romanticizing its dark eccentricity.

When the artist and her production company decided to upgrade the *Monster Ball Tour* from theater stage to arena in a relatively short period of time, Gaga would further play on her "mad artist" persona. While in the first version of *The Monster Ball*, the artist promoted the revamped show as a completely reworked stage with new acts whose concepts were the brainchild of Gaga and her Haus. When she pondered on her risky decision, she dramatically replied: "I'm throwing out the [original] stage. My team thinks I'm completely psychotic. But I don't fucking care" (Montgomery, "Lady Gaga"). Years later, one of her statements in a documentary about Arthur Fogel, the CEO of Live Nation Entertainment (*Who The F**k Is Arthur Fogel*), sparked media interest and helped sustain her self-foddered myth of psychosis: Gaga claimed that the decision to revamp the tour allegedly led her on the verge of bankruptcy simply because she wanted a revolutionary production to attract Fogel's attention. The arena-scale production was almost twice the size of the original one, incorporating a main stage and a long runway that extended to a smaller stage reaching into the audience. Divided into four segments, the show was conceived of as an electro-pop opera with a New York setting wherein Gaga and her friends are en route to the imagined Monster Ball. Gaga's onstage presence was backed by extravagant props, including a large urban setting with fire escapes and neon signs, a subway car, and a replica of Central Park's Bethesda Fountain that spurted blood. Unlike the original production and despite having been conceptualized in a very short period of time, the revamped show displays thematic integrity and a coherent narrative, successfully blending musical performances with actual dramatic action.

A truly camp spectacle, *Monster Ball* 2.0 epitomizes the idea of theatrical(ized) concert. The stage bears a notable resemblance with Broadway productions, such as *Hair* and *Rent*, which feature the urban background of New York City. Its storyline, though, establishes the most obvious allusion to *The Wizard of Oz*. Much like Dorothy and her friends, Gaga wanders in her Manhattan-inspired fantasy world and encounters various fictional creatures. Concert criticism drew out the similarities between the two productions and mainly complimented the configuration of the stage in terms of fashion and props (Concepción; Montgomery "Lady Gaga Goes"; Petridis, "Lady Gaga"). Interestingly, camp as the dominant aesthetic that binds the show together is hardly addressed in these critiques. The closest evaluation of the show's camp factor, but still without any lexical, let alone theoretical reference to camp, is Dan Aquilante's unenthusiastic review, according to which "[the show] was Broadway for the deranged" and "Gaga's attempt to paint the grit and glitz of NYC was cartoonish". Yet, camp fuels the whole spectacle and is exactly what this critique illustrates: a surreally inflated world that reaches the point of ridiculousness wherein derangement is inscribed upon a Dorothy-like Gaga in the most outrageous fashion. Not only does Gaga here perform the campiness of her icon but creates a camp lineage by aligning her persona and her show with the camp classic of *The Wizard of Oz*. Horn makes a well-put argument in comparing Gaga's extravaganza with the MGM musical, underlining not only the interconnected elements of their camp appeal to queer audiences, but also Gaga's continuation of Judy Garland's gay legacy (85–89). Most importantly, according to the writer, "[the show] evokes community, kinship, and non-biological family ties of the freaks and outsiders, in this case known as Little Monsters, into a Broadway show-act" (Horn 89). The reworked *Monster Ball* presents itself as an allegorical Land of Oz, where queer people and, practically, any other marginalized group come together to form communities. Fans gathering at the concert venues responded to the camp praxis of Gaga, fashioning themselves into the star persona and thus creating a colorful community that celebrated the queer spectrum of her spectacle (see more in Chapter 5). Horn notes that, by equating herself with Dorothy/Garland and at some point with *Peter Pan*'s Tinker Bell, Gaga proposes a camp viewing of the world where gender is reduced to wigs and costumes (92). Her allegorical Monster Ball, apparently the Foucauldian heterotopia that exists "somewhere over the rainbow," proposes itself as a gender-spectral utopia and ultimately a cathartic *telos* in a long journey filled with metaphorical monsters.

What is more, camp helps foreground a queer history deeply connected with the city of New York that in time has become quintessential in the queer imagination. Of course, the employment of camp ends up glamorizing this history and manages to centralize it around Gaga's persona. In spite of that, the show succeeds in preserving an underground past and dramatically reintroduces it to younger queer generations. The tour's Park segment is best demonstrative of this dramatization. In the footsteps of *The Wizard of Oz*, Gaga and her friends here are also struck by a twister that lands them on the simulated Central Park. The segment is then introduced with a video vignette where Gaga appears in leather couture and with antlers on head, dancing amid thorny threes. When the performer and the dancers emerge on stage, they are all dressed in fringed black costumes that resemble animal coats. Already a space that has been signaled as ominous, the stage now transforms into a gothic version of the Bethesda Terrace with its angelic Fountain spurting blood instead of water. The segment begins with the song "Monster," wherein Gaga illustrates her physical romance with a carnivorous lover and for the performance of which she is being sexually ravaged by her dancers in a simulation of a gang rape. This performance is then followed by the Dionysian act of "Teeth," which, similarly staged as an orgy, visualizes the lyrical innuendos of the song about oral sex. The segment culminates with the performance of "Alejandro" wherein the artist bids farewell to her fictional lovers while rinsing her body with blood from the Fountain. In consonance with the explicit homage to homosexuality in the song's video,[6] the live version of "Alejandro" lays emphasis on a choreographed romance between dancers and concludes with a male couple kissing.

The staging of Central Park as a gothic space that is queerly eroticized is significantly informed by the city's subcultural past and present. First and foremost, the site of the Park has traditionally been home to sexual intermingling contributing a thriving cruising culture. Theater and film productions, including *Hair* and William Friedkin's *Cruising*, have occasionally featured the park's urban history, establishing it, quite assertively, as a sexually charged scene that allows marginal queerness to emerge: *Hair* envisions the Park as a naturalist haven for countercultural bohemia, while, manifestly darker, *Cruising* proposes a psycho-dramatic view of the Park's perilous queer activity. It is Tony Kushner's *Angels in America*, though, that appears to be most closely associated with

Gaga's Park segment. Kushner's "gay fantasia" has as its point of reference the queer Central Park and, in particular, its Bethesda Terrace with the angel statue, both being symbolic spaces of conflict and resolution in the play that queer up established notions of Christianity. Similarly, Gaga's segment explores queer sexuality via the gothic setting by garishly underlining a moral story with an unorthodox twist. Upon landing onto the Park, Dorothy-Gaga mingles with what legitimately appears to be a lurid saturnalian culture. Strongly influenced by the gore genre, the narrative sees Gaga falling prey to the sexually voracious creatures, ultimately transforming into one herself by succumbing to their instinctual appetite. In the final act, she comes to terms with her nature and, while she is being baptized in the blood pool, focus is shifted upon the emerging queer romance of the dancers as perhaps symbolic of a redemptive finale.

Interestingly, *Monster Ball*'s Park is linked with and perhaps ritualizes, in camp manner, New York's queer tribes. George Chauncey's historical account of the city's queer subcultures reveals a tribal categorization of men who have sex with men into fairies and wolves. In the common lexicon of queer culture, the fairy stands for the effeminate homosexual whose demeanor derives signifying power from the camped-up expression of femininity and whose prominence and plausibility served as a role-model for self-questioning young men (Chauncey 49). At the opposite end, the wolf is the male who identifies with a hypermasculine role and, by extension, assumes a sexually active position. Apart from evoking well-known fairytale archetypes, fairies and wolves reiterate patriarchal gender divisions as their roles constitute a reflection of heterosexual relations between women and men. In this sexual culture, fairies resorted to cruising for pleasure and income, while wolves were renowned for their virility and prowess. It is worth mentioning here that the relationships developed between these two groups were not of sexual interest only; intimacy and long-term relationships—termed "marriages" by Chauncey (90)—were not uncommon. As a truly queer form of kinship, the intimate relations between fairies and wolves might as well extend beyond the culture of cruising. Arguably though, the social stigma imprinted upon such bonding in early twentieth-century New York could not have been eradicated and the extent to which these relationships could have been tolerated remains unexplored.

Gaga's staging of the Park seems to invoke this cult of fairies and wolves and, importantly, invests in the ethical story accruing from the queer narrative. Both appropriated from the fairytale genre, the figures of the fairy and the wolf in queer culture serve as sexual archetypes of androgyny and carnal instinct, respectively, thereby illustrating, possibly in the most basic way, the binary nature of queer male sex. Similarly, the *Monster Ball* segment envisions Gaga in the position of the fairy, who has been lost in Central Park, and her dancers as the predatory wolves who are after her. The acts of "Monster" and "Teeth" make the allusion even more palpable: "Monster" portrays Gaga's love interest as "a wolf in disguise" with evil eyes and paws, "a monster in [her] bed," while prior to every performance of "Teeth," the performer announces that she needs affirmation from the audience, otherwise she could die, much like Tinker Bell. Although mostly dramatizing a culture of rape that is resultant from that of cruising, the Park derives maximal benefit from the staged allegory by paying attention to queer intimacy as performed by the two dancers for the finale of "Alejandro." The act effectively underscores that in the heart of an allegedly voracious culture, whose high sexual drive expresses the pathos that results from the normative pressure impinged upon queer sex, forms of intimacy can also be attained. "Alejandro" imagines and acts upon the queer romance after the climactic series of sexual drama presented in the previous acts, thereby proposing a cathartic world of queer bonding—even in its conventional dyadic form—beyond purely sexual terms, and highlighting the moral inherent in Gaga's camp aesthet(h)ics.

As Gaga's first attempt to explore a storytelling narrative dramatized upon a fantastic stage, *Monster Ball* 2.0 succeeds in delivering a moral on marginality and sexual expression to its audiences. Scoring a commercial triumph, the tour was key in associating Gaga with a camp-fueled notion of spectacle. Its garish play with the genres of gothic and fairytale saw the artist's experimentation with grotesqueness making a felt appeal to her fans who heavily invested, both financially and emotionally, in the artist's new phase. The end of *The Fame Monster* era was rather smooth, since a few months prior to concluding the tour, Gaga already announced a new monstrous era, therefore furthering her play with the well-established gothic formula. Picking up the baton from *The Fame Monster*, the follow-up 2011 album, titled *Born This Way*, a peculiar mix of electronica with metal sounds and rock 'n' roll, heralded "the beginning of a new race, the Little Monsters' race, at the epicenter of which Lady Gaga epitomized what Halberstam accurately describes as 'an erotics of flaws and flows'" (*Gaga Feminism*, xiii). The album with the homonymous lead single and video foregrounds queerness and LGBTQ+ rights by figuratively drawing from Gaga's underdog success story. The cultural impact of *Born This Way* pointed to a liberating body politics expressed through the flaunting of freakish sexualities and gendered transformations. At the same time, its commercial impact was synonymous with Gaga's strategic glorification of a culture of misfits. The success of the album may as well accrue from the openness applied to the term "misfit"; in Gaga's "Born This Way" lyrical lexicon, it stands for any human being, "black, white, beige," "gay, straight, or bi, lesbian, transgender life," who feels or has felt "outcast, bullied, or teased." Practically, the artist's musical mantra here touches upon the essences of human insecurity and queers up traditional narratives of creation, thus offering a rather empowering and convincingly marketable body of work that nonetheless is well supported with a non-normative ethos.

With its glam-gothic aesthetic, the *Born This Way* era outcamps its predecessor in terms of fashion, technology, and the deliberateness of Gaga's moral message. Along with her creative team, the artist drew from the 1980s music scene, amplifying her glam rock profile from *The Fame Monster* to a chic metal persona with an evidently pop apprehension of goth and punk. *Born This Way* exhibits a heavy-metal sensibility that has been contemporaneously adapted to fit the early 2010s electronic dance music (EDM) trends. Similarly, Gaga's look invited a meticulous ornamentation of body and attire, favoring influences from the biker and leather cultures. Most notoriously, the artist toyed with her physical image by adorning her body with prosthetics resembling protruding bones, horns, and scales, which were largely influenced both by performance artists such as Orlan and Stelarc, as well as the rock acts of Alison Cooper and Motley Crüe. The performer also introduced her male alter ego, Jo Calderone, an Italian American macho pianist who was allegedly Lady Gaga's lover. Creatively, the era not only cited references from the dancefloor phases of artists such as Madonna, Michael Jackson, and Whitney Houston, but also followed a tradition of male rock established by the likes of Bruce Springsteen as well as its theatrically tinged form found in the work and persona of Freddie Mercury. Gaga's artistic mining for creative output exemplifies the postmodern nature of her work, which marries seemingly incompatible elements, such as the machismo of heavy metal with the gaiety of bubblegum pop. Always crucial in her oeuvre is also her politics of gender, which here is once again extravagantly staged, this time, though, through a technologically reformulated body. What her *Born This Way* performances demonstrate is the irony inherent in an enhanced and/or compartmentalized body that deviates from biological norms, yet is carefully placed in a camp context.

That having been said, the promotional tour for this era, *The Born This Way Ball* tour, is a spectacular narrative that visualizes the conceptual ethos of its parent album, paying tribute to the diversity of Gaga's Little Monsters. Housing a highly intricate stage with imaginative props and a rapid interchange of acts, the show is a lavish enterprise of mammoth proportions and remains one of the most extravagant productions in touring history alongside U2's *360° Tour* (in 2009–11), Roger Waters/Pink Floyd's *The Wall Live* (in 2010–13), and Madonna's *Sticky & Sweet Tour* (in 2008–09).[7] Gaga and her team created a setting conceived of as a medieval castle, named the Kingdom of Fame, which incorporated multistoried towers and rotating structures, therefore allowing the artist to cover as much of the vertical space of the stage as possible. With an immersive concept similar to Kylie Minogue's Splash Zone for the *Aphrodite Tour, Born This Way Ball* featured the Monster Pit, a trapezoid space that consisted of the stage and its extended runways, the purpose of which was to bring the audience closer to the spectacle. The artist promoted the Monster Pit as the highlight of the show by establishing a contest-like convention according to which the person to arrive first in each played gig would be granted with the "Monster Pit Key," a Gaga-modeled clef that supposedly unlocks the Pit space inside the arena (Mitchell, "Lady Gaga Giving"). As with the previous tour, fans were also encouraged to dress up for the Ball in attire that now incorporated Gaga's recently introduced looks, thus carrying on an established cosplay tradition. With a sturdy cult/camp following, the tour attests to an engaging experience for which Gaga attempts a breaking of the fourth wall by creating an interactive spectacle that extends well beyond the stage and reaches into the audience. Forged with queer allusions and symbolic valences, the show transforms the arena into a space of acceptance wherein Gaga's Little Monsters identify with the diva's ethos of inclusivity and freedom of expression.

As a continuation of the performer's *Monster* repertoire, the acts of *Born This Way Ball* are heavily based on the genres of gothic and science fiction. However, Gaga upped the creative ante for this tour by mixing a space opera narrative with a medieval setting, resulting in an excessive and absurd use of the respective genres. In the show, Gaga appears as a persecuted renegade of an extraterrestrial colony, named Government Owned Alien Territory (G.O.A.T.), fortifying herself in the Kingdom of Fame and seeking out for creative inspiration in order to confront her adversaries. Gaga first introduced the futuristic concept of G.O.A.T. in the video of "Born This Way" (in 2011), in which she was portrayed giving birth to the race of Little Monsters in outer space. Expectedly, birth-giving is a central concept in the concert show since it best highlights Gaga's Mother Monster figure and her cosmogonic vision of a world freed from discrimination and bias, thus becoming an essential starting point of the staged narrative. What is important to underscore here is that it is almost impossible to distinguish between the acts of the show, although, depending on the brief instrumental interludes, they can roughly be estimated to five (encore included). Due to the sequential narrative and rapid change of props and costumes—sometimes serving as a second backstage space, the interior of the castle perfectly facilitates this motion of changes—the acts smoothly blend into one another, providing theatrical coherence. In terms of aesthetics, following the audiovisual palette of the album, Gaga presents her Gothic alien persona in outlandish costumes fashioned out of leather and latex couture with strong metallic tinges as expressive of her heavy metal and S&M affiliations.

Born This Way Ball exemplifies the hyperbole of camp not only with its over-the-top stage, but, importantly, because it sets this stage as a portal to an imagined queer world. Through its network of polysemous acts, the show variably addresses a queer subjectivity. Once again, Gaga stages a storytelling spectacle with its performed moral pointing to a camp utopia. As Michael Bronski argues, "[b]y making things not what they are, camp can also be camouflage to provide an outlet or protection" (43). Gaga's Kingdom of Fame and the accompanied Monster Pit stand for this flamboyantly configured reality that serves as an alternative—read queer—*topos*; in there, conventional gender and sexual identities go topsy-turvy. Establishing referential connections with sci-fi themes of monstrous genesis, outer space, and alien life, the show plays up its narratives of Otherness, wherein queerness is welcomed as part of one's biology, contrary to the centuries-old public perceptions of the queer self as deviant, repulsive, even alien. Here, the images of Mother Monster and her Little Monsters (in all their queer glory) populating both the stage and the space of the arena are the actual reification of *Born This Way*'s moral of acceptance and freedom of expression. Appropriately, the stage becomes a cosmic womb giving birth to androgynous figures as Gaga reenacts a birth-giving scene on a giant prop of legs for the performance of the title song. The show allows for symbolic readings that connect the stage and the Monster Pit with the womb, thus undergirding the show's narrative and aesthetic with mythological, even archetypal discourses.[8]

With regard to the show's space of dramatic action, the Kingdom of Fame undoubtedly dominates throughout. Being perhaps the most recognizable and indeed emblematic site of reference within the genres of gothic, romance, and fantasy, the castle, as an artistic formula here, draws from its generic conventions and provides semiotic relevance to the narrative. As best articulated in romance and gothic fiction, the castle has traditionally been a literary convention that acquires signification through manifold purposes, serving both as a terrain of functionality whereupon narrative action unfolds as well as a symbolic *locus* wherein the fictional heroes explore psychic conflicts. More specifically and in relation to Gaga's invocation of monstrosity, according to Norman Holland and Leona Sherman, the castle "is a nighttime house—it admits all we can imagine into it of the dark, frightening, and unknown" (282). Drawing from Freudian discourse, the writers also assert that "the castle admits a variety of our projections. In particular, because it presents villains and dangers in an archaic language and *mise-en-scéne*, it fits childish perceptions of adult threats" (Holland and Sherman 282, original emphasis). In addition, the space with its "midnight revelry, violence, battles, confusing noises and disturbance" may point to subconscious fears and fantasies of childhood, while, in Western cultures, its iconicity has more often than not been associated with "an idealized past epoch of social history (a nostalgia for romance, chivalry, Christian goodness, and divine order)" (Holland and Sherman 282). Both aesthetically and symbolically, the Kingdom in *Born This Way Ball* realizes the signifying power from its cultural archetype and decidedly braids its gothic tradition with Gaga's themes of queerness and otherness. Yet, the show simultaneously challenges this very tradition by establishing the caste as a welcoming site for gender and sexual outcasts. Gaga's castle, powered by technology, is ultimately a microcosm that remodels, converts, and illuminates itself, functioning thus as a living prop that not only dramatically emphasizes each performed act, but is also attuned with Gaga's understanding of social identities and realities as multimodal and plastic.

Appositely, through the concept of the Kingdom, Gaga's engaging with the subject of camp and, by extension, her politics of queer representation propose a staged reality, which, precisely due to its gaudy and surrealist treatment of the gendered/sexual order, becomes consciously detached from normative molds. It can be argued that the show itself refuses to abide by the established conventions of the concert spectacle format, as its scenic construction and thematic composition prove. The *Born This Way Ball* tour is a deliberately faux concert, faux opera/musical, ultimately verifying its flexible comprehension of generic labeling; its queering of standardized perceptions is where the camp of Gaga resides. Indeed, the Kingdom is an anything-can-happen space: within the two-hour extravaganza, Gaga emerges out of a giant eggshell with ram horns on her head (in "Bad Romance"), becomes a tele-operated apparition (in "Bloody Mary"), and is forced down a meat grinder (in "Poker Face"). Toying with every idea of biologic essentialisms, Gaga wishes to celebrate a grotesque body by putting it through absurdist onstage tasks. While these acts attest to the way in which Gaga employs the power of camp to challenge the very ontology of the human body, there is also an array of camp acts in *Born This Way Ball* that are queer-dictated in their evocation of a gender-spectral fantasia.

The opening act of the show calls upon the camp of a queer imagery by means of fairytale symbolism. Gaga makes her dramatic entrance mounted on a mechanical unicorn and heading to the castle. The artist atop the robotic prop is being carried by two dancers in ritual-like motion along the runway circumference of the Monster Pit. Dancers following the procession hold futuristic machine guns and flags that read "G.O.A.T." Dressed in elaborate metallic attire with a black veil that conceals her face and falls to oversized shoulder-pads giving the impression of wings, Gaga introduces her Gothic alien image and performs the opening song, "Highway Unicorn (Road to Love)". Taking into account the popularity of equestrian themes in female-led acts, Gaga's performance here adds to the tradition of the female performer within an equine imagery.[9] The history of hippodrama, a fusion of circus spectacle and melodrama that established the onstage equestrian theme, attests to a largely male-dominated canon (Banham 168; McArthur 20).[10] However, the image of the female horse-rider, as popularized by the English legend of Lady Godiva, has stood for a feminist symbol that effectively subverts male power. Performance historian Kim Marra argues that the image of the equestrienne became a source of anxiety and desire for men, who were simultaneously threatened and aroused by the assertive female horse-rider

(508). While it is evident that the feminist figure of the equestrienne is also, unsurprisingly so, placed under the scrutiny of the scopophilic gaze, especially if one takes into consideration the emblematic nudity of Lady Godiva and the circulation of her eroticized image across popular culture corpora, the performance of Gaga powered by the surrealist praxis of camp resists any eroticization.

Gaga astride on the unicorn becomes a queer subject of fantastic embodiment. Her metallic costume and veil covering most of her body ultimately frustrate any enforced voyeuristic attempt. The artist clad as a Gothic alien overshadows her human form and tilts more to an animal-like figure. In addition, her conscious choice of playing with the mythology of the unicorn than that of any other type of horse brings thematic integrity to her stage. Gaga had already introduced the unicorn imagery in her video of "Born This Way," placing it in conjunction with a pink triangle, thus foregrounding the queer history of both since they are used by the LGBTQ+ community as signifiers of uniqueness and memory.[11] Therefore, from the very first moment of the show, Gaga marks the entrance into her unapologetically queer world with symbolic cohesion and cultural context.

This ultra-camp kick-off demonstrates that the rest of the show not only eschews subtlety, but wishes to altogether leave normative reality behind. The artist's show envisions corporeality in fluidity by celebrating a play of transformation(s). The body of Gaga, as the central body of the spectacle, is a shape-shifting body that ignores traditional markers of identity, be they gender, sex, ethnicity, or race. She glides through identity modifiers, inhabiting thus multifarious subject positions. Those positions that are energized with camp, though, do not simply imagine a body beyond the signifiers of gender or ethnicity or race. On the contrary, these signifiers are deliberately inflated, with their fluidity streaming out (of) an excessive theatricality. The proposed body of camp is manifestly gendered, molded out of feminine constituents/attributes. In a reversal of normative reality, camp does not envision gender inscribed upon the body, but rather designates a body to a fantastic gender, a gender of theatrical analogies whereupon the body flexes into shape. Effectual as it is to speak of camp's plastic/morphing potential, it does have to be reiterated here that this theatrical treatment of gender relies on the social history of its feminine signifier and those conventional givens that (have) come to constitute the notion of femininity as tantamount to femaleness and its sociocultural variants. The camp body and, by extension, the camp reading of a body absorbs traditional notions of corporeality and produces a pumped-up, parodic view.

Under this premise, the camp body of Gaga may seem to abandon corporeal reality when experimenting with bodily transformations, but, in fact, opts for one where the body is still gendered, or otherwise marked, yet absurdly so. Consider here the artist's animatronic transfiguration into Mother G.O.A.T., the facial replica of which appears inside an illuminated prism hovering above the main stage throughout the show. The prismatic visage is a corrupted form of Gaga's face, carrying monstrous features, while its prosthetic horns make a self-referential nod to the said evil persona that Gaga introduced in the video of "Born This Way". With Mother G.O.A.T. alluding to pagan and occult horned deities, Gaga once again draws from and queers up mythological imagery as a means of maintaining thematic coherence of the show's narrative arc. For the duration of the concert show, the prism of Mother G.O.A.T. serves as the narrator as well as Gaga's antagonist, and occasionally appears between acts to propel the musical narrative. Eventually, in the performance of "Paparazzi" toward the end of the show, Gaga once again uses her disco stick and kills Mother G.O.A.T. The simulacrum speaks in a dramatically slow and ominous manner and her English bears a strong French accent. Her transcendence of bodily form, however, does not signify the erasure of her gender: her prototype is Gaga; her communicative ability is vocalized by Gaga (in the form of prerecorded audio) whose voice is already familiar to the public; and, ultimately, her identification as Mother inevitably delineates her female sex. The artist could altogether dismantle the traditional sex/gender correlation here, since the disembodied form of Mother G.O.A.T. allows such creative opportunity, yet she maintains it and manages to camp it up. In addition, her invocation of an ethnic Other, here the French Other, not only sharpens the dichotomy between a friendly Gaga and the G.O.A.T. adversary but, importantly, relies on the stereotype of a feminized French culture.[12] The staging of Mother G.O.A.T. as an otherworldly creature is thus heavily modeled out of distinct human and cultural markers but is effectively campified by means of parodic exoticization.

The simulacrum also invites a posthumanist reading with regard to Gaga's treatment of a disunified and digitized body. Still, the posthuman body does not necessarily preclude gendered or racial or even ethnic embodiedness. As Sherryl Vint argues, "[t]he human body, like the human subject, is a product of both culture and nature. Both body and subject must maintain a sense of natural and stable boundaries by continually marking out the distance between what is self and what is not" (17). For Gaga, to play with the notion of futurism, both in terms of spectacle and social critique, is to involve her body in the process despite the seemingly radical modifications of it. Camp also cannot and should not be ignored from any discussion on the artist's over-the-top shtick. As was the case with Beyoncé's embodiment of the fembot in the performance of "Diva" (see Chapter 3), here too Gaga imagines a grotesque, albeit still feminized replica of herself, though one that is monstrously configured and, being a Mother, potentially threatening because of its reproductive ability. Her performance as Mother G.O.A.T. demonstrates that the praxis of camp, due to its performative utilization of gender, cannot in any sense omit corporeal expression. For camp, the body becomes the stage upon which gender is dramatically acted out and, because of that, it is essential that the prismatic Mother G.O.A.T. retains some sort of corporeal signification. Of equal importance here is the contribution of technology for Gaga's stage which is fundamental for the materialization of such intricate concepts. It only makes sense that the incorporation of elaborate mechanics can only amplify the performing potential of the show and the artist's delivery while, interestingly enough, it effectively plays up the camp factor through the surplus of extravagant contrivances employed.

Undoubtedly, technology is a driving force behind the spectacle of *Born This Way Ball*. Gaga's performance, in fact, relies on it both practically and aesthetically. The utilization of technology, as a matter of fact, provides alternative approaches to viewing and staging the body, adapting it to the dictates of the fantastic setting. Envisioning therefore a digitized corporeality calls upon the aesthetic power of technology to intervene and creatively remodel the body. The performance of Mother G.O.A.T. epitomizes the compartmentalization and digitization of the body as crafted out of a gothic and sci-fi imagery, reminiscent of Haraway's cyborgian concept.[13] Acts usually vary in contextualizing the technological body, affirming thus both the plurality of it as well as Gaga's imaginative concepts toward embracing fluidity. For instance, the performance of "Heavy Metal Lover" invites the aesthetics of technology to imagine a hybrid form, a mechanical body. This particular act sees Gaga transforming into a motorbike: by fusing herself with a tricycle prop, the artist recreates on stage the artwork from the cover of the *Born This Way* album. With the song Gaga addresses her sexual indulgence into the culture of heavy metal and pays homage to the underground scene of New York. For the dramatization of the song, a leather-clad female dancer rides the Gaga-bike while performing erotic moves on it. The simulated intercourse between the dancer and Gaga here foregrounds the praxis of lesbian sex, simultaneously invoking the queer biker scene, wherein bikers, both female and male, act out a butch aesthetic as an appropriation of an allegedly masculine—read heterosexual male—culture. At the same time, the female rider making love to Gaga's mechanized body widens conventional categories on the practice of sex in its move from human-on-human action to one of human-on-machine. Finally, the sexual treatment and personification of the motorbike are a fetishistic approach to the materiality of the biker cult and, by extension, to its accruing power dynamic. Simultaneously glamorizing the queer scene and camping up the machismo of the biker image, "Heavy Metal Lover" introduces Gaga's part-human/part-machine body as a sexually charged site upon which the erotics of queerness is enacted.

Evidently, both the performance of Mother G.O.A.T. and "Heavy Metal Lover" explore by means of technology the power of camp to play with the theatrics of the gendered body. Steve Dixon corroborates that "[p]erformances by the proponents of flesh and metal symbiosis can be sited frequently within the aesthetics of camp by virtue of their theatrical and computational codes of high-artifice and excess, and through their celebration of 'monstrous' transgression" (22). Undertaking analyses of performance art works by artists such as Guillermo Gómez-Peña, Stelarc, and Momoyo Torimitsu, and within the frame of what he identifies as metal performances—best exemplified in cyborgian narratives, robotic concepts, and portrayals of the mechanized body—the writer proposes the term "metallic camp," a performance-specific ideological and aesthetic play of camp with the abovementioned themes, wherein "metallic" bears denotations with regard to physical substance, as well as connotations of loudness, aggressiveness, and resistance (Dixon 15–16). As best explanative for the stage and acts of Gaga here, the concept of metallic camp is an apt motif that expands and elaborates on camp's specific treatment of the technologically configured reality and the gendered body within it. "Metal performances," Dixon concludes, "exalt in the conjunction of the hard and the soft; the natural and the technological; the metal and the meat," fusing purely contrastive material to underscore ironies inherent in the antithesis, in analogy to camp's conjugation of the serious and the parodic (40). Gaga's spectacle of the techno-body grounds this fusion of dichotomies: her exposed derriere on the tricycle prop is juxtaposed with her metallic limbs fused with the bike's façade, prefiguring the natural versus the artificial; the fetish with the physical versus the fetish with the material; and most importantly, the human versus the machine Other.

Arguably, the imagery of metallic camp appears inextricable with the overall camp panorama of the *Born This Way Ball* stage. The show advocates for a plural body, one that acquires critical potential through each new signification. Mostly risqué in nature, Gaga's camp body veers from ambiguity to assertiveness, to pornography and theatricality, to exoticization and rebelliousness. The camp juxtaposition of the mechanical with the natural body simultaneously repels and invites eroticization in each respective act, without thus clinging to either/or positions. As per Haraway's manifesto, wherein it is established that Western cultures are permeated with corporeal and mental dualities that the high-tech culture has eventually challenged (177), Gaga's cyborgian body, simultaneously too physical and too metallic, wishes to transgress binaries, which is ultimately what marks its queerness: a body that stands for potent camp irony, successfully merging political valence with playfulness, and femme posture with robotic performance.

In what can be legitimately defined as the highlight of the show, the segment with the performances of "Americano," "Poker Face" and "Alejandro"—henceforth referred to as the Meat segment—epitomizes the said irony of Gaga's camp body. Precisely due to its staged critique, but also because it is carefully placed toward the end of the show, the Meat segment is an ethnic and queer amalgam of Gaga's most recognizable high-energy pop tunes. Introducing the Meat act is a Spanish guitar solo for which a simulated wedding ceremony takes place: the bride's face is fully covered with a thick veil before which the groom feels appalled when he attempts to lift it. The bridal couple reenacts a melodramatic conflict as Gaga enters the main stage to perform "Americano." Wearing a variation of her infamous meat dress, the artist exits the castle suspended alongside hanged meat carcasses, while her chorus of female dancers appears similarly dressed. Shortly after, the artist's crew of male dancers enters in military attire, carrying machine guns and committing brutalities on the female crew. Gaga here acts as the performing narrator while occasionally joining the female chorus. Meanwhile, the bride has left the stage and the groom joins the male chorus in their violent acts. For the staged narrative of the song, the female dancers skillfully disarm the military crew and turn the guns against them, chasing them off stage. The dramatic finale of "Americano" sees the bride returning on stage with a machine gun. Having now her veil lifted, she reveals her male identity and vengefully shoots the groom dead.

"Americano" explores the dramaturgy of camp in assaulting patriarchal power. Bearing strong feminist undertones, the performance benefits from generic melodrama in its reversal of power dynamic and instills agency into the female/feminine subjectivities in a deliberately simplistic way. At the same time, the theatrics of drag and its shock value are utilized in the performance of gender. In particular, the striptease act in specific drag shows culminates with the revelation of the performer's male identity, which is employed as a plot twist for the allegedly unaware audiences. By setting up a female illusion and subsequently letting it collapse before the audience, the revelation of the "man" behind the drag as the *effet de surprise* cuts across any gendered stabilizations.[14] Here, although the stripping act is limited in the lifting of the veil, it does qualify as a critical surprise ending, especially when put in the context of homophobic and sexist abuse presented on stage. Importantly, "Americano" bears potent queer resonances in its narration of a lesbian love story developing in the barrios of Los Angeles. *Rolling Stone*'s Jody Rosen identified the song, "[a] disco-fied showtune with a pronounced 'Latin'-flavor, complete with flamenco guitars and castanets," as "the campiest song Gaga's recorded yet" (Rosen). The song's generic mixture of techno with musical theater lyricism and mariachi sounds exemplifies a markedly stylized and joyful pop text that is simultaneously carved with political nuances in its takes on gay marriage and immigration law. As a continuation of the *Monster Ball* tradition, the *Born This Way Ball* rendition follows the conceptual camp of previous-era "Alejandro," this time encompassing a Latin melodrama with bilingual stylizations and Gaga caught in the crossfire of a queer romance.

Nevertheless, contextualizing "Americano" in the Meat segment as the introductory act inevitably strikes one as bizarre. Considering the thematic coherence of previous performances, including "Highway Unicorn" and "Heavy Metal Lover," a Latinx-inspired wedding ceremony with a meatpacking imagery amid the Medieval castle seems incongruous, to say the least. While the staging of "Americano" could perfectly stand outside the *Born This Way* aesthetic, its incorporation into the show's concept is rather challenging for the audience who might struggle to establish any sort of connection between Gaga's futuristic transformations and the act's carnal vicissitudes. On top of that, the follow-up performance of "Poker Face," although thematically attached to "Americano," seems to perpetuate the bizarreness of the overall segment. Before commencing with "Poker Face," Gaga performs a musical monologue in which she states: "In 1978, Larry Flint declared that women will no longer be treated as meat on the cover of *Hustler* magazine, but in *The Born This Way Ball*, meat is precisely how we treat them." Meanwhile two of her military-clad dancers coquet with her and strip her meat dress into a meat leotard—Gaga here goes the extra camp mile. The performance of "Poker Face" is delivered by Gaga half-submerged in a meat-grinder prop and culminates with her male dancers forcing her all the way down. "Alejandro" eventually rounds off the Meat segment and sees the male crew engaging in homoerotic activities, while Gaga reemerges positioned on a meat couch, wearing military attire and having two machine guns attached to her bra as extensions of her breasts. In yet another self-referential act, the artist here evokes the queer imagery as well as her gun-bra costume from the "Alejandro" video.

Although one could argue that the exposition of the meat metaphor in the overall segment provides fertile soil for a politically charged performance, it ends up being incongruous when juxtaposed with the show's conceptual integrity. However, it is this incongruity, which is firmly based on the poetics of camp, that best foregrounds Gaga's stage as a moral battleground. The artist's showcase binds together the dramatics of camp with performance art, a curious mixture of playfulness, surrealism, and political edge. In exploring the denotations and connotation of meat on stage, Gaga's acts draw from the work of performance artists such as Marina Abramović and Carolee Schneemann. More specifically, the former's *Balkan Baroque* addressed issues of memory, pain, and loss caused by the Yugoslavian Wars. Abramović would be seated on a pile of cattle meat, rinsing the animal bones and singing folk dirges as an intracultural homage to those sacrificed during the war period. Schneemann's *Meat Joy*, which Gaga's segment is more akin to, envisions an orgiastic performance where female nudity and sexuality are brought center stage in order to challenge patriarchal perceptions of the female body. With an affinity to Dionysian rituals, Shneemann's performance revels in the rawness of the meat and its various forms, simultaneously becoming emotionally and politically charged. By equating the meat with the human, the body art of Abramović and Schneemann wishes to underline not only the materiality of the flesh and its exposed vulnerability to the scrutinizing gaze, but also its feminist assertiveness to function as a celebratory corpus that survives and transcends narratives of violence and sexism. The Meat segment of *Born This Way Ball*, which musically and theatrically expanded on Gaga's MTV meat dress shtick, aligns the artist with the ethnic and intergenerational legacy of *Balkan Baroque* and *Meat Joy* by dramatizing an ironic performance that collaboratively houses the visceral effect of the meat with the political edge of queerness.

Unlike Abramović's and Schneemann's projects that rely on the critical valence of their performance art to explore the meat concept, Gaga has camp as her performative device, thereby instilling into the seriousness of her subject matter the kitsch of the genres of musical and melodrama. The Meat segment is a multivalent act that raises questions on the—American—politics of gender, sexuality, and ethnicity, and addresses them with camp irony. The juxtaposed dynamics of power, that is, vulnerability and oppression, is absurdly magnified. In the framework of metallic camp, the collision of elements—namely those positions of gender and ethnicity behind the antithetical allusions of the meat and the machine guns or, simply, Gaga's flesh in the giant grinder—reifies the artist's camp aesthet(h)ics: namely, the delivery of a moral story whose political gravity, merging reality and spectacle, is amplified with stylized irony and extravagant theatrics. Here, Gaga vacillates between positions of power and identification: she is simultaneously a Chicana lesbian for "Americano"; a piece of meat in the grinder for "Poker Face"; and an armed combatant femme in "Alejandro". Not only does camp motorize this vacillation, but, importantly, contextualizes it into the overarching concept of the *Born This Way* era to move against traditional archetypes of identity and opt for a vision of gender as role-play. Thus, the specific medley may seem to deviate from the narrative structure of the show, yet it remains steadfast to the ethos of the plural self embraced by Gaga on stage. After all, the fact that the artist's stage consciously supports a surrealist approach of the self that is simultaneously backed by conventions of the fantastic proposes camp incongruity as the show's *raison d'être*.

Free bitch, baby: Queer youth and the politics of childishness

Arguably, the thematic narrative and conceptual staging of *Born This Way Ball* were pregnant with subversive potential as regards performances of gender and sexuality. As a matter of fact, the show upped the ante of what Gaga had already set in motion throughout her previous years of performing and touring. Taking into consideration the global outreach the tour had in promoting its radical theatrics, it is expected that its identity politics would impact differently across its diverse audiences. The queer material as well as the risqué subject matter of the *Born This Way Ball* performances were rather challenging for the conservative spectrum of

Gaga's international itinerary. As was the case with Madonna's *MDNA Tour*, which was met with backlash in Russia because of an allegedly explicit homosexual agenda, Gaga's tour was similarly met with resistance for its overtly homosexual and pornographic content. More specifically, the tour's stop in Jakarta's Gelora Bung Karno Stadium had to be cancelled due to harsh criticism and threats extended to the artist by Islamic groups (Prendergast). In particular, what was targeted were her "provocative choreography and support for gay rights," with conservative and religious authorities proclaiming the artist as "a devil's messenger" and "the destroyer of morals" (Prendergast). In the same vein, earlier on, preceding the tour's grand opening in Seoul were protests from South Korean Christian groups against Gaga's performances that were deemed as "obscene" (Mitchell, "Lady Gaga's Born"). This bias against the yet-to-be-revealed show was grounded on the premise that Gaga's persona and overall attitude would have an immoral impact on the young audiences attending her performance (Mitchell, "Lady Gaga's Born"). As a result, the production team, settling between the protesters' request and not cancelling the concert, decided to rate the show as an event for adult audiences only.

It is true that Lady Gaga has time and again employed pornographic shticks as a means of marketing her persona and, of course, many a time capitalized on her queer appeal. At the same time, however, she has been an ardent promoter of free sexual expression and retained the queer core of her work quite strong. It is this particular revolutionary promotion of gender fluidity and the theatricalized identity in her work that have been embraced by her queer fanbase. The conservative allegations impinged upon Gaga's promotion of homosexuality indeed express not only a concern over homosexuality as social behavior and sexual practice, with all the connotations and specificities that are culturally inscribed upon these terms, but also a deeper fear that exposure to a seemingly homosexual lifestyle, culture, or discourse might negatively influence those exposed. To be more specific, in the abovementioned cases of the Seoul and Jakarta performances, this "negative influence" stands for a perception of an inherently abnormal homosexuality with the contagious potential to dissolve heteronormative structures. It is legitimate that this perception of a tainting homosexuality, when viewed in the broader context of globalized interrelations, is simultaneously linked with the notion of a libertine Western culture whose championing of a liberal politics of gender and sexuality do not align with the cross-culturally varied non-Western identity models. Furthermore, in both incidents and especially the latter, adolescent audiences are framed as the vulnerable receivers of Gaga's titillating expositions. What is presented to be at stake here is the development of a youth that deviates from the established social morals and cultural norms; hence, an imminent threat to the vision of a future generation that is homogeneous in accordance to the dictates of heterodominant culture.

Always connoting an optimistic sociopolitical future, youth is bound to be protected and preserved for the sake of a utopian reality that is yet to come. When the prescribed ethos of the youth is jeopardized and, therefore, the vision of the future is automatically seen as unstable, if ominous, the need to police the youth and the cultural input they receive becomes imperative. Historically, according to Michael Nevin Willard, "'youth' have been located within a logic of moral reform," being contained in safe spaces due to the common assumption that "if left unsupervised, youth will become immoral or delinquent" (470). Inextricably bound to that, however, is the notion of youth as dynamic producers of culture(s) whose creative power comes with the need to harness it. In commercial terms, youth culture lies at the epicenter of market interest not only because of their ability to generate, circulate, and digest lifestyle and trends with considerable velocity, especially in the social media era, but also due to the catalytic intermediateness of their age in the formulation of core tastes and sensibilities that are based on social, cultural, and political stimuli they receive. Willard speaks of a change in the status of youth:

> [F]rom a life stage to be contained and protected [...] to one where coming of age matters much less because youth already engage in labor that, in addition to producing subcultural values, is already a highly sophisticated form of techno-scientific, information management, and value-producing labor within the global information economy. (471)

To incorporate youth in the processes of labor production and culture-making is to instill agency in their supervised status of adolescence, an agency that is inevitably gauged by means of capital, especially when youth consumption is equated with investment and target markets. What the constructive strand of culture-making points to, therefore, is a status of youth as makers and consumers of ideas and morals.

Under this premise and to return to Lady Gaga, the challenge her concert and image brought upon the host cities of Seoul and Jakarta demonstrates that the youth's buying power of an allegedly queer culture might altogether prove devastating for conservative morals. Even though Gaga's radicalness is a meticulously staged performance and her impact rather a playful projection of a truly queer culture, it still manages to contest established rigid norms regarding gender and sexuality. The queerness of Gaga's stage and the political reaction this triggered can be viewed as a veritable thrash against patriarchal standards and reproductive futurism. Elaborating on the latter, Lee Edelman explains how heterosexual culture has ultimately fetishized the process of reproduction as well as the figure of the child, both of which have come to embody idealistic fantasies of a moral future that is culturally and historically perpetuated (11–20). Drawing from Lacanian theory, the writer proposes that queerness and specifically the non-reproductivity of queer sex function as a catalyst, a rupture for the reproductive scheme sanctified by heteronormative discourse (17), and ultimately links queerness with the death drive since "[it] embodies this death drive, this intransigent jouissance, by figuring sexuality's implication in the senseless pulsions of that drive" (27).

The idea of a queer rupture of heteronormative ideology, as this is realized via the instinctual drives of death and sex, is apt here and resonates with Gaga's performance ethics. The camp character of her oeuvre coupled with the absurdist nuances of her persona indeed propose a rupture of the commonsensical evaluation of gender and sexuality. The artist's extravagant realities embody a break from the conventional, a transcendence from the (hetero)norm to the surreal, to the Gaga. The promoted notion of creative expression that allows the diva to play with and distort the gender binary and, by extension, any identity category is that exact moment of freedom that Tristan Tzara imagined in his conception of Dada, as indicated in the chapter's epigraph. The message Gaga conveys to her audience, especially to the queer spectrum of it, is this moment of abandoning the sensible and surrendering to the senseless, which is not exactly the joy derived from the spectacle or the experience of concert-going, but rather the *jouissance* that Edelman sees in imagining identity as a no-future, a dynamic queer-driven force that exists in the moment, outside the frame of provision. Indeed, Gaga's queer affinities endorse a fanbase and youth culture that celebrate the breaking of identity barriers and the temporary formation of a deeply democratic kinship. In other words, her spectacle celebrates community-making as an act that relies on a collective consciousness whose notion of identity spills over or even leaps beyond the boundaries of conventional categorization. As Gaga takes pride in calling herself a "free bitch," we witness at once an erotically charged status with the transgressive potential to channel this sexual energy toward a liberated sense of self.[15]

Gaga's performance agenda after the monstrous era of *The Fame Monster* and *Born This Way* saw her return to the retro-futuristic aesthetics rooted in her debut album, *The Fame*, which, evidently, served as a point of reference for 2013's *ARTPOP* in terms of image and stage performance. What both albums promote is a self-centered image of Gaga whose Warholian treatment of celebrity invokes a sense of identity that revels in its own plasticity. Abiding by the postmodern ethics of pop art, the albums uphold the idea of the fragmented self as well as the preeminence of the copy over the original. Most importantly, the notion of futility is central here: what indeed pervades the discourses of both celebrity and pop is this idea of the exhaustible and replaceable text and/or persona contextualized within the rapid interchangeability of recyclable trends and fashions. *The Fame*, for instance, is indicative of a Bowie-meets-Warhol project that is unapologetically derivative of the pop art movement and is permeated by the discourses of fame and sex in its entirety. With its club-made anthems, the album celebrates the self-absorbed consumption and façade of celebrity lifestyle, presenting Gaga as a superficial and utterly futile pop act, a true Warhol(ian) superstar soon to be exhausted. In the same vein, *ARTPOP*, deemed by Gaga as "a reverse Warholian enterprise,"[16] toys with works of world art by placing them under Gaga's ultra-pop microscope. The project also cites references from the 1990s rave psyche-delia as well as from the Dada and Expressionism movements, particularly from their post-1960s resurgence, as reflected in the performance art of Yoko Ono and Marina Abramović.

In Gaga's *Fame* and *ARTPOP* performances, futility is connected with tempor-ariness, while their postmodern citation indicates a glorification of remodeling past corpora. The poetics of camp are critical here in foregrounding superficiality and artifice as two important driving forces in the conceptualization of a vain selfhood. Gaga's pop art projects are attracted to the past and are built for the present; their relation to the notion of futurity is limited in their play with futurism, which, again, in a postmodern manner, is energized via a retro aesthetic. As with Edelman's queer rupture, Gaga's camp, which toys with the notion of temporality, proposes the here-and-now of performance, be it the actual stage show or the performativity of iden-tity. Camp role-playing, for that matter, points to an experimentation with the social self which is seen as a farce, a nonsensical comedic/dramatic treatment of situations, images, and identities. Camp's comeditization/dramatization of reality and the idea of not taking oneself seriously oppose conventional expectations of the social self to evolve and grow mature, in a conceptual framework that imagines and perhaps requires some sort of progressive linearity. In the context of gendered reality, trad-itional gendering similarly requires from the social self not only to abide by the strict dichotomy of the gendered standards—boys or girls—but also to develop in accord-ance with the future expectations of these standards—boys to men, girls to women. In light of this, camp's decided queer play rejects seriousness and serves as an absurd break in the sequence of established gender identities.

Gaga's camping up of gender, which, as has been made evident here, is ener-gized by pop culture trivia and queer practices, upsets this progressive linearity with its farcical poetics. Consider, for instance, Gaga's performance as Candy Warhol for *The Fame Ball Tour*. Inspired by Warhol's transgender muse Candy Darling, Gaga filmed a series of vignettes featuring her Candy persona that served as visual interludes for the show.[17] In them, the artist appears in an interroga-tion scene reminiscent of the interview scene for the finale of Warhol's *Women in Revolt* movie, starring Darling. Initially, the artist's image and posture resemble those of Andy Warhol, though she introduces herself as "Lady Gaga." As the vignettes unfold, she is presented in her signature hair bow and has her face covered with sheer leggings. Her slow, almost robotic-like manner of speech indicates a challenged stream of consciousness in her tone when narrating to her interrogator, in repetitive motion, how "pop ate [her] heart" and how she craves for the fame. In other shots, the artist casually brushes her hair in front of the mirror, appears with pink blood-like stain on her shirt holding a yellow plastic gun, and has her pantyhose-covered face applied with lipstick by her interrogator. For the last scene, the man asks her: "What did Pop say?" and she replies that "He needed a new face." Ascribing Pop with a male pronoun here makes an interesting, yet ambiguous statement: "He" capitalized foregrounds an authorial or revered figure as in papa (father) or even pope, which by Gaga standards at the time might as well refer to Warhol and his esteemed status in the pop world. Following that, the interrogator asks her to introduce herself to the world and she says "Candy Warhol," but when the man corrects her and asks of her real name, she responds in an oblique manner, saying she does not understand the question.

Representative of the artist's *Fame* phase, the short clips bear a colorful aesthetic and, when put together, they present a small narrative of the Candy persona. While the clips were used as interludes between acts, the songs comprising each act were not always fixed. *The Fame Ball*, being Gaga's debut solo tour, was rather a collage project whose pieces could be reassembled in a different order.[18] Therefore, the videos did not necessarily introduce a new concept for every new act, but rather bound the show together in what appeared to be a pop-music-fashion showcase. As a result, the structural theme of the show verified its pop art lineage and, in it, Gaga starred as the new face of Pop. Importantly, as is indicated in the videos, the artist identifies Pop with the male pronoun—as in the phrase "Pop ate my heart [...] He downed the whole thing in one efficient gulp." Conversely, her persona vacillates between feminine/effeminate identifications, that is, Warhol and Darling. By employing a camp approach of her persona, Gaga manages to unsettle the conventional orders of logic and age here. Her covered face effectively eliminates any accurate time framing of her persona: she embodies the past through Warhol and heralds the future in being the new face of the showbiz industry; simultaneously, she brings these visual accounts into the present setting of the show. In addition to that, her ultra-feminine persona is carefully juxtaposed with the male figures of the interrogator and that of Pop, while her proclamation that she has lost her heart and brains perpetuates the stereotype of the blonde celebrity bimbo. In finding creative lineage with the ethos of pop art and the queer affiliations established in and around the Warholian collective, Gaga's pop camp here underlines the constructedness of the artistic persona who consciously embraces imitation and derivativeness as critical devices for a camped-up performance.[19]

Akin to the concept of Candy Darling for *The Fame Ball*, *The ARTPOP Ball* explored the absurdist nature of Gaga's pop art. While deviating from the dark concepts of the two previous tours, *The ARTPOP Ball* saw the artist returning to her bubblegum pop roots as first presented in her debut tour. Despite departing from the collage aesthetic of *The Fame Ball*, the 2014 tour displayed coherence in its thematic segments. Strongly influenced by the European and Japanese EDM scenes, the show was conceived of as a rave party, featuring psychedelic color-ations and strobe light showcases while Gaga's looks alternated between futur-istic costumes inspired by previous phases of her career. The main stage housed a large Atlantis-esque kingdom with white dome structures that accommodated the light show, while the elevated runways that extended into and above the audi-ence were translucent so as to allow the crowd to take a direct look at the stage action. As is the case with most major corporate arena shows employing various strategies for audience immersion, the American leg of *The ARTPOP Ball*, true to its rave culture origins, featured a bar attached to the front runway where fans could enjoy custom-made Gaga drinks throughout the performance (Kolah). The show's entertaining objective and repeated mantra, after all, was the celebration of art and creativity through the abandoning impulse of the rave.

The frivolous and artificial nature of *ARTPOP Ball*'s concepts seem an appro-priate terrain for Gaga's play with camp. The show once again utilizes elements of the fantastic in its recreation of an underwater world that feature, among other things, dancers dressed as sea-creatures, seahorse-like instruments and Gaga enveloped in a latex costume with tentacles.[20] However, the conjunction of camp with the poetics of the rave, a peculiar combination of hyperbole and transgres-sive performance, are traced in two specific instances of the show. The first one sees Gaga exploring Greco-Roman mythology and galactic explorations in her postmodern embodiment of Aphrodite/Venus. During the second act of the show, Gaga's divine alter ego emerges on stage to perform the song "Venus". Having already introduced the persona in her promotion of the *ARTPOP* album, the artist utilizes familiar stylistic devices for the live performance: her Aphrodite, informed by the traditions of drag and burlesque, sports a seashell bikini outfit and a volu-minous blond wig, creating a simultaneously titillating and cartoonish impression. Likewise, the performed song, which critics saw as "almost parodical" (Cragg) with Gaga "cop[ping] a drag queen's arch humor" (Ganz), is a narrated inter-stellar journey to planet Venus as well as a sexual call to the goddess. The naiveté of "Venus" is effectively brought on the live stage wherein colorful bubbles fill the visual background and large inflatable flower-like props sprout across the runway platforms. Throughout the performance, Gaga, accompanied by her dance crew, extends her arms in V positions and executes a solo with a pink V-shaped guitar while confetti bursts shower the stage.

The vibrant props, the euphoric calls, the lyrics, and Gaga's very own exposed body bring the celebration of (female) sexuality center stage here. The risqué act constitutes a camp tribute to hedonism whose deliberate symbolism to female climax as signified with discursive and dramatic connotations—the pop-up flowers, the V-based gimmicks, and the ejaculatory confetti—is ostentatiously performed. The performance is rather too specific to invite any further interpretation; at the same time, the referential corpus of its camp iconicity is all too dense, making it a nuanced lush spectacle. Contrary to Gaga's grotesque and metal camp in the previous shows, wherein identity politics motorized each performance, the "Venus" act here encapsulates the art of camp in its evocation of a gay—both joyous and queer—temporality. Its retro sensibility establishes artistic lineage with David Bowie's spectacles as well as the 1970s space disco scene in which the voluptuous lyrics and electronic beats were visualized through futuristic aesthetics, while the sexually vibrant performance may even allude to *Hair*'s "Aquarius" in its tribal dialectics of euphoria.[21] Most importantly, considering that *The ARTPOP Ball* epitomizes EDM/house rhythms, Gaga's "divine" act is essentially energized with the diva poetics of the gay disco scene. Similarly with the previously explored cases of Madonna, Kylie, and Beyoncé, Gaga too reiterates the tradition of the worshipped diva within the cultural context of disco, with her performance retaining a frolicsome, self-parodic approach, and perhaps a nod to Studio 54's racy parties.

As "Venus" indicates, the crossing of temporal borders is a key constituent of camp praxis. With the performance sounding and appearing completely detached from the present, temporal incongruity—best envisioned in Gaga's retro-futurism—instills camp an otherworldly edge, while the notion of transcendence inherent in the orgasmic simulation of the performance adds to a complete detachment from reality. Gaga's camp aesthet(h)ics here incorporate a carnivalesque celebration in which the amalgam of role-play, jouissance, and what can be defined as a politics of childishness, a cartoonish engagement with performance that veers from the unserious to the unintelligible, is at work. Camp and the Bakhtinian carnivalesque, in fact, converge in terms of their subversively parodic qualities, for, as Cleto argues,

> the two share hierarchy inversion, mocking paradoxicality, sexual punning and innuendos, and, most significantly, a complex and multilayered power relationship between the dominant and the subordinate (or deviant), and finally the whole problem of how far a "licensed" release can effectively be transgressive (or subversive). (32)

In the context of Gaga's performance, the parodic and sexually charged culmination employs double entendres (again, the climactic confetti showers) as a means of moving far beyond the demarcated line of seriousness, even perhaps that of the conventionally sensible. After all, the absurd logic of camp, a paradox in itself, imagines entropy in the seeming order of the rational reality that surrounds it. For Gaga's stage, the idea of containment can be identified as the source of unease, but at the same time as the ultimate incentive that energizes her camp toward a queer pushing of conventional boundaries.

Apart from "Venus," camp's carnivalesque transgression and the politics of childishness in *The ARTPOP Ball* are better manifest in the rave-themed segment toward the end of the show. Upon concluding the previous act, Gaga abruptly removes her wig and proceeds to an onstage costume change. The artist turns her back to the audience and undresses to a backup sound while her styling crew appears on stage to help her into the next outfit. As a matter of fact, the strip act serves as the interlude to the rave segment and, rather unorthodoxly, the costume change does not occur backstage. The audience witnesses live Gaga's transition into a girlie character inspired by Japanese anime and the rave culture. Similar to Kylie's Manga Girl persona for the *KylieX2008* tour (see Chapter 2), Gaga's fashion is ornate and vivid, albeit comprised of futurist neon colors and plastic garments suggestive of an urban club aesthetic, contrary to Minogue's kabuki references. Solely built on electronic sounds, the segment mainly features the artist executing choreographed performances for the dance singles "Bad Romance" and "Applause." It is the act finale "Swine", though, that best materializes the conjunction of camp with rave dynamism. Throughout the performance Gaga emulates a pig, squealing while holding her nose and walking on all fours. Her dancers act likewise; many of them appear in pig masks and eject paint through canons attached to their back. The artist interacts with them in animalistic poses and casually screams to the audience. Finishing the number, she announces being nauseated and executes a frenetic routine.

In its entirety, the segment successfully stages a climax of/through transformation and transcendence. The decision to perform the costume change as a live act is rather radical not only due to the risqué approach but also in terms of challenging the conventional show structure according to which changes traditionally occur out-of-sight so as to facilitate and carefully delineate the transition to the next segment as well as build on the audience's expectation. Arguably, the backstage space functions as a terrain of technicalities and practicalities, a space that is mythologized because of its ability to store the secret operations of the spectacle and the star performer; if the front stage represents the world of the extraordinary, then, undeniably, the backstage stands for the ordinary, but, simultaneously, the secretive and the revealing. By consciously bringing the dramaturgy of the backstage space to the front and staging it as a striptease act, Gaga debunks any seriousness concerning the constructedness and mythologization of the performer by exposing the mechanics of the spectacle and playing with audiences' suspension of disbelief. Despite being an act that deconstructs the illusion of the spectacle, it really is an homage to the notion of it since it allows the audience to peek through its processes of transition and acknowledge the craftsmanship and challenges behind it. Furthermore, whereas the undressing process here may point to the dramatics of burlesque, it is rather more akin to those of drag and its shocking revelation of the inner self. As a matter of fact, in announcing *ARTPOP*'s lead single "Applause," Gaga released a promotional lyric video that presented her in a drag club alongside popular queens. The show's strip act thus reimagines and consolidates the artist's affiliation with drag culture while congenially making a nod to it in the removal of the wig, commonly known in camp circles as the "weave-snatching," a state of being impressed or shocked.[22]

By playing up the shock value, Gaga sets the camp tone for her audacious anime character to emerge and to ultimately reach a rave rapture in "Swine." The song itself is an EDM track with edgy industrial sounds in which Gaga illustrates a man as a swine. The artist has claimed writing the song about a rape incident she experienced as a young woman entering the music business.[23] Music criticism acknowledged the raw eccentricity of the track, describing it as "*ARTPOP*'s wow-factor centrepiece" (Empire, "Lady Gaga"), "a romping, ridiculous synth blart" (Lloyd), "a shrieking industrial number" wherein "[t]he singer sounds physically disgusted" (Lipshutz). The live performance effectively foregrounds the disjointed aesthetic and trance-inducing rhythm of the song, thus fueling Gaga's hectic rave act. In it, the artist's performance of femininity escalates from cartoonish to mocking to nonsensical, replacing staccatos and high-pitched vocals with squeals and unintelligible cries, thereby reenacting a poetics of disorder and colorful chaos as originally experienced in the rave scene. Also inspired by Japanese anime, Gaga's caricature act alludes to the genre's stock character of the "magical girl," an ultra-feminine heroine renowned for her "psychic abilities and interdimensional traveling" (Newitz 4). In addition, one could underline references to Greek mythology and the Homerian account of Circe, the enchantress that eventually drugged Odysseus' crew and transformed them into swines.[24] Appositely, the artist's "magical girl" aligns with the transcendent ethos of the show and its glamorization of drug culture as already demonstrated in other acts of the show, including those for the songs "Jewels and Drugs," "Dope," and "Mary Jane Holland," which all reference Gaga's substance abuse.

Historically, the rise of rave in the late 1980s was largely perceived as a corruptive culture of narcotics and excessive hedonism whose policing and regulation were resultant of a triggered moral panic (A. Brown 78). Yet, Simon Reynolds highlights its escapism in arguing that "[a]t the heart of rave lies a kernel of tautology: raving is about celebration of celebration" (86). Since Gaga's tour, being a highly commercial event, cannot generate or even replicate the original subcultural edge and spontaneous combustion of the rave culture, it resorts to

164

borrowing its style and mantra in making celebration (of the self, of community) its *raison d'être*. As is the case with her previous shows, the artist's reenactments of colorful utopias, especially those configured with the poetic aid of camp, indicate a disruption of the serious and the orderly normative. The conjunction of camp with rave here is an utterly bizarre collision of queer energy with stylized anarchy, the praxis of which unravels in complete *ataxia*, aptly signifying both disorder and mischief. Gaga's politics of childishness, thus, prefigure a regressive state to being a child, not as in Edelman's teleological figure of a heteronormative future, but rather as a romanticized intermediate stage with the ability to morph in and out of roles and be exempted from the world of seriousness. Throughout *The ARTPOP Ball*, Gaga would call out her audience to let loose and celebrate their diversity and artistic creativity, the two core values nested both within the artist's very own camp aesthet(h)ics as well as in the joints of pop art and rave.

Although Gaga's queer engagement with performance has been steady throughout the abovementioned tour enterprises, the same cannot be argued for the follow-up tour. The conclusion of *The ARTPOP Ball* eventually found the artist taking a brief hiatus from arena extravaganzas before returning with 2017's *Joanne World Tour*. She did manage to keep her camp appeal steady with numerous in-between projects, whether these regard live performance—consider her androgynous transformations into late icons Frank Sinatra and David Bowie for the "Sinatra 100: An All-Star Academy Concert" (in 2015) and the 2016 Grammy Awards, respectively—or television acting—most famously, her Golden Globe-awarded role of The Countess in FX's *American Horror Story: Hotel* (in 2015–16). Touring-wise also, the artist embarked on a jazz concert series with Tony Bennett as part of their collaborative project, *Cheek to Cheek*. The *Cheek to Cheek Tour* (in 2014–15) mainly reached North American music halls and a few European jazz festivals. As opposed to Gaga's major scale enterprises, the production of this show, abiding by the classical/jazz concert tradition and supervised by Robert Wilson, was rather minimal in terms of props, visual effects, and staged narratives. Juxtaposed to Bennett's formal profile, Gaga would simply up the camp ante by alternating between flamboyant gowns and elaborate wigs. The complete omission of her standard hits along with the accustomed theatrics from the show evidently distanced the diva from the camp/queer-inflected agenda of previous extravaganzas. In *Cheek to Cheek*, Gaga mainly drew from the musical and aesthetic catalogue of past and present divas, including Edith Piaf and Cher's, to mention just a few, thus bringing a high camp approach to her performance. Gaga's style was a nostalgic nod to American feminine glamour, with the artist "shape-shifting from approximations of Mae West to Marilyn Monroe to a glittery cat-suited vamp [...] like an old-time burlesque performer" (Holden). The show's dazzling camp factor remains attached to Gaga's costumes in a sense that it foregrounds the artist's play with camp as an era-specific conceptual project which, similar to that of *The Fame Ball*'s Candy Warhol, indulges in anachronistic dramatics in its showcasing of a retro reality. At the same time, her camp praxis semantically draws from the tradition of the torch singer worship, abiding by trends also followed by her contemporaries, such as Adele and Lana Del Rey, who have established their pop personae through high (melo)drama and balladry.

However, these latest works of the artist seem rather distanced from what she had set in motion, at least for the first five years of her career. These projects are bereft of the distinctive absurdism that previously fueled Gaga's notion of spectacle and performance art. *Joanne World Tour*, for that matter, exemplifies the transition from the radicalism of previous shows, wherein Gaga's praxis of camp was simultaneously energized with subcultural references and critical twists, to one that is simplistically nostalgic on stage. Despite being a high-octane production with elaborate staging, the *Joanne Tour* lacks the camp edge that either *Monster Balls* or *The Born This Way Ball* exhibited. Supporting her personal and perhaps most affective album, *Joanne*—titled after her own middle name—the tour lays emphasis on the alleged "real self" through intimate and traditional mini narratives. Gone here are the wigs, the surreal costumes, and the fairytale-like settings. With the album titling to an Americana aesthetic, ranging from generic rock 'n' roll to country, Gaga's Joanne persona(?) is brought on the live stage with a distinct American kitsch, sporting cowboy hats, leather boots, and studded denim. The performances are structured upon an emotional spectrum, veering from pain to joy, to grief to love, while, lyrically, the performed *Joanne* tracks reference cowboy culture ("John Wayne"), Christian religion ("Angel Down," "Come to Mama"), and American exceptionalism ("Diamond Heart," "A-Yo").

Arguably, the *Joanne Tour* sees Gaga moving from camp to kitsch. As Long argues, "[k]itsch is kitsch because it does not recognize contradictions in value [...] Innocent of the world around it, kitsch is art without an immune system. It is created without a sense of context" (86). Conversely, the writer underlines that "[c]amp is a conscious response to a culture where kitsch is ubiquitous. Camp is essentially an *attitude* toward kitsch" (Long 86). Gaga's slip to nostalgic romanticism, whether this is established through the alleged vulnerability in her new sense of the performing persona and/or her championing of traditional values permeating American identity and culture, deviates from her conspicuous campification of corpora, as was the case, for example, with her ultra-camp treatment of the leather biker culture in *Born This Way Ball* or her pop art shenanigans for *The ARTPOP Ball*. While the *Joanne* show could toy with its country theme in a similar manner that Kylie did in her *Golden Tour*, as well as benefit from the camp-inflected potential of songs, such as the tongue-in-cheek "John Wayne" or the risqué "Dancing in Circles,"[25] it resorts to run-of-the-mill choreographies that remain detached from the songs' contexts. Music critic Jon Caramanica accurately noted that "Lady Gaga made her name with ostentation, ironic flamboyance and pseudo performance art. That strangeness once gave her centrist disco-pop real teeth, but it has long since decayed" (Caramanica). Gaga's shift of focus on the seemingly more authentic profile as this is based on and understood by rock('n' roll) culture stands in stark contrast with the plasticity and audacity of her camp approach in all her previous projects. Whereas this shift risks confusing Gaga's audiences, whose appeal, to a certain extent, may originate in camp pleasure, it should be noted that not only has the artist so far sustained a historical camp tradition but, importantly, has left her own imprint in the culture of camp by creating her very own iconic legacy.

Fans attending the *Joanne World Tour* seemed to embrace the artist's Americana turn. Many of them appear in concerts wearing *Joanne*'s signature pink cowboy hat as well as copying Gaga's newly imported looks from recent performances, such as the football-glam style from the artist's 2017 Halftime Super Bowl show or the looks from the "John Wayne" video, while others preserve the artist's iconicity through references to her past phases. Undoubtedly, her Little Monsters revel in the preservation and promotion of Gaga's camp appeal. In other words, even if the artist eventually becomes a nostalgia artist, a kitsch act, her audiences' performative response in emulating her persona will always be a potent praxis of camp forged with the diva's unique camp aesthet(h)ics and the here-and-now communal spaces around her stage. The queer temporality created by the audiences' conscious embodiment of camp in the context and contours of the star performer can in fact underscore camp as a critical performative device that effectively elasticizes a strictly normative reality. With that in mind, let us now delve deeper into divas' fan culture and their materialization of a camp self and space.

NOTES

1. As opposed to the tradition of musical theater in the pre-*Oklahoma!* period, wherein the plot is interrupted by musical numbers providing comic relief or melodramatic accentuation, in the integrated musical—commonly referred to as the book musical, because it is based upon the libretto—the musical numbers propel the plot, therefore displaying narrative continuity (Taylor and Symonds 14).

2. Though this chapter thoroughly deals with most of Gaga's tour shows, I have decided to only briefly touch upon the *Cheek to Cheek Tour* (in 2014–15), her joined collaboration with Tony Bennett in support of their namesake jazz album, since the specific tour follows the music hall format and eschews the arena spectacle aesthetics. The praxis of camp here is limited to Gaga's outfits and dramatic delivery, with the show—a signature creation of Robert Wilson—being consciously minimal as informed by the classical/jazz tradition.

THE MUSIC DIVA SPECTACLE

3. According to Peter Hutchings:

    > [T]he mad artist has become a stock figure in the horror genre, although he (or more rarely, she) has often been overshadowed by his cousin, the mad scientist. Both share a concern to shape reality according to their own self-centered vision, no matter what the consequences for the people around them. (22)

    From the murderous artist in *Mystery of the Wax Museum* to the emblematic genius insanity of Hannibal Lecter in *The Silence of the Lambs*, all of Hutchings's examples attest to a tradition that is conspicuously male centered.

4. David Bergman argues that the grotesque female body holds a central position in camp, especially in the performance of drag wherein queens overemphasize feminine features on body and face (102). The cinema of camp, including films such as *Sunset Boulevard*, *What Ever Happened to Baby Jane?*, and *Mommie Dearest*, to name a few, also depicts monstrous women that usually border on insanity.

5. An alternative performance of "Paparazzi" in *Monster Ball* features Gaga with extremely elongated braids that dominate the stage. Pursuing her are her dancers who wield oversized pairs of scissors, which, ultimately, force upon Gaga's hair.

6. "Alejandro" is a melodramatic mid-tempo song with Hispanic influences, the chorus of which envisions Gaga saying goodbye to three male figures—Alejandro, Fernando, and Roberto. The video of the song features Gaga in a Nazi-inspired setting—perhaps paying homage to musical *Cabaret*—and incorporates erotic scenes between her male dancers. In the same vein as Madonna's play with Catholicism, "Alejandro's" ultra-camp video also sees the artist leading a funeral procession, appearing as a latex-clad nun, and swallowing rosary beads.

7. As of 2015, online press placed Gaga's production among the most expensive concert tours ever created, including the shows of Madonna, Roger Waters, U2, and The Rolling Stones. *The Born This Way Ball* cost $2 million to create and $1 million per venue setup (Drughi; Erbar).

8. One might as well argue that Gaga toys with Jungian archetypes of motherhood, emulating the Terrible Mother that Jung identified with the dark qualities of destruction, seduction, and deviance—as exemplified by the mythological figures of Lilith and Kali, among others, who were associated with the underworld and the abyss (*Four Archetypes*, 15–16). Cf. Carl Jung's *Four Archetypes: Mother, Rebirth, Spirit, Trickster*, and *The Archetypes and the Collective Unconscious: Second Edition*, edited by Sir Herbert Read, Michael Fordam, Gerhard Adler, and William McGuire, translated by R.F.C. Hull.

9. Consider Madonna's Equestrian segment in the *Confessions Tour*; Kylie Minogue's pommel horse performance in *Homecoming* as well as her performing atop a golden Pegasus in *Aphrodite Tour*; and, finally, Katy Perry's Egyptian-themed performance of "Dark Horse" in her *Prismatic World Tour* (between 2014–15).

168

10. A notable exception to this canon was the production of *Mazeppa, or The Wild Horse of Tartary* (in 1910) in which actress Adah Isaacs Menken executed a notoriously risqué performance, riding naked on stage (Banham 168).

11. Both the unicorn and the pink triangle abound in the tradition of Pride parades. The unicorn's elusive and benevolent nature is metonymic of a queer utopia. More tangibly, the pink triangle that had been used in Nazi concentration camps to mark suspects of homosexuality has been reclaimed by the LGBTQ+ community. Consider Richard Plant's *The Pink Triangle: The Nazi War against Homosexuals*.

12. From the American perspective, the viewing of French culture as a feminine one has been a prevalent stereotype. According to Todd Reeser, "US culture has coded French culture as effeminate in its imaginary, in part because French masculinity is regarded as effeminate, as a way to masculinize itself by opposition" (183). "Such codings, however," Reeser suggests,

> often imply the imposition of one nation's definition of masculinity onto another where it may not apply. An American may view French masculinity as effeminate because of, among other traits, its attention to clothing when, in a French context, an emphasis on dress is considered a culturally sanctioned form of masculinity and not necessarily effeminate. (183)

13. Consider Haraway (173–81).

14. In her ethnography of the American drag subculture, Esther Newton argues that

> [t]he trick in stripping is to look and move as much like a "real" stripper as possible and create the same erotic effects on the audience, to sustain the illusion of "reality" down to the bra and g-string, and then, as a climax, to "pull" (slip off) the bra, revealing a perfectly flat chest. Since gay audiences know for a certainty that the drag queen has a flat chest, strip is more often seen in the straight shows. (45)

15. Gaga's songs "Bad Romance" and "Dance in the Dark" feature a variation of the lyrics "I'm a free bitch, baby."

16. For the promotion of *ARTPOP* in 2013, the artist opted for reverse psychology marketing, announcing in a commercial trailer that "[Lady Gaga] is over" and "no longer relevant" (Thorpe). Influenced by Warhol's work to render pop as art, Gaga announced that she would "bring art culture into pop in a reverse Warholian expedition" (Thorpe).

17. The three vignettes, titled "The Heart," "The Brain," and "The Face," are home-made art films that were first showcased during The Pussycat Dolls' *Doll Domination Tour* (in 2009), where Lady Gaga was the opening act. Also known as *Crevette Films*, Gaga named the series after *crevettes* ("*shrimps*" in French), claiming that "shrimps are small, but decadent and tasty, which is how I think my films should be" (Barton).

THE MUSIC DIVA SPECTACLE

18. While one could argue that technically the setlist begins with "Paparazzi" and concludes with "Poker Face," the in-between arrangement of the songs, even those seemingly standard slots after the interlude videos, could occasionally be subjected to changes. This can be explanatory of the show's smaller scale production, which tilted to a small club-like gig show (compared to Gaga's future arena enterprises) and, thus, allowed flexibility.

19. In her essay "Imitation and Gender Insubordination," Judith Butler explicates the inauthenticity of gender which, similarly to the Baudrillardian concept of the simulacrum, bears no original. Butler relied on the practice of drag to postulate that:

> [T]here is no original or primary gender that drag imitates, but *gender is a kind of imitation for which there is no original*; in fact, it is a kind of imitation that produces the very notion of the original as an *effect* and consequence of the imitation itself. (261, orginal emphasis)

20. The concept alludes and may have, in fact, drawn influences from either Janet Jackson's *All for You Tour* (between 2001–02) or Katy Perry's *California Dreams Tour* (between 2011–12), both of which were mostly reminiscent of camp cartoon fantasias.

21. Space or galactic disco, as exemplified in the productions of Giorgio Moroder, Kraftwerk, and Boney M., lays emphasis on heavy synthesizer and arpeggiator beats, repetitive lines, and ambient acoustics (Leone). In terms of fashion, the camp glam of space disco might as well be informed by pop culture and cult corpora, such as *Star Wars* and *Barbarella*, and in terms of lyrics, the allusions to outer space are dominant.

22. *Urban Dictionary* defines "snatched"—as in the "the wig is snatched"—as "a popular term in the gay community referring to good looks, fierceness, or something good." The phrase "to have one's weave snatched" indicates "being astoundingly surprised," while "to snatch a weave" is "an action taken in a girl fight when one grabs the hair weave of the other," which is also common in drag put-downs and catfights. Although there is limited cultural theory regarding the term, it is possible that the term came to wider usage through Black culture.

23. Gaga talked about "Swine" while being interviewed for *The Howard Stern Show*. The artist said: "The song is about rape. The song is about demoralization. The song is about rage and fury and passion and I had a lot of pain that I wanted to release" (Payne). She mainly referred to her performing "Swine" for the 2014 SXSW (South by Southwest) Festival in which she notoriously had performance artist Millie Brown vomit on her on stage.

24. See Robert Fitzgerald's translation of *Odyssey*, Book Ten, "The Grace of the Witch."

25. In "John Wayne" Gaga addresses her quest for real men, having the iconic figure of Wayne as an archetype, while in "Dancing in Circles" she performs an homage to masturbation.

5

Dressed for the Ball:
Audience Drag in the Arena Space

*[D]rag traditionally has been a sampling machine. We have always
taken little bits to piece together a bigger story.*

(RuPaul, *Vulture*)

Having a ball [...] Wish you were here.

(*Paris Is Burning*)

As a mode of entertainment, concert-going entails more than simply attending
and enjoying a gig. One has to think of the concert experience as a climactic process that incrementally builds on the excitement of the attendee-to-be. Starting
with the first organizing steps, such as booking tickets and planning the route to
the site of the concert, and culminating with the actual performance engrossing
the audience, the gig wishes to establish itself as a happening, a marked event in
the attendee's memory. Considering the prospective spectator is both an attendee-
to-be and a devoted fan of the star performer, the climactic process often begins
from the moment a new album is announced, which more often than not signals
or coincides with the announcement of an upcoming tour. Fans may even get
exposed to exclusive rehearsal content that performers might make public prior
to embarking on tour. Inextricably linked with that is the functional role of social
media which only seems to have amplified the event-nature of the concert in manifold ways. Apart from being utilized as promotional platforms by artists and live
entertainment companies, social media is catalytic in bringing communities of fans
together who share their personal experiences of a show or an artist in online fora.
Fans who may attend on a later date have the opportunity to get a glimpse of the
show to be performed thanks to those who were present at an earlier one; likewise,
fans unable to attend at all rely exclusively on the shared material, thus partaking

in the concert experience virtually. Although the overall structure of a show usually remains the same, there might be occasional changes in setlist or costuming that render each concert unique, adding to the fans' enticement and thus offering different perspectives of the supposed "original" production. In odd cases, audiences may even experience a completely different version of the show depending on their locale; for instance, Lady Gaga's two-pieced *Monster Ball Tour* had San Francisco and Toronto as host cities for both versions of the tour, contrary to Mexico City or Sydney whose audiences got to attend only the revamped show. In that case, fans recording and sharing versions of a show online manage to collectively preserve and build on a multifaceted experience.

Undoubtedly, locality and the politics of space play a key role in the audiences' relation to the spectacle. Major-scale tours, including all the productions explored in this work, incorporate space, be it geographical, performative, or communal, as a significant parameter in the overall reception. Large productions are mainly accommodated in arenas or stadia in the vicinity of a metropolitan center. Therefore, they remain attached to the physiognomy of urban cultures and their interconnectedness with the host city, contributing to the latter's micro and macro politics. On a micro level, arena concerts are financial, social, and, at times, quasi-political events that may momentarily influence their social surroundings. Host cities are strategically picked by touring companies not only because of their geographical functionality to attract audiences in their broader radius but also due to their role as consumerist cores. Local market economy may be boosted through businesses catering for concert-goers, from restaurants and convenience stores to lodging and souvenir shops (for attendees coming into the host city). Politics-wise, the character of a show or even the nature of the spectacle, which is connected with the performing persona, impacts variably on certain locales: consider again possible protests or boycotts by local groups against the allegedly provocative spectacles of Madonna and Lady Gaga (see Chapters 1 and 4). On a macro level, concerts brought into a host city on a regular basis may gradually morph the local audiences' taste and sensibility as regards entertainment. In the long run, apart from capital locations with established concert market, such as New York and London, cities like Milan, Osaka, or Tel Aviv have become standard touring destinations whose cosmopolitan audiences may exhibit a more open appreciation of spectacles.

While audiences vary depending on locale, what can safely be argued is that, in their majority, concert-goers share at least one objective: they are all motivated into the spectacle by their relation to the star performer. Attending an arena concert requires that the attendee, in order to be present, has invested emotion, time, and finance—all being aspects linked with the performing artist. Chances are that a person neutrally attached to an artist—meaning that they are not devoted fans, but not entirely indifferent either—would still come to a show driven by the star's magnitude: put simply, one would come to see the latest Madonna show not for the sake of its newness or musical quality, but mainly because Madonna is performing. Emotional, temporal, and financial investment here may exist at a minimum, since the attendee might be content with simply watching Madonna from a random seat in the arena; or, they may have come to hear and see her classic repertoire, driven by nostalgia. On the contrary, hardcore fans' investment usually reaches a maximal level when they go to see both the artist and the new show because they are probably familiar with past concerts and want to upgrade their knowledge on the star performer. These fans often congregate in the arena terrain, the "pit," which means they may be holders of the much-prized front-row and golden-standing tickets or they may have spent hours or even days outside the concert space waiting for the gate opening as was the case with Beyoncé's fans in Sao Paulo (see Chapter 3).

Above all, though, as ardent followers of the performing artist, fans will appear in tune with the character and aesthetic of the presented spectacle. In divas' case, this means adopting a camp aesthetic. Seeing that Kylie Minogue and Lady Gaga as well as other divas inside or outside this work are renowned for a camp spectacle, their audiences embracing the camp quality of their spectacle points to a cognitive way of an active participation in the divas' world displayed on stage. Their coming to the live performance not only signifies the moment when they get to materialize their love for their adored diva but also encourages a more playful and flexible treatment of their social identity. It is true that the conscious embodiment and expression of one's imagined ideal, especially in the collective space of a live concert, constitute important components for the individual's pleasure and self-gratification. As Lawrence Grossberg indicates, "[f]ans' investment in certain practices and texts provides them with strategies which enable them to gain a certain amount of control over their affective life, which further enables them to invest in new forms of meaning, pleasure and identity" (65). For queer fans, in particular, this claiming of agency is deeply connected with a control over their own sexuality and gender that the environment around the diva welcomes. Diva spectacles in fact serve as beacons of queer expression in offering a momentary disengagement from conventional gendered reality.

Transforming themselves by means of styling for the live concert thus is key in fans' materialization of affect and agency. This transformation may range from simply painting one's face or adorning one's body with accessories borrowed from the star performer's visual arsenal, to a complete sartorial reconfiguration of the star herself.[1] A common phenomenon in the diva concerts explicated in this work is witnessing fans, both female and male, dressing up as their favorite divas in a praxis not dissimilar with drag. The attention paid to detail and the meticulous approach taken by fans as regards referencing from the variety of stylistic appearances divas have made in memorable performances or on album covers over the years are in fact akin to the elaborate work done by professional stage impersonators and drag queens. Therefore, what I identify as *audience drag* is this exact performative practice which, informed by the poetics of drag in the camp reconfiguration of the gendered self, sees fans appropriating the looks of the onstage persona as a means of expressing their affinity with the latter's brand and projected culture.

In order to better understand the praxis of audience drag, one has to conceptualize it as a social activity that merges the collective character of mass entertainment with the carnival of camp in light of the performed spectacle-event. In addressing the nature of this activity, we must, first and foremost, examine the theatrical tradition of drag alongside its gradual emergence from its subcultural environment and its relocation into the commercial terrain of popular culture. Inevitably, this motion raises questions with regard to drag's cultural capital as well as the politics of queer culture in the circulation of the community's traditions and practices. In the context of camp, audience drag, which is energized by it, should always be treated contextually; and since camp embodies a parody of (hetero)normative conventions and identities, but is simultaneously bound to pop culture, audience drag, in turn, validates it as a mechanism of resistance, but also follows its cultural clauses. Drag, as stated in the epigraph, "is a sampling machine" whose pieces aid in the formation of a bigger story, according to popular drag mother RuPaul Charles (A. Jung). Taking into consideration that this story is unattached to the evolution of contemporary queer cultures, it becomes imperative to investigate the openness and broader reception of audience drag when put in the framework of the industries of pop and global entertainment. What is addressed further here is fans' attendance in drag, which, although inadequate as an action to solidly verify one's queer sexuality, it does play on camp—itself denoting queerness/gayness. What does it ultimately signify to bring the subcultural praxis of drag out in the public sphere of mass entertainment and see it exercised out of its designated position upon a stage? In light of this, is it legitimate to view audience drag as a theatrical device that transforms the audience into "spect-actors"? Finally, what is the role of the arena space in the housing of audience drag?

Drag beyond the stage

In the long history of music fandom, fashion has played a key role in engaging and acclimating fans with a said music culture. As evident in the variety of music scenes and movements, such as British punk rock or Japanese *kawaii* pop, dressing expresses community belonging with the fans' identity being baptized into a style that stands in concert with the sensibility of each culture. Artists serve as the vessels channeling the fashion of their affiliated music culture, thus becoming creative templates for the fans to draw from. For example, Madonna's style throughout the 1980s, merging ethnic elements with the sensibility of New York's club cultures, exemplified a postmodern urban collage, which, most importantly, carried a second-hand ("thrift-store") aesthetic, therefore immediately becoming accessible to her fans. As John Fisk suggests,

> [t]he Madonna fans who, on MTV, claimed that dressing like Madonna made people take more notice of them as they walked down the streets were not only constructing for themselves more empowered identities than those normally available to young adolescent girls but were putting those meanings into social circulation. (38)

Dressing is a significant component in allowing fans to express, commune, and even politicize their music identities. Madonna's provocative sense of style, which to a large extent employed body exposure as a feminist device, provided at the time a progressive view in understanding female empowerment and volition through fashion.

As a tool that expresses lifestyle, personal taste, and political sensibility, style can become perhaps the most instantly recognizable marker of one's self and identity. The cognitive selection of clothing, accessories, and hair style is what importantly underlines identity as performative. According to Carol Tulloch, everyday style encloses agency in the sense that it becomes part of the self's identity narrative. More specifically, the writer sees "the styling practices of a layperson's articulation of everyday life through their styled body as exercising that agency" (5). Without downplaying exogenous factors influencing a person's formation of style, such as fashion advertising, circulation of trends, and taste of peer groups, agency lies at the kernel of selection and assemblage out of the variety of signifiers. In a postmodern context, fashion is informed by an assortment of styles, be they subculture-related, era-specific, or region-inspired, among other factors, which are made available to consume in what Ted Polhemus identifies as "the Supermarket of Style" (131). Polhemus suggests that postmodern consumers of fashion emphasize the mixing of styles and the incongruity and ironies surfacing from the mixing process (132). Understanding therefore modern prosumers as editors of their personal styles helps us toward conceiving dressing—in our case, dressing as part of the concert-event—as ascribing a purpose to one's narrative of style, especially when placed alongside other individual narratives. To revisit Madonna's American female fans in the 1980s, their style narratives were backed by the purpose of empowerment through gender and body politics against a generally conservative social milieu. The purpose was significantly motivated by Madonna's hyped narrative of success, yet simultaneously required from her female fans to take action in breaking ties with traditional views of femaleness and femininity.

Through the lens of camp, dressing champions the falsehood and artifice that Polhemus attributed to the postmodern fashion supermarket. In camp's world of style, the figures of the dandy, the effeminate man, and that of the drag queen all addressed style as inextricably linked to a consciously stylized image of their social personae, whose destabilizing approach of heteronormative identities would often lead to patriarchy-instigated narratives of risk or even violence. Inasmuch as camp denotes effeminacy, the excessive styles inherent in dandyism and drag have historically become a source of anxiety for heterosexist culture as well as (straight, gay, and bi) masculinity. Drag, as a matter of fact, due to being ubiquitously practiced as an inseparable tradition of Pride parades or as a form of theatrical entertainment, has become a cross-cultural signifier of modern gay culture itself.

Being a performative device and a performed tradition, drag has employed the power of style in its parodying of normative genders. Indeed, the drag-associated camp encloses a dynamic of mockery and artifice that can elasticize traditional understandings of gender, and insofar as camp has infiltrated pop culture and music, drag too has entered those domains by establishing itself as a comedic style of performance. Nevertheless, in the case of audience drag, it is important to imagine the camp practice of drag as indivisible with the queer culture that has surrounded it and significantly contributed to it being shaped and narrativized into the form we currently know. Its practice also attests to the fact that music diva culture has contributed to paving the ground upon which fans enjoy toying with gender stylization. Considering there is an apparent, if evolutionary, development that sees drag moving from its liminal status to it being casually practiced out in public—at least at the site of the arena, as examined here—attention should also be paid as to this evolution in accordance to music cultures.

Historically and prior to becoming synonymous with queer culture, drag had mostly been located in the world of theater. Evolving from religious practices and rituals, drag entered the theatrical stage as an act of magical transformation, mainly of a man into a woman, and rarely vice versa. These practices, according to Laurence Senelick, often entailed same-sex and polyamorous activities as part of their trance-inducing rituals, while cross-identification was commonly identified with prostitution, eventually leading to the popular association of theater-acting with effeminacy and prostitution (23–31). It would not be until the mid-eighteenth century that drag would emerge as a firmly queer expression and, by extension, a symbolic subcultural practice. This more concretized association of drag with queer culture results from the formation of more vibrant, self-identified, and partly visible queer communities, at least in the Western world. Though drag was commonly practiced in variety shows and circuses, thus carefully enveloped within the environment of a stage, it was other subcultural scenes, such as London's molly-houses, as Senelick's account indicates (302), that established a coherent relation of drag with homosexuality.[2] In the public mind, drag quickly grew to be a queer-related praxis, although one that would progressively dissociate itself from cross-dressing and prostitution, and would tilt to a more skillful, if artistic form of gender performance.

Eventually, other drag practices started mushrooming within queer urban centers, such as those of Berlin, Paris, and New York, to name a few. Gradually growing in terms of visibility, frequency, and consistency, not only did those practices cement drag as a queer tradition but significantly aided queer individuals in forming and sustaining communal bonds. The case of New York's drag balls is noteworthy here and one can see how their radicalness has made a felt impact on modern queer culture and, by extension, has successfully reached the music diva stage, as all cases of this work demonstrate. Drag balls, according to George Chauncey, rose to popularity in 1920s Manhattan and derived their festive structure from the tradition of late nineteenth-century masquerade balls (291). Importantly, as the writer argues, queer culture appropriated an allegedly heterosexual convention and gave it a new edge that would later be branded with their own queer insignia (291). In addition to that, by carrying the urban sensibility of queer New York, an amalgam city of racial and ethnic elements, balls welcomed in diversity and cultural convergence. As is currently known, Harlem's Black and Latinx drag balls emerged in the 1920s and became the basis out of which the subsequent voguing scene and Houses were patterned. Despite the auspicious position drag enjoyed within these cultures, though, drag balls were certainly no queer utopias. Adversities within the ball circuit were a given and usually translated into classism, and racism, homophobia, and persecution.[3] With regard to queer life at the time, cross-dressing as well as sodomy constituted a felony (Chauncey 295). Similar to Britain's "gross indecency" laws that prohibited same-sex intercourse but also often incriminated cross-dressers on the basis of immorality and sodomy associations, American legislation tolerated neither homosexuality nor alternative gender expressions. Though at times balls could be legally accessible as long as they were under police surveillance and considering that participants had to present police-initiated license of attendance allowing masquerading, cross-dressing was still regulated to a large extent (Chauncey 295–96). This partial institutional elasticity with the practice of drag demonstrates a tolerance with it because it is a stage performance, contrary to other cross-dressing acts in the street or in prostitution circles.

While trans culture, prior to entering the political umbrella of the modern LGBTQ+ movement, has been closely associated with cruising and prostitution activities, thereby linking cross-dressing with the idea of a fetish that is meant for sexual pleasure, drag has represented its theatrical equivalent which evolved quite differently. Moving from sexual to political and back again, drag in the stage environment challenges the ideological structures of gender and tackles them by means of irony and parody. Ultimately, drag *is* theater, one that simultaneously dons on traditional gender and comically exposes its mechanics and fissures. Politically, even pedagogically speaking, drag, as Roger Baker puts it, "is about anarchy and defiance" (16). Precisely due to its theater roots, though, drag has acquired artistic connotations and, more importantly, it has somehow through its parodic treatment of gendered reality blunted the edges that cross-dressing generated to conventional thought. In this sense, it can be argued that drag, as often located in the sphere of comedy and spectacle, might lack the radicalness of its street counterpart, a fact that points to its political mitigation. By being safely placed in the contours of a stage or within the limits of its subculture, it has grown to popularity in part because, in the public mind, it does not seem to pose any serious threat to systemic gender, contrary to the political, legal, and medical anxiety that trans-associated cross-dressing practices have instigated. The general attitude toward onstage drag or subcultural drag, both exercised in clientele-specific locales, venues, or sites, helped the practice develop rather uniquely and contributes to our knowledge of its evolution and popularization.

As a matter of fact, the politics of space must not be omitted from discussions around the social and historical development of drag. Stage has more often than not functioned both as a protective platform whereupon drag has been safely positioned, as well as an artistic vehicle that smoothly propelled it into mainstream culture. Stage drag, after all, has been in the world of theater globally for centuries, thus allowing audiences to acclimate with the practice of it as a dramatic device meant to satirically upset the gender order and elicit laughter. The stage has thus served as that private, if limited, spatial territory where the camp of drag is commonly welcomed. On the contrary, drag queens taking to the streets seem to have always unnerved the majority of the public, because their flaunting of queerness would make manifest a rampant queer culture. In her mid-century ethnography of drag subculture, Newton explicates the division of female impersonators into stage and street queens: "the street pattern is a *fusion* of the 'street fairy' life with the profession of female impersonation. Street fairies are jobless young homosexual men who publicly epitomize the homosexual stereotype and are the underclass of the gay world" (8, original emphasis). Conversely, Newton argues that "the stage pattern *segregates* the stigma from the personal life by limiting it to the stage context as much as possible. The work is viewed as a profession with goals and standards rather than as a job" (8, original emphasis). Insofar as drag is confined within its controllably delineated and staged environment, its practice is perceived as a knowledgeable profession, whereas street drag remains more akin to trans culture and prostitution. The juxtaposition, thus, created between stage and street, or between the isolated subcultural lifestyle and its clash with the mainstream, is one of a private/public dichotomy.

Public manifestations of queerness, which are usually linked to dressing and posture, have triggered problematic responses by both heterosexual and homosexual cultures. While, historically and cross-culturally, heterosexual culture and, more specifically, conservative groups within it not only have been patronizing queer lifestyle and behavior but have sought ways to incriminate and penalize queer practices, the same also holds true for the conservative spectrum of homosexual cultures, thus pointing to an intra-communal conflict in the perception of queerness itself. These notions seem to accrue from a socially established and institutionally perpetuated fear of the queer Other and its open manifestation (flaunting) of queerness. Standing metonymically for queer culture, drag's closet-defying practice stimulates similar response when taken out of its stage environment and brought into wider view. For instance, popular arguments against the concept of Pride parades often target the conspicuous campiness of drag and, by extension, that of gay culture, proposing instead a more toned-down demonstration of gay pride and identity. Those requests favoring the downplaying of Pride's queerness/gayness, which are still encountered across countries, evince the persistent anxiety that the subject matters of drag and camp can generate. On the contrary, drag may seem more natural or, to put it in a less essentialist manner, more innocuous upon a stage since spectacle has traditionally depended on values of transformation and shock as well as erected the safety of the fourth wall between performance and audience, affirming thus the nature of drag as a purely theatrical act.

Coming to an awareness of drag as a potent, if militant, device against the predominance of the gender binary, queer culture has rather effectively politicized its parodic praxis. The unsettling sentiments cross-dressing has for years inspired in the mainstream public have not only been located in moralist discourse, but, most importantly, they have multifariously materialized through institutional power. The narratives of pathologization and penalization mentioned earlier here attest to the way the gender binary informed the medical and legal system toward punitively regulating practices of cross-dressing, thereby directly and indirectly affecting communities of queer people that failed to meet the imposed gendered standards. According to Andrea Ritchie, "[f]or much of the twentieth century, police used sumptuary laws to punish gender non-conformity among drag queens, transgender women, and butch lesbians of color" (131). "Trans women and self-identified drag queens of color were often rounded up and arrested on the basis of cross-dressing laws" (131), the writer reiterates and argues how "[f]eminine attire worn by transgender women is pervasively cited by police as grounds for suspicion that they are engaged in prostitution or 'lewd contact'" (132). In America, law enforcement raids and pursuits of trans-/cross-identified individuals infamously culminated with the Stonewall riots in the Village, yet the outburst was rather resultant from and indicative of, as the history of drag ball surveillance evinces, a century-long suppression of homosexuality and cross-dressing practices. With the advent of queer collectivity in light of the 1960s liberation movements, the need to depathologize and decriminalize both homosexuality as well as non-conforming gender expressions drove queer communities in America to variably employ cross-dressing as a form of activism that was simultaneously forged with camp parody and political resistance.

Having extensively populated the world of theater and art, drag practitioners, be they glamour queens or male/female impersonators, progressively entered the mainstream terrain of popular culture through which the camp praxis of drag managed to reach a wider audience. Among these first and most important terrains that helped popularize drag are musical theater and cinema, with celebrity culture following suit. The stages of Broadway and the West End, for that matter, have frequently been material sources for the production and diffusion of works that do not simply utilize drag as a dramatic device that ruffles gender on stage, but foregrounds it as inextricably linked with the queer culture drag is affiliated with. By featuring characters in drag as protagonists, productions such as *The Rocky Horror Show*, *Torch Song Trilogy*, and *M. Butterfly*, to name just a few, centralized their narratives around the praxis of drag and the queering of identity; their subsequent film adaptations not only established these works as widely appreciated queer texts—consider the cult reception of *The Rocky Horror Picture Show* (in 1975)—but firmly embedded them in the history of queer art-making. Film-wise, drag has occasionally served as a comic tool employed to provide relief in mainstream movies—a point I will address shortly—but, as a gay-associated tradition, its existence has rather been limited within queer cinema. For instance, films including *Pink Flamingos La Cage Aux Folles*, and *The Adventures of Priscilla, Queen of the Desert* now belong to the filmic canon of camp and have variously been revisited in popular culture and within academic theories of cultural and LGBTQ+ studies. Last but not least, local scenes and celebrity culture have also contributed in popularizing drag, ranging from personae emerging to national and international stardom from their respective locales, such as RuPaul and Lily Savage (aka Paul O'Grady), as well as queer groups and enclaves, including 1980s Manhattan's Club Kids (featuring, among others, the self-proclaimed "celebutantes" James St. James and Amanda Lepore) and House voguers, who assertively enveloped drag with celebrity narratives and made themselves a brand name.

Inasmuch as drag's history has been one of defiance and resistance, to use Baker's words, it has also been a history of cooptation and exploitation. Mainstream cinema has often employed drag in a way that, although at times detached from gay culture, may have in part disseminated misconceptions about cross-dressing, effeminacy, and the queer self. Widely popular films such as *Some Like It Hot*, *Tootsie*, and *Mrs. Doubtfire* have all incorporated cross-dressing (specifically, female drag) as a deceptive practice that assists the men in plot to pass as women. Though not directly drawing from gay drag, these were examples presenting feminized men as intentionally deceiving and exploitative of women's expressive lexicon, an image that seems to pile on stereotypes of effeminate gay men. Conversely, queer artists have extensively utilized drag in their films by drawing from the cultural tank of camp. John Waters, Pedro Almodovar, and Harvey Fernstein are among those directors who have radically portrayed drag on screen and made their names synonymous with its camp valence. Currently, drag enjoys the limelight across various platforms. More specifically, original Broadway hits featuring characters in drag, such as *Rent*, *Victor/Victoria*, and *Kinky Boots*, are frequently running global productions, while RuPaul's contest series, *RuPaul's Drag Race*, has majorly impacted mainstream pop culture by making its way into prime time television and appearing in numerous media formats. It is those crossover productions that can offer effective insights into the actual perception of drag by queer and non-queer audiences alike.

Ultimately, the praxis of drag has been in constant communication with diva culture as it does not only draw from it, but, importantly, feeds it back with discursive, narrative, and performative power, thus serving as a template for the imitation as well as critique of gender. In this mutually foddered relationship, drag and diva culture share an understanding of gender performance and, more specifically, the notions of femininity and masculinity as a site of extraordinariness, an act that willingly breaks ties with conventionality and mundaneness, and opts for grandiose narratives and fabulousness. When Kylie Minogue poses as Marlene Dietrich on the cover of *Sorbet* (*The Glamour Issue*, in 2015), one cannot overlook the fact that her transformation and posture is akin to an approach a drag queen would have taken for a Dietrich impersonation. Similarly, Lady Gaga's alter-ego Jo Calderone, who was introduced in her music video of "Yoü and I" and was subsequently brought on the live stage of 2011's MTV Awards, is a full-on male drag act for which the artist completely erases any feminine traits of performance in favor of a meticulous masculine emulation. Cases of other divas notoriously camping up their gender performance, including Cher (especially, her Elvis impersonation for the 2002 *VH1 Divas Las Vegas*), Christina Aguilera, and Lana Del Rey, who exhibit particular fondness for extravagant hairdo and makeup as well as dramatic kinesis and delivery on stage, testify to drag's influence on female music artists.

Discourse-wise, drag culture has steadily been informing the expressive lexicon of divas, proving that the latter are finding queer slang captivating and arguably thinking of it as a relevant and effective vehicle of communication with their queer audiences. Consider how divas like Beyoncé, Jennifer Lopez, or Cardi B bring into their personae and performances catchphrases borrowed from the vogue scene.

Seeing therefore how the camp of drag has made inroads into the diva stage, one witnesses a motion through time in which drag gradually starts losing its concrete association of a man impersonating a woman, and becomes a praxis of toying with gender. Faux queens are a noteworthy example here. Similarly to most divas examined in this work, these queens (also known as bio queens) are non-queer women adopting the stylistic and expressive arsenal of drag queens (Harrington 218). Their performance of femininity is a deliberate parody of their cisgender status which ends up being a double female parody or, in other words, female-to-female drag.[4] As the usage of the terms indicates, the *faux* (i.e., artificial, fake) in *faux queen* presumes that the drag of women performing as women is only an imitation of the "original" drag in which the "real" *queens* are always males—specifically, queer ones—impersonating women. However, the culture of faux queens falls under the umbrella of drag with which it does not want to dissociate itself. Because of their affiliation with "original" drag to which they pay homage to, faux queens are well received within gay culture and, more often than not, appear to be LGBTQ+ allies. For example, celebrity faux queens, such as Michelle Visage and Ana Matronic of Scissor Sisters, have each forged their personae with the camp of drag while always remaining in close liaison with their respective queer scene. In this way, not only do their takes on gender presentation retain a camp valence, but are also steadfastly grounded in queer culture. After all, as Madison Moore notes in his astute *Fabulous: The Rise of the Beautiful Eccentric*, "[a]ll forms of drag practiced by all genders and non-binary people are equally potent critiques of gender" (12).

A camp fandom

In light of the above and in order to conceptualize audience drag and, in particular, drag performed by queer audiences in the context of the diva spectacle, one must take into consideration this leap that the camp of drag has taken from stage to audience, from subculture to popular culture, and, ultimately, from private to public sphere. Camp's infiltration into mainstream pop provided the latter with colorful multiplicity and thus geared it toward favoring, even celebrating, identity flux and lush styles. Camp has traditionally reveled in the alternation of images as well as the queering of popular texts by means of humor, irony, and artifice. The popularity drag has attained in the past few years—not only manifest in the queens achieving celebrity status but also in the widespread dissemination of drag culture, expressed through the high usage of camp talk and the gender play—seems to mount the influential surge of camp in pop. In other words, camp has elasticized pop in becoming flexible enough to accommodate the praxis of drag and allow for its circulation. Such attainment would not have been achieved had Western LGBTQ+ movements not paved the way for queer visibility and flexibility of gender expression. To a large extent, queer culture has extensively relied on pop to move out of its peripheral position toward an epicenter—though still the prevalence of homophobia and sexism prove that this motion center stage has a glass ceiling. It might as well be argued that the politics of the LGBTQ+ movement sought to underline the uniqueness of modern gay culture by promoting it as a vibrant and, most importantly, productive source of fashions, trends, and expressions. At the same time, inasmuch as gay culture has marketed its way into mainstream culture, the latter has also benefited from and largely cultivated the socioeconomic capital carried in practices of the former. Therefore, drag making inroads into popular culture is simultaneously a demonstration of queer culture's progress-making as well as a result of savvy marketing by the mainstream and queer culture alike.

At the time being, drag in pop, as a practice emerging from and attached to gay culture, rejoices in its trend-setting position as well as the years of historical liminality it has withstood (or still withstands). As contemporary pop embraces gender fluidity, its prosumers adopt a more plastic, certainly playful, and fashion-conscious image of gender identity. In light of this, the trend of drag has interestingly spawned a wave of styles and fashions whose cultural roots are ingrained in its gendered philosophy of transformation. While the future of drag's popularity undoubtedly invites more debate, especially if factored in is the futility of trends within the pop industry, what should be noted is that practices of gender transformation by means of style are increasingly becoming popular among prosumers of pop. Fans from a variety of popular culture domains, including music and film, express their affinity with their accustomed field not only through fashion, but also through role-playing and identity reconfiguration. The pop text fans engage themselves in provides an array of cultural and aesthetic options that allows them to mold themselves into their favorite pop persona or even come up with their own personae.

Demonstrative of the abovementioned process is cosplay, a practice that has grown in popularity over the past decades. Embracing role-playing through costuming, the practice has flourished within genre conventions, such as manga/anime, comic literature, fantasy, and science fiction, whose prosumers enjoy dressing up and acting out popular characters while interacting with each other.[5] Fans of *Harry Potter*, *Naruto*, and Marvel superheroes, to name a few, have each established their own cosplay conventions where many of them get to cosplay their favorite character regardless of their gender, thus ascribing a drag character to the practice itself. The idea of a pop terrain which allows fans to freely experiment with gender stylization and, by extension, any clause of their identity, makes cosplay and its conventions a veritable site of inclusion and community building that moves beyond binary perceptions, contrary to the fact that many of the aforementioned fantasy products perpetuate traditional gender roles. The practice of cosplay and, in fact, any similar drag/costuming praxis akin to pop attests to the fact that, in terms of reception, audiences have sought new ways of identification with the pop text/characters they invest in. At the same time, this proves that pop, the paradigm of financially driven *modus operandi*, will infinitely offer new ways of audience immersion.

Arguably, music fandom does not deviate from this pattern. With regard to the costuming of the self, music fans have likewise channeled their love of pop icons into stylistic transformations. The public persona of pop artists, as this is presented and mediated to their audiences, is always already a performed identity with particularly expressive vocabulary, aesthetic sensibility, and social kinesis. As a result, this cultural lexicon surrounding the persona is readable and can become accessible to fans. The latter may select through a variety of codes offered by their adored persona and incorporate them into aspects of daily life, as explained earlier in Madonna's case. Apparently, though, there exists a distinguishing line between dressing, say, like Madonna and immersing oneself fully in the performable aspect of the Madonna persona. While adopting elements from the persona's stylistic vocabulary and fusing them with one's own everyday style narrative is rather mundane in nature, a full-on drag act requires an estimated amount of fan investment and largely points to a ritual-like practice. Not only do fans craft elaborate costumes out of divas' fashion arsenal, but they are also attentive to supportive details, such as props, as well as kinesis, thus rendering the drag performance a meticulous and certainly painstaking process.

Space and temporality are also two important factors that add up to this differentiation. Fans in drag will either seek or create an occasion, such as a concert-event or a thematic convention, wherein they will act out the persona, whereas simple stylistic appropriations may smoothly integrate with the individual's social routine and surroundings. It can be argued that impersonation, as perhaps the ultimate manifestation of fan devotion, binds the artistic persona with the fan—or, in other words, the spectacle with the audience—in an act that strategically immaterializes the artist into pure iconicity and renders her/him performable and, by extrapolation, available to the fan. Tribute acts are exemplary of that: consider how Elvis impersonators have for years preserved the performative legacy and star icon of Presley. As Matt Hills argues:

> Elvis impersonation is a project; it represents recourse to an archive (the precisely catalogued set of jumpsuits and outfits worn on-stage by Elvis; images of Elvis; setlists and conventionalised details of his stage show), and recourse to a powerful set of memories; those of the fan's lived experience *as a fan*. (165, original emphasis)

Similarly, audience drag sees fans immersing themselves into the cultural body of the star performer, paying particular attention to all kinds of trivia that surround the performer in order to instill accuracy, precision, and devotion into their performance. The amount of detail and expertise pertinent to this dramatic reconfiguration of the social self into a popular persona not only points to maximal levels of emotional investment, but also underlines the praxis of drag as a skillful craft.

Approaching audience drag as a craft aligns the practice with camp's philosophy of transformation and resistance. Camp has traditionally been an expressive mode attached to dominant culture, though existing as a rather distorted reflection of it. The images and discourses promoted by high culture as serious, or those crudely enjoyed by low culture, are filtered by camp in manifold ways, ending up being playful, grotesque or risqué. Such distortion requires that camp knowingly absorb the details of dominant culture in order to mold its own version of it by means of irony and parody. Simultaneously, the need to do so points to a desire for an alternative reality that divests itself the veil of seriousness and embraces frivolity. Queer men, as a matter of fact, have employed camp as a feint attack against heterodominant culture. The strategies of double entendres in camp talk or the queer appropriation of texts and images indicate how queer culture has strategically camouflaged its practices under those of the dominant one. Drag, in particular, has been a camp praxis that has paid scrutinizing attention to the heterodominant gender formation so as to achieve a consciously artificial performance of it by imitating or subverting every gendered detail. The ability of genderqueer people to utilize fashion for either cross-identification or radical subversion attests to drag's inherently plastic power to toy with gender.

Likewise, audience drag performances, which to a great extent are a celebration of the spectacle of gender—at times, a political one as well—are tasks that in a way tap into camp's reservoir of knowledge. In camp's perception of a theatricalized reality, the dramatic reconfiguration of the self accrues from acknowledging and reiterating the mechanisms of gender ideologies. The discursive pool of femininity that camp so endlessly plunges into has served as the tank wherefrom drag derives its histrionic expression, as well as the sociocultural position which the camp self identifies with. Practitioners of drag and female impersonators, in general, have acquired and exercised the skill to interpret the performative lexicon of femininity before reenacting it on stage. Similarly, the camp self has learned to operate the poetics of flamboyance, such as effeminate body posture, highly stylized vocabulary or risqué humor, both as a queering praxis as well as a defense mechanism.[6] The esteemed status of the many diva icons and their worship within queer culture attest to the fact that camp—and drag, in particular—sees the highly constructed image of the diva as a terrain of dramatic action that has grown into form through role-playing. Simply put, the icon of the diva is a set of performative pieces assembled in glamorous craftsmanship. Fans, therefore, take pleasure in tracing the joints of the star body and having the opportunity to direct and reassemble the diva text into new narratives. The identification with or impersonation of the diva instill into the fans' camp self an agency by granting access in this (re)construction of glamour.

Audience drag is ultimately demonstrative of a meta-textual camp performance, especially when we consider how fans devote themselves to their character of interest. Fans act upon their investment in and familiarization with specific gimmicks of the star persona, including her sensibility, her own performance of femininity as well as her social demeanor in and out of stage. Apart from the metonymic understanding of craft as skill and knowledge, there is a corporeal aspect that goes into audience drag. Stylistic transformation is above all a physical process that practically sees the fan of the star persona becoming *the* star persona. The material needed for this transformation, from wigs and makeup to costumes and signature props, makes the fans' experiential presumption of the star persona tangible. Their embodiment of the diva, thus, is physical through and through. For instance, Lady Gaga's fandom has notoriously seen costuming and impersonation as part and parcel of the diva's stage theatrics. Fans who decide to show up in a concert in full-on Gaga drag will seek to interpret her visual vocabulary, which is often extravagant, in their own do-it-yourself way. In utilizing every kind of material, they can create a homemade version of Lady Gaga that successfully imitates the prototype in appearance, manner, and posture.[7] When fans eventually coalesce in the communal space of the concert, the diva's artistry becomes a performed canvas expanding from the stage to the audience.

The reason why audience drag, more often than not, flourishes within the diva spectacle is a testament to the fact that the personae, stage, and cultural appeal of divas are in constant interaction with the domains of gender and sexuality. Though a typical concert from touring male artists, such as Justin Timberlake, Bruno Mars, or Justin Bieber, are generally more gig-oriented, the diva concert embraces theatrical elements which, to a great extent, allow for dramatic fluidities when it comes to gender performance. The diva audiences are, thus, in tune with that gender-fluid aesthetic of the performed show. As a matter of fact, the diva's stage is a veritable playground of gender which, as the artists' performances explicated previously in this work indicate, encourages audiences to toy with the very structures of it. With diva audiences experimenting with and thereby questioning gender itself,

186

the diva concert practically transforms into a space and/or event that can arguably be read as a critical social performance that opens a liberating portal to queer expression. In addition to that and contrary to many of their male counterparts, divas' remaining in close proximity to queer culture constantly galvanizes their persona and performance with a queer sensibility, which not only reassures queer fans of their favorite divas' ally status, but also guarantees an aesthetic pleasure, be it aural, visual, or physical, which is custom-made for them. Divas' theatrics of costume-changing, for instance, which is rapidly plural in nature, bespeaks of a queer and camp understanding of persona and spectacle as these actively resist any fixity in terms of roles, and go for the wow factor of the surface, while simultaneously shielding divas behind glamour. These are all aspects of sociality that have relentlessly been informing the modern queer self with regard to its designated position within heterodominant realities, and have subsequently made their way into queer performance. As such, audience drag reiterates and realizes these ideological clauses of the diva praxis in a way though that is intelligible and dynamic.

In camp culture, the desire to act upon the diva text has been an identificatory practice which has for years nurtured queer individuals with a sense of empowerment and community. Enclosed in camp's kernel, transformation and resistance are those quintessential qualities that have energized the diva identification and have thus been transferred into the practice of audience drag. The diva emulates an empowering role-model who champions narratives of emotionality, vulnerability, and passion alongside highly stylized looks and assertive attitude. What queer audiences, specifically, find appealing in divas is also partly linked with the rejection of an identification with the male stars whose impossible masculinities may indeed serve as objects of queer desire, yet they seldom allow for effective queer identification. Conversely, the diva's feminine pathos does serve as an expressive position wherefrom queer individuals can draw symbolic power and interpret their life narratives through the diva praxis. Being a celebrity star, the diva presents her own life narrative to the fans in mediated forms, which rather function as magnifying lens and may distort the reality around her; hence, the diva narrative in and out of stage becomes a meta-reality, a fantasy. Fans, of course, are aware of the celebrity artifice in which they consciously indulge. Yet, what arguably fuels the queer appeal of the diva lies at the trading of conventional reality for an alternative one wherein the queer self is freed, perhaps partly and momentarily so, from imprisoning binaries and imposed futures.

This is nowhere felt more tangibly than in the actual live space of the diva show, where diva worshipping acquires a communal character and the audience's embodied queerness becomes a collective performance. Traditionally, the spaces where divas' fans congregate have been sites of queer exchange and community formation. In the past, those spaces were the discos, queer bars, and even gay baths, where divas frequently performed—the case of Bette Middler in New York's Continental Baths is one out of many. Most importantly, though, concerts have primarily been the communal space of divas' queer fandom par excellence due to the divas' live immediacy and the gig's event-nature. In them, the communal character of diva worshipping is even more concrete as it operates within the framework of space and temporality. Sites of congregation where queer/camp expression converges and is provided with the necessary affective ground, aid toward a corporeal manifestation of collective queerness. Judy Garland and her gay male fandom serves here as an interesting case in point as the artist's concerts would attract numerous queer men for whom these were occasions and spaces of free queer expression and interaction. As Daniel Harris argues, "[a]lthough Garland was in many ways a brilliant performer, homosexuals came to regard her simply as the catalyst for the raucous, gay pride 'love-ins' that erupted spontaneously during her concerts"(17). Harris also underlines that:

> [Garland's] uncritical mass appeal helped overcome our fragmentation to create for only a few hours, within the safe confines of the auditorium, an ephemeral, transitory "community" that lured us out of the closets in order to experience the unforgettable thrill of a public celebration of homosexuality. (17)

The writer makes a critical point in establishing the site of the concert as a public space that creates temporary communal bonds and offers its contours for emotional interplay. Considering the time frame of Garland's performing career, homosexuality, let alone a public manifestation of it, remained largely under the radar, and in order for queer men to be able to freely interact with each other in public, a sort of safety net was required. The fact that Garland's concerts could function as such bespeaks of an empowerment stemming both from the tangible queer kinship formed among these men as well as their relationship with the performing diva. The diva concert, thus, offered itself as a spatiotemporal occasion during which the dream of an out-and-proud manifestation of queerness, indeed a utopia at the time, could become a reality.

In the context of the contemporary diva spectacle, the arena is this space that is conducive to queer expression and collectivity. As the diva stage encourages all sorts of gender playfulness and identity fluidity, fans see the concert site as the ideal space to exercise queer bonding as well as feel free to toy with gender. Here, the camp of drag may come across as radical when taken out of a theatrical environment and brought out into public space. Fans in drag attending a concert most of the times appear already dressed up at the concert site, which means that the costuming transformation happens elsewhere, possibly at a domestic environment. The itinerary from one's starting point to the concert means that a part of the drag performance takes place in the openness of the streets, which at times can be an unpredictable environment for camp expression. A person in drag, especially drag that is not utilized for "passing," but to flaunt one's queerness, can often be vulnerable to conservative attitude and condemn. In defining fabulousness as an act that is transgressive as well as a potent critique of gender, Madison Moore corroborates that "[b]eing fabulous in public space is risky" (19); homophobic and transphobic behaviors are, in fact, not uncommon acts against queers challenging traditional gender. This is always locale-specific, though, and should be examined as such; some urban centers appear to be more acclimated with flamboyant styles and queer fashions than others depending on local politics and social configuration. While diva drag alludes to a fan culture and may come across as less radical because of its playful theatricality, it is still a practice run with a certain degree of risk and is directly connected to the fan's repository of emotional strength needed to accomplish it out in public. Cross-dressing largely remains connected to queer sex and cruising activity, a fact that instills radicalness in drag acts performed in public, outside their stage or cultural environment.

Juxtaposed to the above, the space of the arena seems to compensate for the potentially hostile environment of the streets. As Robert Edgar et al. argue, "[t]he arena concert does not offer a picaresque experience, of walking the site of a musical happening, but an enveloping, communal experience across a vast space, as arranged around a central performance" (9). The performing persona and the content of the show per se are indicative of the sensibilities of an estimated majority of the attending audience as they are quintessential markers of the audience's musical appeal, fashion sense, and expressive tastes. In a diva show, where audiences are predominantly female and queer, the aesthetics of the stage theatrically orchestrate the surrounding environment by setting the camp tone in action. Hence, flamboyance, choreographed structures, dramatic ballads as well as dance-inflected tunes are those core elements that fill the audiovisual space of the venue and will, thus, nest within the spectatorship. The here-and-now of the performed show instills in queer fans a sense of sociocultural relevance since they potentially see themselves as part of a camp utopia wherein queerness vividly fits into place. Examining performance sites as utopic spaces, Jill Dolan perceives

> the audience as a group of people who have elected to spend an evening or an afternoon not only with a set of performers enacting a certain narrative arc or aesthetic trajectory, but with a group of other people, sometimes familiar, sometimes strange. (10)

The writer adds that "[a]udiences form temporary communities, sites of public discourse that along with the intense experiences of utopian performatives, can model new investments in and interactions with variously constituted public spheres" (10). Dolan underlines here the pedagogic character of theater and performance in suggesting that audiences might bring into their social routines the empathy and sensibilities they receive from their participatory activity (10–11). Likewise, diva audiences partaking in a queer-embracing spectacle develop a broader understanding of gender performance and become familiar with aspects of queer culture.

As a social practice, audience drag demonstrates that divas can motivate queer fans toward acquiring a self-assertive gender expression even by means of camp. With drag's popular surge, the dissemination of camp aesthetic has much vitalized queer identities and has in fact recuperated the campy queen, that is, either the drag queen or the effeminate man, both of whom are figures loathed within heterosexist culture, as vital components of queer culture. Being the aesthetic and political embodiment of camp, the drag queen specifically—drag kings, perhaps worriedly, have remained in her shadow[8]—is a dual template that reflects both heterosexual and queer culture: with a rather unquestionably "gay" sensibility, her mockery of femininities and masculinities expresses all those gendered fantasies, fears, desires, and anxieties that heterosexual culture has projected upon the queer one, and vice versa. Approaching racial drag in the spaces of subcultural bars and clubs as well as through *Paris Is Burning*, Daniel Contreras sees

> drag as emblematic of unrequited love and dreams of utopia. This is drag as pathos; drag as *Hollywood* pathos is perhaps the most compelling consideration [...] The "suffering woman" occupies much of [the writer's] thought about gay men of color and their relationship to the world at large. (76, original emphasis)

The concept of audience drag proposed here wishes to acknowledge the said pathos of the drag queen alongside the frivolity and gaiety of drag entertainment as quintessential resources that energize its praxis. Moving beyond the confines of a subcultural stage into the openness of the diva concert as well as trading the notion of a vulnerable queerness with a self-empowering one, audience drag attests to a modern and certainly updated view of queer culture that has grown intimate with its flamboyant side. For as Moore notes, "it's about making a spectacle of yourself not merely to be seen but because your body is constantly suppressed and undervalued" (M. Moore 8). Queer fans in drag thus organically help to envision a queer utopia within the microcosm of the diva spectacle through their channeling of their inner divas and their tactile response to the theatrics of gender which radically camp up their performance of self as well as the space around them. This ultimately constitutes audience drag a spectactorial practice through which fans, being both consumers and performers of spectacle, have come to somatically respond to its dramatization.

To be able to celebrate the camp of drag out of its subcultural liminality is undoubtedly demonstrative of a progress with regard to gender appreciation and the politics of gay culture. What would have been unthought-of no more than 30 years ago, when the anti-queer rhetoric accompanying the HIV/AIDS epidemic had reached a climax, currently enjoys a public spot and is a practice favored by both queer and fan cultures. Arguably, drag and diva worship have proven to be lasting shared traditions in the history of camp. Though the role-models upheld may often be locale-specific and thus unique, the practices themselves are cross-culturally adapted and performed. What has to be understood, though, is that divas are flexible marketable models. The fact that they inhabit an esteemed place within queer cultures should by no means point to absolutisms. Divas are after all pop brands created to cater to all possible audiences. It would be erroneous to claim that audience drag, for that matter, as a diva identification practice, is queer-specific. The diva adoration praxis is flexible enough to accommodate both queer and non-queer identificatory practices like impersonation. For instance, Beyoncé and Lady Gaga's fanhood equally comprises heterosexual women who share the same amount of emotional and financial investment in their adored star personae as queer fanbases do. Undoubtedly, though, divas' camp appeal has widely connected them with queer culture, a fact that renders the practice of audience drag a potent camp praxis whose roots remain attached to performances of queerness.

The popularity of audience drag, indeed a convergence of drag praxis with music fandom, is inextricable with consumer and celebrity cultures and its future (or futility) in part depends on the mechanics of the latter. Referring to professional impersonation, Nightingale argues that

> impersonation generates another experience, a re-creation of the star not as an image but as a story about capitalism, often as the story of a contradiction in capitalism. As the "star's" personal narrative is recreated and explored by the impersonator, another performance, another personal narrative is pursued—the impersonator's life as the star. (qtd. in Hills 160)

The desire for star materiality and star material per se are noticeable objectives in the practice of fan drag which sees fans perform their own prosumer status since audience drag plays upon both the commercial and emotional link developed between them and divas. Fan practices cannot possibly be conceived of outside the framework of pop market economy because this is what practically gives birth to them. Hence, the contract established between divas and fans will always be of consumerist, if fetishistic, nature. Seeing also camp's indulgence in celebrity narratives and images of glamour, one cannot help but notice the contradiction, as Nightingale points out, behind the practice of fan drag. Diva narratives and models serve as source material for camp which thrives and feeds on them; at the same time, camp responds by sanctioning the means of exchange, thus perpetuating a circulation of the sociocultural capital powering the relationship.

In Livingston's seminal *Paris Is Burning*, the queens seem to face daily struggles in their subcultural environment and while they practically enjoy impersonating stars celebrated by the vogue scene, they do not seem to eschew from the pursuit of glamorous lifestyle they so fervently oppose. The paradox lies at the core of their camp praxis, which simultaneously criticizes and idolizes celebrity culture. On the one hand, when we juxtapose the performance of drag within the vogue Houses to the one performed in the openness of an arena concert, another paradox surfaces. Though the leap from liminal to public space as regards flamboyant performances is demonstrative of a progressive appreciation of queer expression, one has to reassess the means by which the camp of diva worship is realized. Space is important here: the subcultural position of the ballroom queens had been a daily challenge that continually contested their relationship to diva culture. On the contrary, the fan practice of drag is celebrated in the arena concert environment, the entrance to which presupposes financial and emotional investment, thereby endorsing the diva spectacle without actually challenging it. As a matter of fact, diva culture is habitually idolized, but barely criticized. Audience drag, thus, is indicative of how the camp of drag has largely been accommodated by and into mainstream popular culture. On the other hand, the coming-of-age of queer culture and its moving toward a more visible place are facts that should be neither underestimated nor downplayed. The fact that diva concerts provide welcoming ground for queer expression and collectivity serves as a reminder of the sociohistorical trajectory of queer communities from oppression and liminality to a less peripheral and self-loathing position. Rather than being the sole result of finding relief from oppressive narratives and realities, as was the case with camp reception models of the past, queer expression in the concert space points to a liberating spectacle of queerness and a collective sense of queer entertainment. To cite from the epigraph of this chapter, *Paris Is Burning* stars "were having a ball" and addressed all those outside their circle with an ambisemy: "wish you were here" is inviting (i.e., *we* wish you were here) and taunting (i.e., *you* wish you were here), at the same time. Celebratory and flaunting, communal and simultaneously glitzy, the diva concert upholds the said mantra and carries on the tradition of camp.

NOTES

1. I use the female pronoun here since the project deals with female performers. I would also like to underline the cultural process of transformation, itself associated with the domains of aesthetics and beautification, as a process of feminization, an argument that I will later address in the context of campification. It is not unusual to see fans of male stars transforming into their icons, such as those of Michael Jackson or the glam rock band Kiss. Yet, contrary to the male performer or showman, a female artist may offer a diverse pool of ever-changing styles and fashions that fans can draw from, always depending on the occasion. For instance, performers like Rihanna or Katy Perry are renowned for their chameleonic style in comparison to their male contemporaries, such as Justin Timberlake or Drake, whose style hardly ever deviates significantly from the urban/hip-hop agenda.

2. Much like brothels, molly-houses were inns and clubs catering to men's sexual proclivities, but instead of female prostitutes, young men in drag provided service.

3. Although most of the times drag balls were events of mixed groups, it can be argued that an invisible racial barrier existed between the ball culture of Greenwich Village and that of Harlem. Both being neighborhoods with sensible queer flair and artistic production, Harlem and the Village became renowned for attracting bohemian queers, whose lifestyle, though vivid and art-oriented, faced the socioeconomic challenges Manhattan's urban milieu posed to working-class and marginal communities. For more information, consult Chauncey's analysis of the two districts (227–36).

4. Interestingly, the female-to-female performance of faux queens also points to the plastic performance of femininity within neo-burlesque practices as their performative devices seem to overlap. See more on the neo-burlesque performances in Claire Nally's essay "Grrrly Hurly Burly: Neo-Burlesque and the Performance of Gender."

5. For more information on the practice of cosplay, consult Suzanne Scott's " 'Cosplay Is Serious Business': Gendering Material Fan Labor on *Heroes of Cosplay*; Joel Gn's "Queer Simulation: The Practice, Performance, and Pleasure of Cosplay;" and, John Bainbridge and Craig Norris' "Posthuman Drag: Understanding Cosplay as Social Networking in a Material Culture.".

6. For instance, camp talk has notoriously been used as a defense mechanism against heterodominant culture. By utilizing extremely formal vocabulary to the point of incongruity or by humorously renaming people or situations, the speaker wishes to parody and neutralize certain aspects of the oppressive mainstream culture. For more, consider Keith Harvey's "Translating Camp Talk: Gay Identities and Cultural Transfer."

7. Music videos and album covers usually serve as the commonest sources of the cited performance and are indicative of a plurality of looks, each signifying a different phase of the artist that best expresses the fan's personal relationship with her.

8. See Halberstam's essay on "Oh Behave! Austin Powers and the Drag Kings" (pp. 125–51) in *In a Queerer Place and Time: Transgender Bodies, Subcultural Lives*.

Conclusion

In approaching contemporary diva shows and queer audiences, this work has explicated the correlation between the two with respect to camp performance. My exploration of tour shows by leading female pop artists and queer icons, including Madonna, Kylie Minogue, Beyoncé, and Lady Gaga, proves that the diva stage is a potent field of study as its plethora of themes and its often unconventional structure point to a direct connection with queer culture. What this study establishes is that music diva concerts largely draw from queer practices, items, and fashions as a means of queer-baiting their audiences, while simultaneously serving as sociopolitical sites that promote freedom of sexual and gender expression through a politics of diversity and inclusion. In terms of production, the diva spectacle operates on camp praxes, which not only bring the subject of queerness center stage but, most importantly, toy with and thereby challenge notions of gender. In terms of reception, it has been demonstrated that queer audiences endorse the diva spectacle by immersing themselves in the camp culture presented through the diva persona and her stage, thus carrying on a legacy of camp passed down through queer praxes of the past as well as generating novel camp narratives and images. This is mostly evinced in the practice of audience drag, a costuming transformation of the fan body into the adored diva in light of the concert that has its origins in drag culture, yet also exemplifying a contemporary pop/camp praxis akin to cosplay. My analysis of the aforementioned artists and their shows as well as of the queer praxes blooming around the latter points to a queer culture that does not simply revel in the sounds of their favorite diva but actively channel her image and praxis into more visible, empowered, and collective queer identities.

Seeing that the music diva has emerged as the dominant diva model within camp culture and (Western) queer culture in general, the study of diva performance and music becomes all the more intriguing and at times quite complex. Though diva adoration prior to the rise of an out and proud queer culture was almost exclusively connected to Classical Hollywood female stars, with queers indulging in and identifying with the camp icons of, say, Bette Davis and Joan Crawford, in my work I argue that the music diva has largely replaced her filmic counterpart as demonstrative of a contemporary model of adoration. Contrary to the film text, which usually offered female models driven by pathos and punishment, music and, specifically, music videos and live performances present more self-assertive and empowering role-models as exemplified by female artists such as Diana Ross, Cher, and Madonna. With queer focus gradually shifting on this newly emerged model, music divas, acknowledging their queer appeal, have managed to directly link their icons with queer culture, yet simultaneously retaining those elements that guaranteed them a crossover mainstream career. Delving deeper in this connection between music divas and queer audiences, this project deconstructs divas' queer-inflected performances by annotating common artistic sources, intertextual references, and, most importantly, an active employment of camp poetics. As opposed to the diva models of the past, their modern music counterparts seem to claim authorial positions in terms of image promotion and show production (at least partly so, considering that it is the entertainment companies that monitor tour productions depending on popular demand and trends). Divas' active engagement with queer culture marks the nature of their spectacle with inclusivity and openness and it is for this reason why music diva camp has been consistently popular with queer audiences over the past four decades.

To these we must add that the diva spectacle, heavily drawing from the realm of musical theater, features queer narrative acts and promotes role-playing. This is an important component in queer pleasure since alternating settings and the fluidity of identity are effective in foregrounding a plural self in terms of gender and sexuality. Manifestly different from a typical male pop show, let alone a traditional rock concert, the diva show theatricalizes the concept of the music concert in a way that thematic arcs ultimately give creators the opportunity to play with conventions of all kind as well as stage acts that are socially and politically relevant. Traditionally, the female pop concert has been deemed as feminine/-izing, apolitical, and lite, contrary to its male counterpart and, especially, the male rock concert, which, following the discursive steps of its musical genre, has been viewed as masculine, serious, and bearing political edge. This work challenges this very idea in establishing that the diva spectacle, though never eschewing a frivolous approach, is governed by a sociopolitical ethos that wishes to inform and often, instruct its audiences. With regard to queer culture, diva spectacles have time and again engaged in showcasing queer topics on stage, ranging from romance and sex to identity and advocacy, thereby remaining sensitive to queer reality and, of course, in close proximity with queer audiences.

Of primary importance for this work has been to historicize, contextualize, and, at times, challenge praxes of diva camp as well as critically assess their reception from a broader social perspective. Since all divas and spectacles examined as case studies in this work are pervaded with concepts and views (especially those pertaining to gender and sexuality) of a generally Western perspective, it has been imperative to place each act and praxis into a cultural context that takes into account local and global politics, understandings of gender expression, specificities as regards the origins of queer practices and traditions in tandem with processes of cultural appropriation, borrowing, homage, and, last but certainly not least, the impact of each diva's icon. More specifically, the camp of Madonna has served as a dense cultural body of work in approaching topics of camp nostalgia and tribute acts as well as delving further into the queer scenes of disco and vogue. Following that, the persona and spectacle of Kylie Minogue has raised some important questions with respect to gendered transformations and the cult of glamorous femininity; this case also provided critical insights into camp's gender-coded system in which aspects of femininity, including effeminacy, collide and simultaneously coexist with masculinity. Coming to Beyoncé's diva praxis, we have seen how the artist's performance of Black camp is crucial in tracing racial inflections, traditions, styles, and mannerisms inherent in camp's queer lexicon, a fact that leads toward a more nuanced evaluation of the politics and poetics of camp beyond its conspicuously White canon. Finally, a camp politics of inclusion and radical opposition against normative molds was the focal point of Lady Gaga's camp acts, whose narrative structures with their moral concepts as well as their elaborate staging that draws from the genres of fantasy and musical theater have proved to significantly vitalize camp's entertaining frivolity with sociopolitical edge. All things considered, this work has explicated the practice of audience drag by historicizing its camp praxis in drag culture and evaluating it as a creative and potent critique of gender that not only asserts queer audiences' diva appeal but, most importantly, encourages a liberating performance of selfhood while promoting queer collectivity.

To conclude, this work has been carried out with the ethos of critical gender studies which it hopes to bolster further. The idea of a stigmatized camp culture that has for years been guilt/shame-ridden, with queer individuals being of course the recipients of those feelings and attitudes, is what this project seeks to challenge. Without overlooking ills and flaws behind the very nature of camp, my approach aligns with the queer school of thought and thus turns a critical eye both outside and inside queer culture and its ideological underpinnings. In seeing camp being recuperated as an assertive performance, as exemplified by the contemporary diva models, and an artistic weapon against dominant cultural norms, as variably exercised by queer generations globally, this work highlights the importance of carrying on the legacy of camp, which despite its co-optation by mainstream culture or its commodification by its very own affiliates still manages to raise questions on gender and the queer identity. With that in mind, it is in the high hopes of queer and gender studies along with pop culture and performance scholarship that this book will contribute to critical dialogues on camp and diva culture as well as welcome readers into the ever-captivating world of the music spectacle.

Coda

As this work was completed prior to the COVID-19 outbreak, it does not pay attention to the fact that public events and performances have been significantly limited. It is true that the pandemic has brought along radical changes in all circles of everyday life, live entertainment included, and the impact and extent to which these novel changes will apply cannot be accurately measured because of the precarious nature of the condition. As such, this study cannot possibly attend to conundrums rising at its wake, let alone reach legitimate conclusions. At present, most live entertainment artists seem to have taken a digital turn introducing their projects in synchronous and asynchronous online events. Live touring has been brought to a halt with all acts set to perform live in 2020 rescheduling for the following year or canceling altogether due to regulations enforcing public safety measures.[1] A lot of concert and theater venues went on to reduce seat availability to help keep distance among audience members. Simultaneously, though, prices for events and performances soared so as to compensate for the decreased number of attendees. Right now, online outlets have proved all the more instrumental in preserving the relationship of artists with their fans amid the crisis to a point where streamed entertainment has provisionally substituted the live productions, not only because digital events are one of the few alternatives but most importantly because they require little cost. Whether and how live entertainment, especially gigs encompassing large crews and mass crowds, will remain as we currently know is yet to be seen.

Certainly, it will be interesting to watch how divas' extravaganzas will adapt in the current situation and if the changes made will impact their future. For now, digital performances, music videos, and home studio sessions seem to be the alternative route. Kylie Minogue, for instance, came up with a prerecorded special event, named *Kylie: Infinite Disco*, in light of her 2020 album, *Disco*, which was made available for streaming a day before the scheduled performance. Fans had to purchase code tickets in advance that would enable them to access Kylie's visual presentation of old and new material as they would regularly do for a physical concert. Regardless, concert touring has been a profitable venture for music artists as well as a direct and material validation of the artist–audience relationship. It is well understood, though, that live events are not out of the table. Lady Gaga is among many artists who rescheduled her upcoming *Chromatica Ball*, the tour supporting her album *Chromatica*, for 2021, which means entertainment companies remain optimistic and flexible with regard to touring artists getting back on the live stage as soon as possible. As it seems, artists and companies still cherish and are far from abandoning live performance since it still is a potent medium that reaches out to audiences, in terms of finance as well as emotion.

NOTE

1. *Billboard* is currently updating a list of the concerts that are cancelled or rescheduled for later dates. See more on the following link: https://www.billboard.com/articles/business/touring/9323647/concerts-canceled-coronavirus-list/. Accessed March 22, 2021.

References

A Streetcar Named Desire. Written by Tennessee Williams, produced by Irene Mayer Selznick, December 3, 1947, Ethel Barrymore Theatre, New York City. Performance.

ABBA. ABBA: The Tour, September 13, 1979–March 27,1980, North America, Europe, and Asia.

ABBA. "Gimme! Gimme! Gimme! (A Man after Midnight)." *Greatest Hits Vol*. 2, Polar Music, 1979.

Adams, Cameron. "First Review: Kylie Minogue's X2008 Tour in Melbourne." *Herald Sun*, December 19, 2008, https://www.heraldsun.com.au/entertainment/kylies-show-is-out-of-her-comfort-zone/news-story/4caa2e70211a5ad061ba7e4a314f41ca?sv=c656339d1b6fe9359fe433ffd7f0e3c0. Accessed July 25, 2016.

Adichie, Chimamanda Ngozi. "We Should All Be Feminists." TEDxEuston, https://www.ted.com/talks/chimamanda_ngozi_adichie_we_should_all_be_feminists?language=en. Accessed April 27, 2021.

Adorno, Theodor. The *Culture Industry: Selected Essays on Mass Culture*. London: Routledge, 2001.

The Adventures of Priscilla, Queen of the Desert. Directed by Stephan Elliot, PolyGram Filmed Entertainment, and Specific Films, 1994.

All About Eve. Directed by Joseph L. Mankiewicz, 20th Century Fox, 1950.

Allen, Robert C. *Horrible Prettiness: Burlesque and American Culture*. Chapel Hill: University of North Carolina Press, 1991.

Altman, Dennis. *The End of the Homosexual?* Brisbane: University of Queensland Press, 2013.

American Horror Story: Hotel. Created by Ryan Murphy, and Brad Falchuk, FX, 2015–2016.

Amnesty International. "Moscow Authorities Ban Gay Pride Event." Press Release, May 18, 2011, https://www.amnesty.org/en/press-releases/2011/05/moscow-authorities-ban-gay-pride-event/. Accessed August 5, 2018.

Annandale, David. "Rabelais Meets Vogue: The Construction of Carnival, Beauty and Grotesque." *The Performance Identities of Lady Gaga: Critical Essays*, edited by Richard J. Gray II, Jefferson, NC: McFarland, 2012, pp. 142–59.

Apple, Dawn. "NUS Women Conference: 'Gay White Men Should Stop Appropriating Black Women.'" *Inquisitr*, March 26, 2015, https://www.inquisitr.com/1953764/nus-women-conference-gay-white-men-should-stop-appropriating-black-women/. Accessed October 29, 2016.

Aquilante, Don. "Madison Sq. Ga-Garden." *New York Post*, July 7, 2010, http://nypost.com/2010/07/07/madison-sq-ga-garden/. Accessed May 5, 2018.

Auslander, Philip. "Barbie in a Meat Dress: Performance and Mediatization in the 21st Century." *Mediatization of Communication*, edited by Knut Lundby, Berlin: De Gruyter, 2014, pp. 505–24.

Auslander, Philip. *Liveness: Performance in a Mediatized Culture*. New York: Routledge, 1999.

Auslander, Philip. "Musical Personae." *TDR: The Drama Review*, vol. 50, no. 1, 2006, pp. 100–119. *Project Muse*, https://muse.jhu.edu/article/197242. Accessed April 27, 2015.

Auslander, Philip. *Performing Glam Rock*. Ann Arbor: University of Michigan Press, 2006.

Azzopardi, Chris. "Beyoncé Opens Up to Gay Fans." *Pride Source*, July 12, 2011, https://pridesource.com/article/48242/. Accessed October 15, 2016.

Babuscio, Jack. "Camp and the Gay Sensibility." *Camp Grounds: Style and Homosexuality*, edited by David Bergman, Amherst: University of Massachusetts Press, 1993, pp. 19–38.

Babuscio, Jack. "The Cinema of Camp (*aka* Camp and the Gay Sensibility)." *Camp: Queer Aesthetics and the Performing Subject: A Reader*, edited by Fabio Cleto, Ann Arbor: University of Michigan Press, 1999, pp. 117–35.

Bailey, Marlon M. *Butch Queens Up in Pumps: Gender, Performance, and Ballroom Culture in Detroit*. Ann Arbor: University of Michigan Press, 2013.

Bailey, Marlon M. "Gender/Racial Realness: Theorizing the Gender System in Ballroom Culture." *Feminist Studies*, vol. 37, no. 2, 2011, pp. 365–86. *JSTOR*, www.jstor.org/stable/23069907. Accessed May 17, 2016.

Bainbridge, John, and Craig Norris. "Posthuman Drag: Understanding Cosplay as Social Networking in a Material Culture." *Research Gate*, August, 2013, https://www.researchgate.net/publication/305882533_Posthuman_Drag_Understanding_Cosplay_as_Social_Networking_in_a_Material_Culture. Accessed April 27, 2021.

Baker, Roger. *Drag: A History of Female Impersonation in the Performing Arts*. London: Cassell, 1994.

Baker, William. Personal interview. June 11, London, 2016.

Baldwin, Michelle. *Burlesque and the New Bump-n-Grind*. Fort Smith: Speck, 2004.

Balkan Baroque. Directed by Pierre Coulibeuf, Institut National de l'Audiovisuel (INA), Regards Productions and Scarabee Filmproducties Nederland, 1997.

Banham, Martin, editor. *The Cambridge Guide to Theatre*. Cambridge: Cambridge UP, 2000.

Barbarella. Directed by Roger Vadim, Marianne Productions, Dino de Laurentiis, and Cinematografica, 1968.

Barron, Lee. "The Seven Ages of Kylie Minogue: Postmodernism, Identity and Performative Mimicry." *Nebula*, vol. 5, no. 4, 2008, pp. 46–63, http://nrl.northumbria.ac.uk/2463/. Accessed June 28, 2016.

REFERENCES

Barthes, Roland. "The Death of the Author." *Image Music Text*, London: Fontana, 1977, pp. 142–48.

Barton, Laura. "I've Felt Famous My Whole Life." *The Guardian*, January 21, 2009, https://www.theguardian.com/music/2009/jan/21/lady-gaga-interview-fame. Accessed May 2, 2017.

The Bee Gees. "You Should Be Dancing." *Saturday Night Fever*, RSO, 1977.

Bennett, Lucy. "'If We Stick Together We Can Do Anything': Lady Gaga Fandom, Philanthropy and Activism through Social Media." *Celebrity Studies*, vol. 5, no. 1–2, 2013, pp. 138–52. https://doi.org/10.1080/19392397.2013.813778. Accessed November 20, 2020.

Bennett, Tony, and Lady Gaga. *Cheek to Cheek*, Streamline, Interscope, and Columbia, 2014.

Bennett, Tony, and Lady Gaga. *Cheek to Cheek Tour*, December 2014–August 2015, North America, and Europe.

Bergman, David. *Camp Grounds: Style and Homosexuality*. Amherst: University of Massachusetts Press, 1993.

Beyoncé. *4*, Parkwood, and Columbia, 2011.

Beyoncé. *B'Day*. Parkwood, and Columbia, 2006.

Beyoncé. *The Beyoncé Experience Live*. Directed by Nick Wickham, Columbia, 2007.

Beyoncé. *Beyoncé (The Visual Album)*, Parkwood, and Columbia, 2013.

Beyoncé. *BEYONCÉ: x 10–The Mrs. Carter Show*. Directed by Ed Burke and Beyoncé Knowles. HBO, 2014, https://www.beyonce.com/tour/the-mrs-carter-show-world-tour/videos/. Accessed September 29, 2016.

Beyoncé. *Beyoncé: Year of 4*. Directed by Beyoncé Knowles, and Ed Burke. *YouTube*, uploaded by Beyoncé, July 1, 2011, https://www.youtube.com/watch?v=3vXXiku0580. Accessed September 29, 2016.

Beyoncé. "Bow Down/I Been On." *Flawless*, Parkwood, and Columbia, 2013.

Beyoncé. *Dangerously in Love*, Columbia, and Music World, 2003.

Beyoncé. "Déjà Vu." *B'Day*, Parkwood, and Columbia, 2006.

Beyoncé. "Diva." *I Am… Sasha Fierce*, Parkwood, and Columbia, 2008.

Beyoncé. "Drunk in Love." *Beyoncé (The Visual Album)*, Parkwood, and Columbia, 2013.

Beyoncé. "Formation." *Lemonade*, Columbia, 2016.

Beyoncé. "Flawless." *Beyoncé (The Visual Album)*, Parkwood, and Columbia, 2013.

Beyoncé. *The Formation World Tour*, April 27–October 7, North America, and Europe, 2016.

Beyoncé. "Get Me Bodied." *B'Day*, Parkwood, and Columbia, 2006.

Beyoncé. *I Am… Sasha Fierce*, Parkwood, and Columbia, 2008.

Beyoncé. *I Am… World Tour*. Directed by Beyoncé Knowles, Ed Burke, and Frank Gatson Jr, Parkwood, and Columbia, 2010.

Beyoncé. "If I Were a Boy." *I Am… Sasha Fierce*, Parkwood, and Columbia, 2008.

Beyoncé. "Irreplaceable." *B'Day*, Parkwood, and Columbia, 2006.

Beyoncé. *Lemonade*, Columbia, 2016.

Beyoncé. *Life Is But a Dream*. Directed by Ed Burke, and Beyoncé Knowles, HBO, 2013.

Beyoncé. *The Mrs. Carter Show*, April 2013–March 2014, Europe, Latin America, North America, and Oceania.

Beyoncé. "Naughty Girl." *Dangerously in Love*, Columbia, and Music World, 2003.

Beyoncé. "Partition." *Beyoncé (The Visual Album)*, Columbia, 2013.

Beyoncé. "Run the World (Girls)." 4, Parkwood, and Columbia, 2011.

Beyoncé. "Single Ladies (Put a Ring on It)." *I Am... Sasha Fierce*, Parkwood, and Columbia, 2008.

Beyoncé. "Sorry." *Lemonade*, Columbia, 2016.

Beyoncé. "Why Don't You Love Me." *I Am... Sasha Fierce*, Parkwood, and Columbia, 2008.

Beyoncé, and Jay-Z. *On the Run Tour: Beyoncé and Jay Z*. Directed by Jonas Åkerlund, HBO, 2014.

Biddle, Ian, and Freya Jarman-Ivens. "Introduction: Oh Boy! Making Masculinity in Popular Music." *Oh Boy! Masculinities and Popular Music*, edited by Freya Jarman-Ivens, New York: Routledge, 2007, pp. 1–20.

Booth, Mark. "*Campe-toi!*: On the Origins and Definitions of Camp." *Camp: Queer Aesthetics and the Performing Subject: A Reader*, edited by Fabio Cleto, Ann Arbor: University of Michigan Press, 1999, pp. 66–79.

"Boycott of Madonna Moscow concert urged." *JWeekly.com*, August 18, 2006, https://www.jweekly.com/2006/08/18/boycott-of-madonna-moscow-concert-urged/. Accessed May 3, 2016.

Brennan, Mark. "The Best Pop Princess: Kylie Minogue." *Beautiful Things in Popular Culture*, edited by Alan McKee, London: Blackwell, 2007, pp. 178–92.

Britton, Andrew. "For Interpretation: Notes against Camp." *Camp: Queer Aesthetics and the Performing Subject: A Reader*, edited by Fabio Cleto, Ann Arbor: University of Michigan Press, 1999, pp. 136–42.

Brooks, Peter. "The Melodramatic Imagination." *Imitations of Life: A Reader on Film and Television Melodrama*, edited by Murcia Landy, Detroit: Wayne State University Press, 1991.

Bronski, Michael. *Culture Clash: The Making of Gay Sensibility*. Boston, MA: South End Press, 1984.

Brown, Adam. "Let's All Have a Disco? Football, Popular Music and Democratization." *The Clubcultures Reader: Readings in Popular Cultural Studies*, edited by Steve Redhead, Derek Wynne, and Justin O'Connor, Oxford: Blackwell, 1997, pp. 61–83.

Brown, Helen. "Madonna: The Mother of Reinvention." *The Telegraph*, August 25, 2008, https://www.telegraph.co.uk/culture/music/rockandjazzmusic/3559140/Madonna-the-mother-of-reinvention.html. Accessed May 3, 2016.

Butler, Judith. *Bodies that Matter: On the Discursive Limits of "Sex."* New York: Routledge, 1993.

Butler, Judith. *Gender Trouble: Feminism and the Subversion of Identity*. New York: Routledge, 1990.

REFERENCES

Butler, Judith. "Imitation and Gender Insubordination." *Cultural Theory and Popular Culture: A Reader*, edited by John Storey, London: Pearson Education Limited, 2006, pp. 255–70.

Butsch, Richard. *The Citizen Audience: Crowds, Publics, and Individuals*. New York: Routledge, 2008.

Cabaret. Music and book by Joe Masteroff, lyrics by Fred Ebb, premiered November 20, Broadhurst Theatre, Midtown Manhattan, 1966.

Cagle, Van M. *Reconstructing Pop/Subculture: Art, Rock, and Andy Warhol*. Thousand Oaks, CA: Sage, 1995.

Cante, Richard. *Gay Men and the Forms of Contemporary US Culture*. Farnham: Ashgate, 2008.

Caramanica, Jon. "Review: Lady Gaga, the Flashy Provocateur, Battles Lady Gaga, the Raw Voice." *New York Times*, August 6, 2017, https://www.nytimes.com/2017/08/06/arts/music/lady-gaga-joanne-tour-review.html?mcubz=3. Accessed May 10, 2018.

Carroll, Michelle. "Why Beyoncé's 'Flawless' Is Not a Feminist Anthem." *Fembot*, December 12, 2015, http://fembotmag.com/2015/12/12/why-beyonces-flawless-is-not-a-feminist-anthem/. Accessed October 10, 2016.

The Carters. *Everything Is Love*, Parkwood, Sony, and Roc Nation, 2018.

CBC. "Madonna's Rome Show Crosses Religious Leaders." *CBC.ca*, August 7, 2006, https://www.cbc.ca/news/entertainment/madonna-s-rome-show-crosses-religious-leaders-1.615273. Accessed April 27, 2021.

Chapman, Simon, Kim McLeod, Melanie Makefield, and Simon Holding. "Impact of News of Celebrity Illness on Breast Cancer Screening: Kylie Minogue's Breast Cancer Diagnosis." *MJA*, vol. 183, no. 5, 2005, pp. 247–50, https://www.ncbi.nlm.nih.gov/pubmed/16138798. Accessed July 3, 2016.

Chasin, Alexandra. *Selling Out: The Gay and Lesbian Movement Goes to Market*. New York: St. Martin's Press, 2000.

Chatzipapatheodoridis, Constantine. "Strike a Pose, Forever: The Legacy of Vogue and Its Re-Contextualization in Contemporary Camp Performances." *European Journal of American Studies*, April 24, 2017, pp. 11–13, https:// doi.org/ 10.4000/ ejas.11771. Accessed April 27, 2021.

Chauncey, George. *Gay New York: Gender, Urban Culture and the Making of the Gay Male World, 1890–1940*. New York: Basic Books, 1994.

Cher. "If I Could Turn Back Time." *Heart of Stone*, Geffen Records, 1989.

Cher. "Walking in Memphis." *It's a Man's World*, WEA, 1995.

Cleto, Fabio, editor. *Camp: Queer Aesthetics and the Performing Subject: A Reader*. Ann Arbor: University of Michigan Press, 1999.

Collins, Patricia Hill. *Black Sexual Politics: African Americans, Gender, and the New Racism*. New York: Routledge, 2004.

Collinson, Dawn. "Concert Review: Kylie Minogue at the MEN Arena." *Liverpool Echo*, April 2, 2011, https://www.liverpoolecho.co.uk/news/liverpool-news/concert-review-kylie-minogue-men-3376429. Accessed April 29, 2021.

Concepción, Mariel. "Lady Gaga / 6 July, 2010 / New York, NY (Madison Square Garden)." *Billboard*, July 6, 2010, https://www.billboard.com/articles/news/live/957486/lady-gaga-july-6-2010-new-york-ny-madison-square-garden. Accessed May 4, 2017.

Contreras, Daniel T. *Unrequited Love and Gay Latino Culture*. New York: Palgrave Macmillan, 2005.

Cook, Pam. "Melodrama and the Women's Pictures." *Imitations of Life: A Reader on Film and Television Melodrama*, edited by Murcia Landy, Detroit: Wayne State University Press, 1991.

Cooper, Carol. "Disco Knights: Hidden Heroes of the New York Dance Music Underground." *Social Text*, vol. 45, no. 1, 1995, pp. 159–65. *JSTOR*, http://www.jstor.org/stable/466679. Accessed April 10, 2016.

Core, Philip. *Camp: The Lie That Tells the Truth*. London: Plexus, 1984.

Corliss, Richard. "Madonna Goes to Camp." *The Madonna Companion: Two Decades of Commentary*, edited by Carol Benson, and Allan Metz, New York: Schirmer, 1999, pp. 1–21.

Cragg, Michael. "Lady Gaga: 10 Things We Learned from Hearing ARTPOP." *The Guardian*, November 4, 2013, https://www.theguardian.com/music/musicblog/2013/nov/04/lady-gaga-10-things-learned-artpop. Accessed May 7, 2017.

Crawford, Trish. "Beyoncé's Single an Anthem for Women." *Toronto Star*, January 23, 2009, https://www.thestar.com/life/2009/01/23/beyonces_single_an_anthem_for_women.html. Accessed September 27, 2016.

Crosley, Hillary. "Beyoncé Says She 'Killed' Sasha Fierce." *MTV*, February 26, 2010, http://www.mtv.com/news/1632774/beyonce-says-she-killed-sasha-fierce/. Accessed September 18, 2016.

Cruising. Directed by William Friedkin, CiP-Europaische, Treuhand, Lorimar Film, and Entertainment, 1980.

Cupid, Jamila A., and Nicole Files-Thompson. "*The Visual Album*: Beyoncé, Feminism and Digital Spaces." *The Beyoncé Effect: Essays on Sexuality, Race, and Feminism*, edited by Adrienne Trier-Bienek, Jefferson, NC: McFarland, 2016, pp. 94–108.

Currid, Brian. "'We Are Family': House Music and Queer Performativity." *Cruising the Performative: Interventions into the Representation of Ethnicity, Nationality, and Sexuality*, edited by Sue-Ellen Case, Philip Brett, and Susan Leigh Lester, Bloomington: Indiana UP, 1995, pp. 165–96.

D'Emilio, John. "Capitalism and Gay Identity." *Making Trouble: Essays on Gay History, Politics, and the University*, edited by John D'Emilio, New York: Routledge, 1992, pp. 3–16.

Davis, Angela. *Blues Legacies and Black Feminism: Gertrude "Ma" Rainey, Bessie Smith, and Billie Holiday*. New York: Pantheon, 1998.

De Lauretis, Teresa. *Technologies of Gender: Essays on Theory, Film, and Fiction*. Bloomington: Indiana UP, 1987.

REFERENCES

Destiny's Child. *Destiny Fulfilled*, Columbia, and Sony Urban, 2004.

Destiny's Child. "Independent Woman, Pt. 1." *Survivor*, Columbia, 2001.

Destiny's Child. "Survivor." *Survivor*, Columbia, 2001.

Dittrich, Boris. "Turkey Has No Excuse to Ban Istanbul Pride March." *Human Rights Watch*, June 28, 2018, https://www.hrw.org/news/2018/06/28/turkey-has-no-excuse-ban-istanbul-pride-march. Accessed August 25, 2018.

Dixon, Steven. "Metal Performance: Humanizing Robots, Returning to Nature, and Camping about." *TDR* vol. 48, no. 4, 2004, pp. 15–46. *JSTOR*, www.jstor.org/stable/4488593. Accessed May 7, 2017.

Dolan, Jill. *Utopia in Performance: Finding Hope at the Theater*. Ann Arbor: University of Michigan Press, 2005.

Dollimore, Jonathan. "Post/Modern: On the Gay Sensibility, or the Pervert's Revenge on Authenticity." *Camp: Queer Aesthetics and the Performing Subject: A Reader*, edited by Fabio Cleto, Ann Arbor: University of Michigan Press, 1999, pp. 221–36.

Drake, Simone C. *Critical Appropriations: African American Women and the Construction of Transnational Identity*. Baton Rouge: Louisiana State UP, 2014.

Dreamgirls. Directed by Bill Condon, DreamWorks, and Paramount, 2006.

Drughi, Octavia. "Rock On! The Most Expensive Concert Stages Ever." *The Richest*, December 1, 2014, http://www.therichest.com/luxury/most-expensive/rock-on-the-most-expensive-concert-stages-ever/. Accessed April 9, 2016.

Drukman, Steven. "The Gay Gaze, or Why I Want My MTV." *A Queer Romance: Lesbians, Gay Men and Popular Culture*, edited by Paul Burston, and Colin Richardson, London: Routledge, 1995, pp. 89–105.

Duan, Noel Siqi. "Policing Beyoncé's Body: 'Whose Body Is This Anyway?'" *The Beyoncé Effect: Essays on Sexuality, Race, and Feminism*, edited by Adrienne Trier-Bienek, Jefferson, NC: McFarland, 2016, pp. 55–74.

Dyer, Richard. *The Culture of Queers*. London: Routledge, 2001.

Dyer, Richard. *Heavenly Bodies: Film Stars and Society* (Second Edition). London: Routledge, 2004.

Dyer, Richard. "It's Been So Camp as Keeps Us Going." Camp: Queer Aesthetics and the Performing Subject: A Reader, edited by Fabio Cleto, Ann Arbor: University of Michigan Press, 1999, pp. 110–16

Dyer, Richard. *White*. London: Routledge, 1997.

Edelman, Lee. *No Future: Queer Theory and the Death Drive*. Durham: Duke UP, 2004.

Edgar, Robert, Kirtsy Fairclough-Isaacs, Benjamin Halligan, and Nicola Spelman, editors. *The Arena Concert: Music, Media and Mass Entertainment*. London: Bloomsbury, 2005.

Elder, Miriam. "Pussy Riot Case: Madonna Labeled Moralizing 'Slut.'" *The Guardian*, August 9, 2012, https://www.theguardian.com/music/2012/aug/09/pussy-riot-madonna-called-moralising-slut. Accessed May 5, 2016.

Elder, Miriam. "Russia Passes Law Banning Gay Propaganda." *The Guardian*, June 11, 2013, https://www.theguardian.com/world/2013/jun/11/russia-law-banning-gay-propaganda. Accessed May 6, 2016.

Empire, Kitty. "Kylie–Review." *The Guardian*, April 2, 2011, https://www.theguardian.com/music/2011/apr/03/kylie-minogue-aphrodite-folies-glasgow. Accessed June 30, 2016.

Empire, Kitty. "Lady Gaga: Artpop–Review." *The Guardian*, November 10, 2013, https://www.theguardian.com/music/2013/nov/10/lady-gaga-artpop-review. Accessed May 7, 2017.

Empire, Kitty. "Mama Don't Preach." *The Guardian*, August 31, 2008, https://www.theguardian.com/music/2008/aug/31/madonna.popandrock. Accessed April 30, 2016.

Erbar, Melanie. "Most Expensive Concert Stages." *Insider Monkey*, January 20, 2015, http://www.insidermonkey.com/blog/most-expensive-concert-stages-338094/. Accessed March 15, 2016.

Evans, David. "From Bumble Bee Slim to Black Boy Shine." *Ramblin' on My Mind: New Perspectives on the Blues*, edited by David Evans, Urbana: University of Illinois Press, 2008, pp. 179–221.

Ewing, Tom. "Kylie Minogue X." *Pitchfork*, November 30, 2007, https://pitchfork.com/reviews/albums/10947-x/. Accessed July 1, 2016.

Faludi, Susan. *Backlash: The Undeclared War Against American Women*. New York: Anchor Books, 1992.

Farmer, Brett. *Spectacular Passions: Cinema, Passions, Gay Male Spectatorships*. Durham, NC: Duke UP, 2000.

Fiske, John. "The Cultural Economy of Fandom." *The Adoring Audience: Fan Culture and Popular Media*, edited by Lisa A. Lewis, New York: Routledge, 1992, pp. 30–49.

FKA Twigs. *Congregata*, May 17–19, Red Bull Music Academy Festival, Brooklyn Hangar, New York, 2015.

Flinn, Caryl. "The Deaths of Camp." *Camp: Queer Aesthetics and the Performing Subject: A Reader*, edited by Fabio Cleto, Ann Arbor: University of Michigan Press, 1999, pp. 433–57.

Foucault, Michel. *The History of Sexuality Vol. 1: An Introduction*. New York: Pantheon, 1978.

Fouz-Hernández, Santiago, and Frey Jarman-Ivens. *Madonna's Drowned Worlds: New Approaches to Her Cultural Transformations 1983–2003*. Aldershot: Ashgate, 2004.

Frank, Gillian. "Discophobia: Antigay Prejudice and the 1979 Backlash against Disco." *Journal of the History of Sexuality*, vol. 16, no. 2, 2007, pp. 276–306. *JSTOR*, www.jstor.org/stable/30114235. Accessed May 9, 2016.

Franklin, Aretha. "Respect." *I Never Loved a Man the Way I Love You*, Atlantic, 1967.

Friess, Steve. "Dear Black Women: White Gays Are Your Allies, So Don't Push Us Away." *Time*, July 16, 2014, http://time.com/2988033/white-gays-black-women-allies/. Accessed September 27, 2016.

Friess, Steve, and Courtney Jones-Stevens. "A White Gay Man and a Black Woman Hug It Out." *Time*, August 20, 2014, https://time.com/3148567/white-gay-man-black-woman/. Accessed April 27, 2021.

REFERENCES

Frith, Simon, Anfrew Goodwin, and Lawrence Grossberg, editors. *Sound and Vision: The Music Video Reader*. London: Routledge, 1993.

Gairola, Rahul. "Re-worlding the Oriental: Critical Perspective on Madonna as Geisha." *Madonna's Drowned Worlds: New Approaches to Her Cultural Transformations, 1983–2003*, edited by Santiago Fouz-Hernández and Freya Jarman-Ivens, Aldershot: Ashgate, 2004, pp. 104–19.

The Gang's All Here. Directed by Busby Berkeley, 20th Century Fox, 1943

Ganz, Caryn. "Lady Gaga 'Artpop' Review." *The Rolling Stone*, November 13, 2013, https://www.rollingstone.com/music/music-album-reviews/artpop-86653/. Accessed May 28, 2021.

Gaynor, Gloria. "I Will Survive." *Love Tracks*, Polydor, 1978.

Geen, Jessica. "Kylie Minogue: My Gay Fans Looked after Me." *Pink News*, August 20, 2009, https://www.pinknews.co.uk/2009/08/20/kylie-minogue-my-gay-fans-looked-after-me/. Accessed June 29, 2016.

Geller, Theresa. "Trans/Affect: Monstrous Masculinities and the Sublime Art of Lady Gaga." *Lady Gaga and Popular Music: Performing Gender, Fashion, and Culture*, edited by Martin Iddon, and Melanie L. Marshall, New York: Routledge, 2014, pp. 209–30.

Gettlemen, Jeffrey. "Ugandan Who Spoke Up for Gays Is Beaten to Death." *New York Times*, January 27, 2011, https://www.nytimes.com/2011/01/28/world/africa/28uganda.html. Accessed August 19, 2018.

Gillespie, Nick, and Todd Krainin. "Everything's Awesome and Camille Paglia Is Unhappy!" *Reason*, March 19, 2015, https://reason.com/reasontv/2015/03/19/everythings-amazing-and-camille-paglia-i. Accessed April 28, 2016.

GLAAD Media Awards. "Boy George Intros Amazing Kylie Minogue Performance at #glaadawards." *YouTube*, uploaded by GLAAD, May 4, 2014, https://www.youtube.com/watch?v=2ZYkpLslUU8. Accessed June 26, 2016.

"The Glamour Issue." *Sorbet*, Spring, 2015, https://read.sorbetmagazine.com/product/issue-7/. Accessed April 27, 2021.

Glazek, Christopher, "The Many Heresies of Madonna Louise Ciccone." *OUT*, March 10, 2015, https://www.out.com/out-exclusives/2015/3/10/many-heresies-madonna-louise-ciccone/. Accessed April 17, 2016.

Glendhill, Christine. *Home Is Where the Heart Is: Studies on Melodrama and the Woman's Film*. London: British Film Institute, 1987.

Gn, Joel. "Queer Simulation: The Practice, Performance, and Pleasure of Cosplay." *Research Gate*, August, 2011, https:// www.researchgate.net/ publication/ 233442086_ Queer_ simulation_ The_ practice_ performance_ and_ pleasure_ of_ cosplay/. Accessed April 27, 2021.

Good, Dan. "Madonna Kissed Drake Onstage at Coachella, and Drake's Reaction Was Interesting." *ABC News*, April 13, 2015, https://abcnews.go.com/Entertainment/madonna-kissed-drake-onstage-coachella-drakes-reaction-interesting/story?id=30275354. Accessed April 17, 2016.

Goodall, Nigel, and Jenny Stanley-Clarke. *Kylie Naked: A Biography*. London: Ebury, 2002.

Gray II, Richard J. editor. *The Performance Identities of Lady Gaga: Critical Essays*. Jefferson, NC: McFarland, 2012.

Gray, Sally, and Anusha Rutnam. "Her Own Real Thing: Lady Gaga and the Haus of Fashion." *Lady Gaga and Popular Music: Performing Gender, Fashion, and Culture*, edited by Martin Iddon, and Melanie L. Marshall, New York: Routledge, 2014, pp. 44–66.

Grossberg, Lawrence. "Is There a Fan in the House? The Affective Sensibility of Fandom." *The Adoring Audience: Fan Culture and Popular Media*, edited by Lisa A. Lewis, London: Routledge, 1992, pp. 50–68.

Hair. Directed by Miloš Forman, United Artists, 1979.

Hajdu, David. *Heroes and Villains: Essays on Music, Movies, Comics, and Culture*. Cambridge: Da Capo Press, 2009.

Halberstam, Jack. *Gaga Feminism: Sex, Gender, and the End of Normal*. Boston, MA: Beacon Press, 2012.

Halberstam, Jack. *In a Queer Time and Place: Transgender Bodies, Subcultural Lives*. New York: New York UP, 2005.

Hall, Stuart. "What Is This 'Black' in Black Popular Culture?" *Popular Culture: A Reader*, edited by Raiford Guinz, and Omayra Zaragoza Cruz, Thousand Oaks, CA: Sage, 2005, pp. 285–93.

Halperin, David M. *How to Be Gay*. Cambridge, MA: Belknap Press of Harvard UP, 2012.

Haraway, Donna J. "A Cyborg Manifesto: Science, Technology, and Socialist-Feminism in the Late Twentieth Century." *Simians, Cyborgs, and Women: The Reinvention of Nature*, edited by Donna Haraway, New York: Routledge, 1991, pp. 149–81.

Harper, Philip Brian. "'The Subversive Edge:' Paris Is Burning, Social Critique, and the Limits of Subjective Agency." *Diacritics*, vol. 24, no. 2–3, 1994, pp. 90–103. *JSTOR*, www.jstor.org/stable/465166. Accessed April 10, 2016.

Harrington, Lee. *Traversing Gender: Understanding Transgender Realities*. Anchorage, AK: Mystic Productions Press, 2016.

Harris, Daniel. *The Rise and Fall of Gay Culture*. New York: Hyperion, 1997.

Harvey, Keith. "Translating Camp Talk: Gay Identities and Cultural Transfer." *The Translation Studies Reader*, edited by Lawrence Venuti, London: Routledge, 2000, pp. 446–67.

Harwood, Erica. "Madonna is 57 and Will Continue to Proudly Show Off Her Body. Thanks!" *MTV*, May 5, 2016, http://www.mtv.com/news/2877374/madonna-met-gala-critics/. Accessed May 10, 2016.

Hawkins, Stan. "Dragging Out Camp: Narrative Agendas in Madonna's Musical Production." *Madonna's Drowned Worlds: New Approaches to Her Cultural Transformations, 1983–2003*, edited by Santiago Fouz-Hernández, and Freya Jarman-Ivens, Aldershot: Ashgate, 2004, pp. 3–21.

Hawkins, Stan. "'I'll Bring You Down, Down, Down': Lady Gaga's Performance in 'Judas.'" *Lady Gaga and Popular Music: Performing Gender, Fashion, and Culture*, edited by Martin Iddon, and Melanie L. Marshall, New York: Routledge, 2014, pp. 9–26.

REFERENCES

Hawkins, Stan. *Queerness in Pop Music: Aesthetics, Gender Norms, and Temporality*. New York: Routledge, 2016.

Hawkins, Stan. "[Un]Justified: Gestures of Straight-Talk in Justin Timberlake's Songs." *Oh Boy! Masculinities and Popular Music*, edited by Freya Jarman-Ivens, New York: Routledge, 2007, pp. 197–212.

Hebdige, Dick. "Subculture." *Popular Culture: A Reader*, edited by Raiford Guins, and Omayra Zaragoza Cruz, Thousand Oaks, CA: Sage, 2005, pp. 355–71.

Herbst, Philip. *Wimmin, Wimps, and Wallflowers an Encyclopædic Dictionary of Gender and Sexual Orientation Bias in the United States*. Yarmouth, ME: Intercultural Press, 2001.

Herndon, Jessica. "Inside Story: The Making of Beyoncé's 'Single Ladies.'" *People*, January 1, 2010, https://people.com/celebrity/inside-story-the-making-of-beyoncs-single-ladies/. Accessed September 25, 2016.

Herr, Corina. "Where Is the Female Body? Androgyny and Other Strategies of Disappearance in Madonna's Music Videos." *Madonna's Drowned Worlds: New Approaches to Her Cultural Transformations, 1983–2003*, edited by Santiago Fouz-Hernández, and Freya Jarman-Ivens, Aldershot: Ashgate, 2004, pp. 36–54.

Hiatt, Brian. "Live to Tell… An Exclusive Interview with Madonna." *Independent.ie*, March 23, 2015, https://www.independent.ie/entertainment/music/live-to-tell-an-exclusive-interview-with-madonna-31074485.html. Accessed May 4, 2016.

Hills, Matt. *Fan Cultures*. London: Routledge, 2002.

Hobson, Janell. "Feminists Debate Beyoncé." *The Beyoncé Effect: Essays on Sexuality, Race, and Feminism*, edited by Adrienne Trier-Bienek, Jefferson, NC: McFarland, 2016, pp. 11–26.

Holden, Stephen. "Lady Gaga Brings Thrill to Tony Bennett's Immutable Style." *New York Times*, June 20, 2015, https://www.nytimes.com/2015/06/22/arts/music/lady-gaga-brings-thrill-to-tony-bennetts-immutable-style.html?mcubz=3. Accessed May 10, 2017.

Holland, Norman N, and Sherman, Leona F. "Gothic Possibilities." *New Literary History*, vol. 8, no. 2, 1977, pp. 279–94. JSTOR, www.jstor.org/stable/468522. Accessed April 10, 2017.

hooks, bell. *Black Looks: Race and Representation*. Boston, MA: South End, 1992.

hooks, bell. "Moving Beyond Pain." *Bell Hooks Institute: Berea College*, May 9, 2016, http://www.bellhooksinstitute.com/blog/2016/5/9/moving-beyond-pain. Accessed October 10, 2016.

Horkheimer, Max, and Theodor Adorno. *Dialectic of Enlightenment*. New York: Herder and Herder, 1973.

Horn, Katrin. "Follow the Glitter Way: Lady Gaga and Camp." *The Performance Identities of Lady Gaga: Critical Essays*, edited by Richard J. Gray II, Jefferson, NC: McFarland, 2012, pp. 85–106.

Horrocks, Roger. *Male Myth and Icons: Masculinity in Popular Culture*. Basingstoke: Palgrave Mcmillan, 1995.

Hubbs, Nadine. "'I Will Survive': Musical Mappings of Queer Social Space in a Disco Anthem." *Popular Music*, vol. 26, no. 2, 2007, pp. 231–44. *JSTOR*, www.jstor.org/stable/4500315. Accessed April 18, 2016.

Hughes, Dave. "Kylie Minogue X." *Slant Magazine*, February 18, 2008, https://www.slantmagazine.com/music/review/kylie-minogue-x. Accessed July 7, 2016.

Humann, Heather Duerre. "What a Drag: Lady Gaga, Jo Calderone, and the Politics of Representation." *The Performance Identities of Lady Gaga: Critical Essays*, edited by Richard J. Gray II, Jefferson, NC: McFarland, 2012, pp. 74–84.

Hutchings, Peter, editor. *The A to Z of Horror Cinema*. Lanham, MD: Scarecrow, 2009.

Iddon, Martin, and Melanie L. Marshall, editors. *Lady Gaga and Popular Music: Performing Gender, Fashion, and Culture*. New York: Routledge, 2014.

Indeep. "Last Night a D.J. Saved My Life." Single, Sound of New York, 1982.

INXS. "Need You Tonight." *Kick*, Atlantic, 1987.

Isherwood, Christopher. *Goodbye to Berlin*. London: Hogarth Press, 1939.

Isherwood, Christopher. *The World in the Evening*. New York: Noonday, 1954.

Jackson, Janet. *All for You Tour*. July 2001–February 2002, North America.

Jackson, Michael. "Bad." *Bad*, Epic, 1987.

Jackson, Michael. *Dangerous*, Epic, 1991.

Jackson, Michael. "The Way You Make Me Feel." Directed by Joe Pytka, 1987. *YouTube*, October 3, 2009 https://www.youtube.com/watch?v=HzZ_urpj4As. Accessed April 27, 2021.

Jameson, Fredric. *Postmodernism; or, the Cultural Logic of Late Capitalism*. London: Verso, 1992.

Jennex, Craig. "Diva Worship and the Sonic Search for Queer Utopia." *Popular Music and Society*, vol. 36, no. 3, 2013, pp. 343–59, http://dx.doi.org/10.1080/03007766.2013.798544. Accessed September 3, 2018.

Johnson, E. Patrick. *Appropriating Blackness: Performance and the Politics of Authenticity*. Durham: Duke UP, 2003.

Johnson, E. Patrick. *No Tea, No Shade: New Writings in Black Queer Studies*. Durham, NC: Duke UP, 2016.

Johnson, E. Patrick. "SNAP! Culture: A Different Kind of Reading." *Performance: Critical Concepts in Literary and Cultural Studies*, edited by Philip Auslander, Abingdon: Routledge, 2003, pp. 173–98.

Jung, Alex. "Real Talk with Rupaul." *Vulture*, March 23, 2016. http://www.vulture.com/2016/03/rupaul-drag-race-interview.html. Accessed July 30, 2017.

Jung, Carl. *The Archetypes and the Collective Unconscious: Second Edition*, edited by Sir Herbert Read, Michael Fordam, Gerhard Adler, and William McGuire, translated by R.F.C. Hull, Princeton, NJ: Princeton UP, 1968.

Jung, Carl. *Four Archetypes: Mother, Rebirth, Spirit, Trickster*, translated by R.F.C. Hull, London: Routledge, 2003.

REFERENCES

Kafka, Peter. "Live Nation's $120 Million Bet: Breaking Down Madonna Deal." *Business Insider*, October 12, 2007, https://www.businessinsider.com.au/live-nations-12–2007–10/. Accessed May 3, 2016.

Kehrer, Lauron. "Who Slays? Queer Resonance in Beyoncé's *Lemonade*." *Popular Music and Society*, vol. 42, no. 1, 2019, pp. 82–98, https://doi.org/10.1080/03007766.2019.1555896. Accessed September 20, 2016.

Kelly, Ben. "Watch 200 Dancers Re-create Madonna's Vogue for Sydney Mardi Gras." *Attitude*, March 17, 2016, https://www.vulture.com/2016/03/rupaul-drag-race-interview.html. Accessed May 7, 2016.

Kill Bill: Vol. 1. Directed by Quentin Tarantino, A Band Apart, 2003.

Kinky Boots. Music and lyrics by Cyndi Lauper, book by Harvery Fierstein, Bank of America Theatre, Chicago, 2012.

Kohlman, Marla H. "Beyoncé as Insntersectional Icon? Interrogating the Politics of Respectability." *The Beyoncé Effect: Essays on Sexuality, Race, and Feminism*, edited by Adrienne Trier-Bienek, Jefferson, NC: McFarland, 2016, pp. 27–39.

Kolah, Ardi. *Improving the Performance of Sponsorship*. London: Routledge, 2015.

Kostenbaum, Wayne. *The Queen's Throat: Opera, Homosexuality, and the Mystery of Desire*. New York: Da Capo Press, 1993.

Kutulas, Judy. "'You Probably Think This Song Is about You': 1970s Women's Music from Carole King to the Disco Divas." *Disco Divas: Women and Popular Culture in the 1970s*, edited by Sherrie A. Inness, Philadelphia, PA: University of Pennsylvania Press, 2003, pp. 172–93.

Kushner, Tony. *Angels in America: A Gay Fantasia on National Themes. Part One: Millennium Approaches. Part Two: Perestroika*. London: Nick Hern, 2007.

La Cage Aux Folles. Directed by Édouard Molinaro, Les Productions Artistes Associés, 1978.

Lady Gaga. "A-Yo." *Joanne*, Streamline, and Interscope, 2016.

Lady Gaga. "Alejandro." Directed by Steven Klein, 2010. *YouTube*, uploaded by Lady Gaga, June 8, 2010, https://www.youtube.com/watch?v=niqrrmev4mA. Accessed May 10, 2017.

Lady Gaga. "Americano." *Born This Way*, Streamline, Kon Live, and Interscope, 2011.

Lady Gaga. "Angel Down." *Joanne*. Streamline, and Interscope, 2016.

Lady Gaga. "Applause." Directed by Inez and Vinoodh, 2013. *YouTube*, uploaded by Lady Gaga, August 19, 2013, https://www.youtube.com/watch?v=pco91kroVgQ. Accessed May 21, 2017.

Lady Gaga. *ARTPOP*. Streamline, and Interscope, 2013.

Lady Gaga. *ArtRave: The ARTPOP Ball*, May–November, North America, Asia, Oceania, and Europe, 2014.

Lady Gaga. "Bad Romance." *The Fame Monster*, Streamline, Kon Live, Cherrytree, and Interscope, 2009.

Lady Gaga. "Bloody Mary." *Born This Way*, Streamline, Kon Live, and Interscope, 2011.

Lady Gaga. *Born This Way*. Streamline, Kon Live, and Interscope, 2011.

Lady Gaga. "Born This Way." Directed by Nick Knight, 2011. *YouTube*, uploaded by Lady Gaga, February 28, 2011, https://www.youtube.com/watch?v=wV1FrqwZyKw. Accessed May 11, 2017.

Lady Gaga. *Born This Way Ball*, April 2012–February 2013, Africa, Asia, Europe North America, Oceania and South America.

Lady Gaga. *Chromatica*, Interscope, 2020.

Lady Gaga. *Chromatica Ball*, July–August, Europe, and North America, 2021 (upcoming).

Lady Gaga. "Come to Mama." *Joanne*, Streamline, and Interscope, 2016.

Lady Gaga. "Dance in the Dark." *The Fame Monster*, Streamline, Kon Live, Cherrytree, and Interscope, 2009.

Lady Gaga. "Dancing in Circles." *Joanne*, Streamline, and Interscope, 2016.

Lady Gaga. "Diamond Heart." *Joanne*, Streamline, and Interscope, 2016.

Lady Gaga. "Dope." *ARTPOP*, Streamline, and Interscope, 2013.

Lady Gaga. "Jewels and Drugs." *ARTPOP*, Streamline, and Interscope, 2013.

Lady Gaga. *Joanne*, Streamline, and Interscope, 2016.

Lady Gaga. *Joanne World Tour*, August 2017–February 2018, North America, and Europe.

Lady Gaga. "John Wayne." *Joanne*, Streamline, and Interscope, 2016.

Lady Gaga. *Lady Gaga Presents the Monster Ball Tour: At Madison Square Garden*. Directed by Laurieann Gibson, Mermaid Films, HBO Entertainment, and Media Blasters, 2011.

Lady Gaga. "Love Game." Directed by Joseph Kahn, 2009. *YouTube*, uploaded by Lady Gaga, June 16, 2009, https://www.youtube.com/watch?v=1mB0tP1I-14. Accessed May 10, 2017.

Lady Gaga. *The Fame*. Streamline, Kon Live, Cherrytree, and Interscope, 2008.

Lady Gaga. *The Fame Monster*. Streamline, Kon Live, Cherrytree, and Interscope, 2009.

Lady Gaga. *The Fame Ball Tour*, March–September, North America, Oceania, Europe, and Asia, 2009.

Lady Gaga. "Heavy Metal Lover." *Born This Way*, Streamline, Kon Live, and Interscope, 2011.

Lady Gaga. "Highway Unicorn (Road to Love)." *Born This Way*, Streamline, Kon Live, and Interscope, 2011.

Lady Gaga. "The Manifesto of Mother Monster." "Born This Way." Directed by Nick Knight, 2011. *YouTube*, uploaded by February 28, 2011, https:// www.youtube.com/watch?v=wV1FrqwZyKw. Accessed April 27, 2021.

Lady Gaga. "Mary Jane Holland." *ARTPOP*, Streamline, and Interscope, 2013.

Lady Gaga. "Monster." *The Fame Monster*, Streamline, Kon Live, Cherrytree, and Interscope, 2009.

Lady Gaga. "Paparazzi." *The Fame*, Streamline, Kon Live, Cherrytree, and Interscope, 2008.

Lady Gaga. "Poker Face." *The Fame*, Streamline, Kon Live, Cherrytree, and Interscope, 2008.

Lady Gaga. "Swine." *ARTPOP*, Streamline, and Interscope, 2013.

Lady Gaga. "Teeth." *The Fame Monster*, Streamline, Kon Live, Cherrytree, and Interscope, 2009.

Lady Gaga. "Venus." *ARTPOP*, Streamline, and Interscope, 2013.

REFERENCES

Lady Gaga. "Yoü and I." Directed by Laurieann Gibson, 2011. *YouTube*, uploaded by Lady Gaga, August 17, 2011, https://www.youtube.com/watch?v=X9YMU0WeBwU. Accessed April 27, 2021.

Lady Gaga, and Beyoncé. "Telephone." Directed by Jonas Âkerlund, 2009. *YouTube*, uploaded by Lady Gaga, March 16, 2010, https://www.youtube.com/watch?v=EVBsypHzF3U/. Accessed May 11, 2017.

Landy, Murcia, editor. *Imitations of Life: A Reader on Film and Television Melodrama.* Detroit: Wayne State UP, 1991.

Lawrence, Tim. "Disco and the Queering of the Dance Floor." *Cultural Studies*, vol. 25, no. 2, 2011, pp. 230–43, https://doi.org/10.1080/09502386.2011.535989. Accessed November 23, 2020.

Le Grand, Fedde. "Put Your Hands Up for Detroit." Single. Flamingo Recordings, 2006.

Legendary. Directed by Rik Reinholdtsen, Scout Productions, May 27, 2021–Present.

Leiter, Samuel L. *Historical Dictionary of Japanese Traditional Theatre.* Landham, MD: Scarecrow, 2006.

Lennox, Annie. "Little Bird." *Diva*, BMG, Columbia, and Arista, 1993.

Lennox, Annie. "Why." *Diva*, RCA, 1992.

Leone, Dominique. "Space Disco." *Pitchfork*, February 6, 2006, http://pitchfork.com/features/article/6252-space-disco/. Accessed June 1, 2017.

Levine, Martin P. *Gay Macho: The Life and Death of the Homosexual Clone*, edited by Michael S. Kimmel, New York: New York UP, 1998.

Levine, Nick. "Kylie: Revised #7: 'Light Years.'" *Digital Spy*, June 21, 2010, https://www.digitalspy.com/music/a229821/kylie-revisited-7-light-years/. Accessed July 2, 2016.

Lieb, Kristin. "I'm Not Myself Lately: The Erosion of the Beyoncé Brand." *The Beyoncé Effect: Essays on Sexuality, Race, and Feminism* edited by Adrienne Trier-Bienek, Jefferson, NC: McFarland, 2016, pp. 75–93.

Lipshutz, Jason. "Lady Gaga, 'Artpop': Track-By-Track Review." *Billboard*, November 5, 2013, http://www.billboard.com/articles/review/5778227/lady-gaga-artpop-track-by-track-review. Accessed May 20, 2017.

Lloyd, Kate. "Lady Gaga–'Artpop.'" *NME*, November 22, 2013, https://www.nme.com/reviews/reviews-lady-gaga-14977-318026. Accessed May 20, 2017.

Long, Scott. "The Loneliness of Camp." *Camp Grounds: Style and Homosexuality*, edited by David Bergman, Amherst: University of Massachusetts Press, 1993, pp. 78–91.

Lorde, Audre. *Sister Outsider: Essays and Speeches*. Berkeley: Crossing, 2004.

Loza, Susana. "Sampling (Hetero)Sexuality: Diva-Ness and Discipline in Electronic Dance Music." *Popular Music*, vol. 20, no. 3, 2001, pp. 349–57. *JSTOR*, https://www.jstor.org/stable/853626. Accessed April 16, 2016.

Lush, Rebecca M. "The Appropriation of the Madonna Aesthetics." *The Performance Identities of Lady Gaga: Critical Essays*, edited by Richard J. Gray II, Jefferson, NC: McFarland, 2012, pp. 173–87.

M. *Butterfly*. Written by Henry Hwang. National Theatre, Washington, DC, 1988.

Madonna. "4 Minutes." Featuring Justin Timberlake. *Hard Candy*, Warner Bros, 2008.

Madonna. *American Life*, Warner Bros, 2003.

Madonna. *Blond Ambition World Tour Live*. Directed by David Mallet, Pioneer Artists, 1990.

Madonna. *Confessions on a Dance Floor*, Warner Bros, 2005.

Madonna. *Confessions Tour*. Directed by Jonas Akerlund, Warner Bros, 2007.

Madonna. *Drowned World Tour 2001*. Directed by Hamish Hamilton, Maverick, 2001.

Madonna. *Erotica*, Maverick, 1992.

Madonna. *The Girlie Show*, September–December, Europe, North America, South America, Oceania, and Asia, 1993.

Madonna. "Express Yourself." *Like a Prayer*, Sire Records, 1989.

Madonna. *Hard Candy*, Warner Bros, 2008.

Madonna. "Holy Water." Rebel Hearts, Interscope, 2015.

Madonna. "Human Nature." Bedtime Stories, Maverick, 1994.

Madonna. "Hung Up." Directed by Johan Renck, 2005. *YouTube*, uploaded by Madonna, October 27, 2009, https://www.youtube.com/watch?v=EDwb9jOVRtU. Accessed April 29, 2016.

Madonna. "I Love New York." *Confessions on a Dance Floor*, Warner Bros, 2005.

Madonna. "Justify My Love." *The Immaculate Collection*, Sire Records, 1990.

Madonna. "Like a Virgin." *Like a Virgin*, Sire, 1984.

Madonna. "Live to Tell." *True Blue*, Sire, 1986.

Madonna. "Living for Love." Directed by Julien Choquart, and Camille Hirigoyen, 2015. *YouTube*, uploaded by February 6, 2015, https://www.youtube.com/watch?v=u9h7Teiyvc8. Accessed May 2, 2016.

Madonna. *Madame X*, Interscope, 2019.

Madonna. "Madonna–COADF Promotion–John Norris Interview, 2005." *YouTube*, uploaded by Veronica Electronica, April 18, 2020, https://www.youtube.com/watch?v=wLSXlrJrMT4&t=373s&ab_channel=VeronicaElectronica. Accessed April 29, 2016.

Madonna. "Madonna–Making of Hung Up." Directed by Johan Renck, 2005. *YouTube*, uploaded by Anastás Chakarov, Spetember 8, 2010, https://www.youtube.com/watch?v=S0ZODfxKR7o. Accessed April 29, 2016.

Madonna."Material Girl." *Like a Virgin*, Sire, 1984.

Madonna. *MDNA World Tour*, Interscope, 2013.

Madonna. "Music." *Music*, Warner Bros, 2000.

Madonna. "Open Your Heart." *True Blue*, Sire, 1986.

Madonna. *Ray of Light*, Maverick, 1998.

Madonna. *Rebel Heart*, Interscope, 2015.

Madonna. *Rebel Heart Tour*, directed by Danny Tull, and Nathan Rissman, Eagle Vision, 2017.

Madonna. *SEX*, Warner Books, Maverick, and Callaway, 1992.

REFERENCES

Madonna. "She's Not Me." *Hard Candy*, Warner Bros, 2008.

Madonna. *Sticky & Sweet Tour*. Directed by Nathan Rissman, and Nick Wickham, Warner Bros, 2010.

Madonna. "Sorry." Directed by Jamie King, 2006. *YouTube*, uploaded by Madonna, October 27, 2009, https://www.youtube.com/watch?v=B5OPMI13qng. Accessed April 29, 2016.

Madonna. *The Girlie Show: Live Down Under*. Directed by Mark "Aldo" Miceli, Warner Bros, 1994.

Madonna. *Madonna: Truth or Dare*. Directed by Alek Keshishian, Boy Toy, Inc, 1991.

Madonna. "Vogue." *I'm Breathless*, Sire Records, 1990.

Madonna. "Vogue." Directed by David Finch, 1991. *YouTube*, uploaded by Madonna, October 27, 2009, https://www.youtube.com/watch?v=GuJQSAiODqI. Accessed May 2, 2016.

Manghani, Sunil. "Performance Kylie: Looks Divine." *The Arena Concert: Music, Media and Mass Entertainment*, edited by Benjamin Halligan, Kirsty Fairdough-Isaacs, Robert Edgar, and Nicola Spelman, London: Bloomsbury, 2015, pp. 247–68.

Manilow, Barry. "Copacabana." *Even Now*, Arista, 1978.

Mannie, Sierra. "Dear White Gays: Stop Stealing Black Female Culture." *Time*, July 9, 2014, http://time.com/2969951/dear-white-gays-stop-stealing-black-female-culture/. Accessed October 10, 2016.

Marra, Kim. "Riding, Scarring, Knowing: A Queerly Embodied Performance Historiography." *Theatre Journal*, vol. 64, no. 4, 2012, pp. 489–511, *ProjectMuse*, https://muse.jhu.edu/article/494442. Accessed May 15, 2017.

McArthur, Benjamin. *The Man Who Was Rip Van Winkle: Joseph Jefferson and Nineteenth-Century American Theatre*. New Haven: Yale UP, 2007.

McMahon, Kyle. "Madonna, Ageism and Sexism." *Huffington Post*, April 6, 2015, https://www.huffpost.com/entry/madonna-ageism-and-sexism_b_7510552 Accessed April 29, 2016.

McMillan, Uri. "Nicki Aesthetics: The Camp Performance of Nicki Minaj." *Women and Performance: A Journal of Feminist Theory*, vol. 24, no. 1, 2014, pp. 79–87, https://doi.org/10.1080/0740770X.2014.901600. Accessed November 20, 2020.

McRobbie, Angela. *Postmodernism and Popular Culture*. London: Routledge, 1994.

McRobbie, Angela. "Second-Hand Dresses and the Role of the Ragmarket." *Popular Culture: A Reader*, edited by Raiford Guinz, and Omayra Zaragoza Cruz, Thousand Oaks, CA: Sage, 2005, pp. 372–82.

Meat Joy. Directed by Carolee Schneemann, Carolee Schneemann, 1964.

"Meme." *Merriam-Webster*, https://www.merriam-webster.com/dictionary/meme. Accessed April 27, 2021.

Metropolis. Directed by Fritz Lang, UFA, 1927.

Meyer, Moe. *The Politics and Poetics of Camp*. New York: Routledge, 1994.

Miller, Janice. *Fashion and Music*. Oxford: Berg, 2011.

Miller, Matt. *Bounce: Rap Music and Local Identity in New Orleans*. Amherst: University of Massachusetts Press, 2012.

Minogue, Kylie. "All the Lovers." *Aphrodite*, Parlophone, 2010.

Minogue, Kylie. *Anti Tour*, March–April, Australia, and United Kingdom, 2012.

Minogue, Kylie. *Aphrodite*, Parlophone, 2010.

Minogue, Kylie. *Aphrodite Les Folies: Live in London*. Directed by William Baker and Marcus Viner, Parlophone, and EMI, 2011.

Minogue, Kylie. "Better the Devil You Know." *Rhythm of Love*, PWL, and Mushroom Records, 1990.

Minogue, Kylie. "Can't Get You Out of My Head." *Fever*, Parlophone, 2001.

Minogue, Kylie. "Come into My World." *Fever*, Parlophone, 2001.

Minogue, Kylie. "Dancing." *Golden*, Darenote, and BMG, 2018.

Minogue, Kylie. *Disco*, Darenote, and BMG, 2020.

Minogue, Kylie. *Golden Live in Concert*, BMG, 2019.

Minogue, Kylie. *Golden Tour*, September 2018–March 2019, Europe, and Australia.

Minogue, Kylie. "Hand on Your Heart." *Enjoy Yourself*, PWL, 1989.

Minogue, Kylie. "I Believe in You." *Ultimate Kylie*, Parlophone, 2004.

Minogue, Kylie. "I Got to Be Certain," *Kylie*, Mushroom Records, 1988.

Minogue, Kylie. "I Should Be So Lucky." Directed by Chris Langman, 1988. *YouTube*, uploaded by PWL, December 2, 2016, https://www.youtube.com/watch?v=3_TvpBwSZDM. Accessed July 23, 2016.

Minogue, Kylie. *Impossible Princess*, Deconstruction, BMG, and Mushroom Records, 1997.

Minogue, Kylie. *Intimate and Live*. Directed by Mark Adamson, BMG, 1998.

Minogue, Kylie. *Kiss Me Once: Live at the SSE Hydro*. Directed by William Baker, Warner Bros, 2015.

Minogue, Kylie. *Kylie: Infinite Disco*. November–December, LH3 Studios, London, 2020.

Minogue, Kylie. "Kylie Minogue–Apple Music 'DISCO' Interview." *YouTube*, uploaded by Kylie Minogue, November 2, 2020, https://www.youtube.com/watch?v=lpIc3pfUEDI&ab_channel=KylieMinogue. Accessed November 25, 2020.

Minogue, Kylie. *Kylie Showgirl*. Directed by Russell Thomas, EMI, 2005.

Minogue, Kylie. *KylieFever2002*, April–August, Europe, and Australia, 2002.

Minogue, Kylie. *KylieX2008*. Directed by William Baker, EMI, 2008.

Minogue, Kylie. *Light Year*, Parlophone, 2000.

Minogue, Kylie. "Locomotion." *Kylie*, Mushroom Records, 1988.

Minogue, Kylie. "Love Boat." *Light Years*, Parlophone, 2000.

Minogue, Kylie. "Please Stay." *Light Years*, Parlophone, 2000.

Minogue, Kylie. "Never Too Late." *Enjoy Yourself*, PWL, 1989.

Minogue, Kylie. "Nu- Di-Ty." X, Parlophone, 2007.

Minogue, Kylie. "Red Blooded Woman." *Body Language*, Parlophone, 2003.

Minogue, Kylie. "Shocked." *Rhythm of Love*, PWL, and Mushroom Records, 1990.

Minogue, Kylie. *Showgirl: The Greatest Hits Tour*, March—May, Europe, 2005.

REFERENCES

Minogue, Kylie. *Showgirl: The Homecoming Tour*, November 2006—January 2007, Australia, and United Kingdom.

Minogue, Kylie. "Spinning Around." Directed by Dawn Shadforth, 2000. *YouTube*, uploaded by Kylie Minogue, April 8, 2010, https://www.youtube.com/watch?v=t1DWBKk5xHQ. Accessed July 23, 2016.

Minogue, Kylie. "Slow." *Body Language*, Parlophone, 2003.

Minogue, Kylie. "Too Much." *Aphrodite*, Parlophone, 2010.

Minogue, Kylie. "White Diamond." *Showgirl Homecoming Live*, Parlophone, 2007.

Minogue, Kylie. *White Diamond: A Personal Portrait of Kylie Minogue*. Directed by William Baker, EMI, 2007.

Minogue, Kylie. "Wow." *X*, Parlophone, 2007.

Minogue, Kylie. *X*, Parlophone, 2007.

Minogue, Kylie and Dannii Minogue. "100 Degrees." *Kylie Christmas*, Parlophone, 2015.

Mitchell, Anne M. "Beyoncé as Aggressive Black Femme and Informed Black Female Subject." *The Beyoncé Effect: Essays on Sexuality, Race, and Feminism*, edited by Adrienne Trier-Bienek, Jefferson, NC: McFarland, 2016, pp. 40–54.

Mitchell, John. "Lady Gaga's *Born This Way* Ball Kicks Off Amid Protests." *MTV*, April 27, 2012, http://www.mtv.com/news/1684062/lady-gaga-born-this-way-ball-seoul/. Accessed May 6, 2017.

Mitchell, John. "Lady Gaga Giving Away 'Monster Pit Key' to Hardcore Fan at Each Tour Stop." *MTV*, April 27, 2012, https://ladydeldiamondis.wordpress.com/2012/05/04/lady-gaga-giving-away-monster-pit-key-to-hardcore-fan-at-each-tour-stop/. Accessed May 6, 2017.

Mitchell, John Cameron, and Stephen Trask. *Hedwig and the Angry Inch: Broadway Edition*. New York: Duckworth Overlook, 2014.

von Moltke, Johannes. "Camping in the Art Closet: The Politics of Camp and Nation in German Film." *Camp: Queer Aesthetics and the Performing Subject: A Reader*, edited by Fabio Cleto, Ann Arbor: University of Michigan Press, 1999, pp. 409–32.

Mommie Dearest. Directed by Frank Perry, Paramount Pictures, 1981.

Monroe, Marilyn. "Diamonds Are a Girl's Best Friend." *Gentlemen Prefer Blondes*, directed by Howard Hawks, 20th Century Fox, 1953.

Montgomery, James. "Lady Gaga Goes the Distance at Montreal Monster Ball Tour Kickoff." *MTV*, June 29, 2010, http://www.mtv.com/news/1642603/lady-gaga-goes-the-distance-at-montreal-monster-ball-tour-kickoff/. Accessed May 18, 2017.

Montgomery, James. "Lady Gaga Reveals Details of Revamped Monster Ball Tour for 2010." *MTV*, December 21, 2009, http://www.mtv.com/news/1628689/lady-gaga-reveals-details-of-revamped-monster-ball-tour-for-2010/. Accessed May 14, 2017.

Moore, John. "'The Hieroglyphics of Love': The Torch Singers and Interpretation." *Popular Music*, vol. 8, no.1, 1989, pp. 31–58. *JSTOR*, https://www.jstor.org/stable/853481. Accessed October 20, 2018.

Moore, Madison. *Fabulous: The Rise of the Beautiful Eccentric*. New Haven: Yale UP, 2018.

THE MUSIC DIVA SPECTACLE

Moore, Suzanne. "Postmodernism Killed the Avant-Garde. Lady Gaga Is No Substitute for Lou Reed." *The Guardian*, October 30, 2013, https://www.theguardian.com/commentisfree/2013/oct/30/postmodernism-avant-garde-lady-gaga-lou-reed-x-factor. Accessed May 8, 2017.

Morris, Mitchell. "Reading as an Opera Queen." *Musicology and Difference: Gender and Sexuality in Music Scholarship*, edited by Ruth A. Solie, Berkeley: University of California Press, 1995, pp. 184–200.

Mrs. Doubtfire. Directed by Chris Columbus, 20th Century Fox, 1993.

Mulvey, Laura. "Visual Pleasure and Narrative Cinema." *Film Theory and Criticism: Introductory Readings*, edited by Leo Braudy, and Marshall Cohen, Oxford: Oxford UP, 1999, pp. 833–44.

Muñoz, José Esteban. *Disidentifications: Queers of Color and the Performance of Politics*. Minneapolis: University of Minnesota Press, 1999.

Murray, David A. B., editor. *Homophobias: Lust and Loathing across Time and Space*. Durham: Duke UP, 2009.

Naiman, Tiffany. "Resisting the Politics of Aging: Madonna and the Value of Female Labor in Popular Music." *Popular Music and the Politics of Hope: Queer and Feminist Interventions*, edited by Susan Fast, and Craig Jennex, New York: Routledge, 2019, pp. 267–82.

The Naked Civil Servant. Directed by Jack Gold. United Kingdom: Thames Television, 1975.

Nally, Claire. "Grrrly Hurly Burly: Neo-burlesque and the Performance of Gender." *Textual Practice*, vol. 23, no. 4, 2009, pp. 621–43, https://www.tandfonline.com/doi/abs/10.1080/09502360903000554. Accessed July 3, 2016.

Neighbours. Created by Reg Watson, Grundy Television, 1985—Present.

Nestruck, Kelly. "Lady Gaga's Monster Ball, Reviewed by a Theatre Critic." *The Guardian*, November 30, 2009, https://www.theguardian.com/music/musicblog/2009/nov/30/lady-gaga-monster-ball. Accessed May 15, 2017.

The New School. "bell hooks–Are You Still a Slave? Liberating the Black Female Body | Eugene Lang College." *YouTube*, uploaded by The New School, May 7, 2014, https://www.youtube.com/watch?v=rJk0hNROvzs. Accessed October 10, 2016.

Newitz, Annalee. "Magical Girls and Atomic Bomb Sperm: Japanese Animation in America." *Film Quarterly*, vol. 49, no. 1, 1995, pp. 2–15. *JSTOR*, http://www.jstor.org/stable/1213488. Accessed May 26, 2017.

Nick Cave and the Bad Seeds, and Kylie Minogue. "Where the Wild Roses Grow." *Murder Ballads*, Mute Records, 1996.

Newton, Esther. *Mother Camp: Female Impersonators in America*. Chicago: University of Chicago Press, 1972.

O'Brien, Lucy. "Not a Piece of Meat: Lady Gaga and *that* Dress. Has Radical Feminism Survived the Journey?" *Lady Gaga and Popular Music: Performing Gender, Fashion, and Culture*, edited by Martin Iddon, and Melanie L. Marshall, New York: Routledge, 2014, pp. 27–43.

REFERENCES

O'Grady, Alice. "Being There: Encounters with Space and the Affective Dimension of Arena Spectacle." *The Arena Concert: Music, Media and Mass Entertainment*, edited by Robert Edgar, Kirtsy Fairclough-Isaacs, Benjamin Halligan, and Nicola Spelman, London: Bloomsbury, 2005, pp. 111–22.

"The Grace of the Witch." *The Odyssey*. Translated by Robert Fitzgerald, Heinemann, 1962, pp. 147–64.

Paglia, Camille. *Sex, Art, and American Culture: Essays*. New York: Vintage Books, 1992.

Paglia, Camille. *Sexual Personae: Art and Decadence from Nefertiti to Emily Dickinson*. New Haven: Yale UP, 1990.

Pareles, Jon. "Lavish Worlds, and the Headwear to Match." *New York Times*, January 21, 2010, http://www.nytimes.com/2010/01/22/arts/music/22gaga.html?mcubz=3. Accessed August 19, 2018.

Paris Is Burning. Directed by Jennie Livingston, Miramax, 1990.

"Pat your weave." *Urban Dictionary*, posted by Bonnie Jackson, June 29, 2008, https://www.urbandictionary.com/define.php?term=pat%20your%20weave. Accessed April 27, 2021.

Payne, Chris. "Lady Gaga Discusses Rape in Howard Stern Interview." *Billboard*, December 2, 2014, https://www.billboard.com/articles/columns/pop-shop/6334807/lady-gaga-rape-howard-stern-interview-swine. Accessed April 29, 2021.

Pells, Richard. "From Modernism to the Movies: The Globalization of American Culture in the Twentieth Century." *European Journal of American Culture*, vol. 23, no. 2, 2004, pp. 143–55, https://rauli.cbs.dk/index.php/assc/article/view/4435. Accessed September 4, 2018.

Peñaloza, Lisa. "Consuming Madonna Then and Now: An Examination of the Dynamics and Structuring of Celebrity Consumption." *Madonna's Drowned Worlds: New Approaches to Her Cultural Transformations, 1983–2003*, edited by Santiago Fouz-Hernández and Freya Jarman-Ivens, Aldershot: Ashgate, 2004, pp. 176–92.

People Staff. "Madonna's Rome Concert Outrages Vatican." People, August 7, 2006, https://people.com/ celebrity/ madonnas- rome- concert- outrages-vatican/. Accessed April 27, 2021.

Perry, Katy. *California Dreams Tour*, February 2011–January 2012, Europe, Oceania, Asia South America, and North Americas.

Perry, Katy. "Dark Horse." Featuring Juicy J., *Prism*, Capitol, 2013.

Perry, Katy. *Prismatic World Tour*, May 2014–October, North America, Europe, Oceania, Latin America, and Asia, 2015.

Petridis, Alexis. "Kylie Minogue, X." *The Guardian*, November 23, 2007, https://www.theguardian.com/music/2007/nov/23/popandrock.shopping. Accessed July 7, 2016.

Petridis, Alexis. "Lady Gaga: Weirdly Wonderful, with Shoulderpads." *The Guardian*, February 19, 2010, https://www.theguardian.com/music/2010/feb/19/lady-gaga-concert-review. Accessed May 5, 2017.

Pink Flamingos. Directed by John Waters, Dreamland,1972.

Pisters, Patricia. "Madonna's Girls in the Mix: Performance of Femininity Beyond the Beautiful." *Madonna's Drowned Worlds: New Approaches to Her Cultural Transformations*,

1983–2003, edited by Santiago Fouz-Hernández, and Freya Jarman-Ivens, Aldershot: Ashgate, 2004, pp. 22–35.

Plant, Richard. *The Pink Triangle: The Nazi War against Homosexuals*. New York: Henry Holt, 1988.

Polhemus, Ted. "In the Supermarket of Style." *The Clubcultures Reader: Readings in Popular Culture Studies*, edited by Steve Redhead, Derek Wynne, and Justin O'Connor, Oxford: Blackwell, 1997, pp. 131–33.

Pollock, David. "Kylie Minogue, SECC, Glascow." *Independent*, July 7, 2008, https://www.independent.co.uk/arts-entertainment/music/reviews/kylie-minogue-secc-glasgow-861261.html. Accessed June 30, 2016.

Power, editor. "Kylie Minogue, the O2, Review." *The Telegraph*, March 24, 2011, https://www.telegraph.co.uk/culture/music/rockandpopreviews/8402213/Kylie-Minogue-The-O2-Dublin-review.html. Accessed June 30, 2016.

Prendergast, Lara. "Lady Gaga Uses Twitter to Express 'Disappointment' at Cancelled Indonesia Concert." *The Telegraph*, May 28, 2012, http://www.telegraph.co.uk/culture/music/music-news/9295960/Lady-Gaga-uses-Twitter-to-express-disappointment-at-cancelled-Indonesia-concert.html. Accessed May 18, 2017.

Prodigy, Jamel (Derek Auguste). Personal interview. March 1, 2016.

The Pussycat Dolls. *Doll Domination Tour*, January–July, Europe, Oceania, Asia, and North America, 2009.

Queen. "Radio Ga Ga." *The Works*, EMI, and Capitol, 1984.

Reeser, Todd W. *Masculinities in Theory: An Introduction*. Chichester: Wiley-Blackwell, 2010.

Reich, June L. "Genderfuck: The Law of the Dildo." *Camp: Queer Aesthetics and the Performing Subject: A Reader*, edited by Fabio Cleto. Ann Arbor: University of Michigan Press, 1999, pp. 255–65.

Rent. Written by Jonathan Larson, New York Theatre Workshop, 1994.

Reynolds, Simon. "Rave Culture: Living Dream or Living Death." *The Clubcultures Reader: Readings in Popular Cultural Studies*, edited by Steve Redhead, Derek Wynne, and Justin O'Connor, Oxford: Blackwell, 1997, pp. 84–93.

Reynolds, Simon, and Joy Press. *The Sex Revolts: Gender, Rebellion, and Rock'n'Roll*. London: Serpent's Tail, 1995.

Rich, Adrienne C. "Compulsory Heterosexuality and Lesbian Existence." *Blood, Bread and Poetry: Selected Prose 1979–1985*, New York: Norton, 1986, pp. 23–75.

Rihanna. *Anti*, Westbury Road, and Roc Nation, 2016.

Rihanna. *Anti World Tour*, March–November, Europe, North America, and Asia, 2016.

Ritchie, Andrea J. *Invisible No More: Police Violence against Black Women and Women of Color*. Boston, MA: Beacon, 2017.

Ritzer, George, and Nathan Jurgenson. "Production, Consumption, Prosumption: The Nature of Capitalism in the Age of the Digital 'Prosumer.'" *Journal of Consumer Culture*, vol. 10, no. 1,

REFERENCES

2010, pp. 13–36, *Sage*, https://journals.sagepub.com/doi/abs/10.1177/1469540509354673. Accessed September 1, 2018.

Riviere, Joan. "Womanliness as a Masquarade". *Psychoanalysis and Woman: A Reader*, edited by Shalley Sagauro, New York: New York UP, 2000, pp. 70–78.

The Rocky Horror Show. Written by Richard O'Brien, Royal Court Theatre, London, 1973.

The Rocky Horror Picture Show. Directed by Jim Sharman, 20th Century Fox, 1975.

Robertson, Pamela. *Guilty Pleasures: Feminist Camp from Mae West to Madonna*. London: I. B. Tauris, 1996.

Robertson, Pamela. "Mae West's Maids: Race, 'Authenticity,' and the Discourse of Camp." *Camp: Queer Aesthetics and the Performing Subject: A Reader*, edited by Fabio Cleto, Ann Arbor: University of Michigan Press, 1999, pp. 393–408.

Robinson, Amy. "Is She or Isn't She?: Madonna and the Erotics of Appropriation." *Acting Out: Feminist Performances*, edited by Lynda Hart and Peggy Phelan. Ann Arbor: University of Michigan Press, 1993, pp. 337–61.

Robinson, Paul. *Opera, Sex and Other Vital Matters*. Chicago: University of Chicago Press, 2002.

Rodríguez-Salas, Gerardo, and Sara Martín-Alegre. "Forget Madonna: The Many Metamorphoses of Kylie Minogue, Showgirl and Survivor." *Proceedings from the 33rd Annual Conference of the Spanish Association for Anglo-American Studies*, Cádiz: Servicio de Publicaciones de la Universidad de Cádiz, 2010, pp. 156–65. Accessed June 29, 2016.

Rosen, Jody. "Lady Gaga's Born This Way; A Track-by-Track Breakdown." *Rolling Stone*, May 18, 2011, https://www.rollingstone.com/music/music-news/lady-gagas-born-this-way-a-track-by-track-breakdown-254582/. Accessed May 19, 2017.

Ross, Andrew. "Used of Camp." *Camp: Queer Aesthetics and the Performing Subject: A Reader*, edited by Fabio Cleto, Ann Arbor: University of Michigan Press, 1999, pp. 302–07.

Ross, Marlon B. "Camping the Dirty Dozens: The Queer Resources of Black Nationalist Invective," *Callaloo*, vol. 23, no. 1, 2000, pp. 290– 312, JSTOR, www.jstor.org/ stable/ 3299563. Accessed March 30, 2016.

RuPaul's Drag Race. Directed by Nick Murray, World of Wonder, February 2009–Present.

Saturday Night Fever. Directed John Badham, Robert Stigwood Organization, 1977.

Sasaki, Maana. "Gender Ambiguity and Liberation of Female Sexual Desire in Fantasy Spaces in *Shojo* Manga and *Shojo* Subculture." *Critical Theory and Social Justice/Journal of Undergraduate Research, Occidental College*, vol. 3, no. 1, 2013, pp. 1–26, https://scholar.oxy.edu/bitstream/handle/20.500.12711/4277/Sasaki.pdf?sequence=1. Accessed August 14, 2018.

Savage, Jon, and Ewan Pearson. "How Donna Summer's I Feel Love Changed Pop." *The Guardian*, May 18, 2012, https://www.theguardian.com/music/musicblog/2012/may/18/donna-summer-i-feel-love. Accessed August 14, 2018.

Schechner, Richard. *Performance Theory*. New York: Routledge, 1977.

Schneemann, Carolee. *More Than Meat Joy: Performance Works and Selected Writings*. New York: McPherson, 1997.

Scott, Suzanne. "'Cosplay Is Serious Business': Gendering Material Fan Labor on Heroes of Cosplay." *Cinema Journal*, vol. 54, no. 3, 2015, pp. 146–54, JSTOR, www.jstor.org/ stable/ 43653443. Accessed April 27, 2021.

Sedgwick, Eve Kosofsky. "From 'Wilde, Nietzsche, and the Sentimental Relations of the Male Body.'" *Camp: Queer Aesthetics and the Performing Subject: A Reader*, edited by Fabio Cleto, Ann Arbor: University of Michigan Press, 1999, pp. 207–20.

Sehgal, Paula. "How 'Flawless' Became a Feminist Declaration." *New York Times*, March 28, 2015, https://www.nytimes.com/2015/03/29/magazine/how-flawless-became-a-feminist-declaration.html. Accessed October 10, 2016.

Senelick, Laurence. *The Changing Room: Sex, Drag and Theatre*. New York: Routledge, 2000.

The Sex Pistols. "Anarchy in the U.K." *Never Mind the Bollocks, Here Come the Sex Pistols*, Virgin, 1977.

The Sex Pistols. "God Save the Queen." *Never Mind the Bollocks, Here Come the Sex Pistols*, Virgin, 1977.

Sex and the City 2. Directed by Michael Patrick King, New Line Cinema, HBO Films, Village Roadshow, and Pictures, 2010.

The Sex Pistols. "New York." *Never Mind the Bollocks, Here Come the Sex Pistols*, Virgin, 1977.

The Sex Pistols. *Never Mind the Bollocks, Here Come the Sex Pistols*. Virgin, 1977.

Shugart, Helene A., and Catherine Egley Waggoner. *Making Camp: Rhetorics of Transgression in U.S. Popular Culture*. Tuscaloosa: University of Alabama Press, 2008.

"Snatched." *Urban Dictionary*. https://www.urbandictionary.com/define.php?term= snatched&page=2. Accessed April 27, 2021.

Some Like It Hot. Directed by Billy Wilder, Mirisch Company, 1959.

Sontag, Susan. "Notes on 'Camp.'" *Camp: Queer Aesthetics and the Performing Subject: A Reader*, edited by Fabio Cleto, Ann Arbor: University of Michigan Press, 1999, pp. 53–65.

The Sound of Music. Directed by Robert Wise, Argyle Enterprises, 1965.

Spears, Britney. *Blackout*, Jive Records, 2007.

Springer, Kimberly. "Third Wave Black Feminism?" *Signs*, vol. 27, no. 4, 2002, pp. 1059–82, JSTOR, www.jstor.org/ stable/ 10.1086/ 339636. Accessed April 27, 2021.

Stallings, L. H. *Mutha' Is Half a Word: Intersections of Folklore, Vernacular, Myth and Queerness in Black Female Culture*. Columbus: Ohio State UP, 2007.

Stein, Karen F. "Monsters and Madwomen: Changing Female Gothic." *The Female Gothic*, edited by Juliann E. Fleenor, Montreal: Eden, 1983, pp. 123–37.

Stucky, Nathan, and Cynthia Wimmer, editors. *Teaching Performance Studies*. Carbondale: Southern Illinois UP, 2002.

Sullivan, Caroline. "Yoko Ono and Madonna Both Fight Ageism—in Radically Different Ways." *The Guardian*, February 27, 2015, https://www.theguardian.com/music/musicblog/2015/feb/27/ yoko-ono-and-madonna-both-fight-ageism-in-radically-different-ways. Accessed May 15, 2017.

Star Wars. Directed by George Lucas, Lucasfiln Ltd., 1977.

Summer, Donna. "I Feel Love." *I Remember Yesterday*, Casablanca, 1977.

REFERENCES

Summer, Donna. "*Love to Love You Baby*." Love to Love You Baby, Casablanca, and Oasis, 1975.

Sunset Boulevard. Directed by Billy Wilder, Paramount Pictures, 1950.

Sweet Bird of Youth. Written by Tennessee Williams, March 10, Martin Beck Theatre, New York City, 1959.

Sweet Charity. Directed by Bob Fosse, Universal, 1969.

Taylor, Millie, and Dominic Symonds. *Studying Musical Theatre: Theory and Practice*. London: Palgrave-Macmillan, 2014.

That B.E.A.T. Directed by Abteen Bagheri, 2012. *Vimeo*, uploaded by Abteen Bagheri, https://vimeo.com/58423297. Accessed May 15, 2017.

Thompson Drewal, Margaret. "The Camp Trace in Corporate America." *The Politics and Poetics of Camp*, edited by Moe Meyer, New York: Routledge, 1994, pp. 128–56.

Thorpe, Vanessa. "Pop Star or Avant-Garde Artist? Lady Gaga Wants to Be the Next Warhol." *The Guardian*, August 18, 2013, https://www.theguardian.com/music/2013/aug/18/lady-gaga-artpop-album-avant-garde. Accessed April 29, 2017.

Timberland. "Give It to Me." Featuring Nelly Furtado, and Justin Timberlake, *Shock Value*, Mosley, Blackground Records, and Interscope, 2007.

Toffler, Alvin. *Third Wave*. New York: William Morrow, 1980.

Tony, Bennett, and Lady Gaga. *Cheek to Cheek Tour*, December 2014–August 2015, Europe, and North America.

Tootsie. Directed by Sydney Pollack, Mirage Enterprises, 1982.

Torch Song Trilogy. Written by Harvey Fierstein, Actors' Playhouse, Greenwich Village, New York City, 1982.

Torrusio, Ann T. "The Fame Monster: The Monstrous Construction of Lady Gaga." *The Performance Identities of Lady Gaga: Critical Essays*, edited by Richard J. Gray II, Jefferson, NC: McFarland, 2012, pp. 160–72.

The Trammps. "Disco Inferno." *Disco Inferno*, Atlantic, 1976.

Trier-Bienek, Andrienne, editor. *The Beyoncé Effect: Essays on Sexuality, Race and Feminism*, edited by Adrienne Trier-Bieniek, Jefferson, NC: McFarland, 2016.

Tulloch, Carol. *The Birth of Cool: Style Narratives of the African Diaspora*. London: Bloomsbury, 2016.

Turner, Tina. "Acid Queen." *Acid Queen*, United Artists, and EMI, 1975.

Tzara, Tristan. "Dada Manifesto." *Theatre of the Avant-Garde, 1890–1950: A Critical Anthology*, edited by Robert Knopf, New Haven: Yale UP, 2001, pp. 257–64.

U2. *U2 360° Tour*, June 2009–July 2011, Europe, North America, Oceania, Africa, and South America.

Valocchi, Steve. "Individual Identities, Collective Identities, and Organizational Structure: The Relationship of the Political Left and Gay Liberation in the United States," *Sociological Perspectives*, vol. 44, no. 4, 2001, pp. 445–67, JSTOR, http://www.jstor.org/stable/10.1525/sop.2001.44.4.445. Accessed April 27, 2021.

Valocchi, Steve. "The Class- Inflected Nature of Gay Identity," *Social Problems*, vol. 46, no. 2, 1999, pp. 207–24, JSTOR, https://www.jstor.org/stable/3097253?seq=1. Accessed April 27, 2021.

Vena, Jocelyn. "Beyoncé 'Nailed It' in 'Girls' Video, Choreographer Says." *MTV*, May 19, 2011, http://www.mtv.com/news/1664223/beyonce-run-the-world-girls/. Accessed October 9, 2016.

Vena, Jocelyn. "Madonna Owns 'Girl Gone Wild' Title in New Video." *MTV*, March 20, 2012, http://www.mtv.com/news/1681471/madonna-girl-gone-wild-video/. Accessed April 29, 2016.

Vena, Jocelyn. "Minaj's Alter Ego Roman Zolanski Makes Grammy Debut." *MTV*, February 13, 2012, http://www.mtv.com/news/1679156/nicki-minaj-roman-zolanski-grammys/. Accessed October 10, 2016.

Vertigo. Directed by Alfred Hitchcock, Alfred J. Hitchcock Productions, 1958.

Victor/Victoria. Written and directed by Blake Edwards, Endemol Theatre Productions, and Polygram Broadway Venctors, New York City, 1995.

Vint, Sherryl. *Bodies of Tomorrow: Technology, Subjectivity, Science Fiction*. Toronto: University of Toronto Press, 2007.

VH1 Divas Las Vegas. Directed by Louis J. Horvitz, VH1 Television, May 23, 2002.

Waiting for B. Directed by Paulo Cesar Toledo, and Abigail Spindel, Popcon - Pop Content Films, 2017.

Wallace-Sanders, Kimberly. *Skin Deep, Spirit Strong: The Black Female Body in American Culture*. Ann Arbor: University of Michigan Press, 2002.

Walley-Jean, J. Celeste. "Debunking the Myth of the 'Angry Black Woman': An Exploration of Anger in Young African American Women." *Black Women, Gender & Families*, vol. 3, no. 2, 2009, pp. 68–86, Project Muse, https://doi.org/10.1353/bwg.0.0011. Accessed July 26, 2021.

Water, Roger (Pink Floyd). *The Wall Live*. North America, Europe, Oceania and South America, September 2010–September 2013.

Watkins, Mel. *On the Real Side: Laughing, Lying, and Signifying: The Underground Tradition of African American Humor that Transformed American Culture*. New York: Simon and Schuster, 1994.

Watney, Simon. *Imagine Hope: AIDS and Gay Identity*. Abingdon; Routledge, 2002.

What Ever Happened to Baby Jane? Directed by Robert Aldrich, The Associates & Aldrich Company, 1962.

Whiteley, Sheila. *Too Much Too Young: Popular Music, Age and Gender*. London: Routledge, 2005.

Whiteley, Sheila. *Women and Popular Music: Sexuality, Identity, and Subjectivity*. London: Routledge, 2000.

Whitelock, Anna. *Elizabeth's Bedfellows: An Intimate History of the Queen's Court*. London: Bloomsbury, 2013.

Who the F**k Is Arthur Fogel. Directed by Rod Chapman, ET Chapman Productions, 2013.

REFERENCES

Widawski, Maciej. *African American Slang: A Linguistic Description*. Cambridge: Cambridge UP, 2015.

Willard, Michael Nevin. "Séance, Tricknowlogy, Skateboarding, and the Space of Youth." *Popular Culture: A Reader*, edited by Raiford Guins, and Omayara Zaragoza Cruz, Thousand Oaks, CA: Sage, 2005, pp. 462–78.

Wilson, James. *Bulldaggers, Pansies, and Chocolate Babies: Performance, Race, and Sexuality in the Harlem Renaissance*. Ann Arbor: University of Michigan Press, 2010.

The Wizard of Oz. Directed by Victor Fleming, King Vidor, George Cukor, and Norman Taurog, Metro-Goldwyn-Mayer, 1939.

Women in Revolt. Directed by Paul Morrissey, Andy Warhol, 1971.

Woodard, Jennifer Baily, and Teresa Mastin. "Black Womanhood: 'Essence' and Its Treatment of Stereotypical Images of Black Women." *Journal of Black Studies*, vol. 36, no. 2, 2005, pp. 264–281, JSTOR, www. jstor.org/stable/40034332. Accessed April 27, 2021.

Youngs, Ian. "Stadium Rock, from Beatles to Bono." *BBC News*, August 13, 2009, http://news.bbc.co.uk/2/hi/entertainment/8188140.stm. Accessed April 10, 2016.

Zwick, Detlev, Samuel K. Bonsu, and Aron Darmody. "Putting Consumers to Work: Co-creation and New Marketing Govern-Mentality." *Journal of Consumer Culture*, vol. 8, no. 1, 2008, pp. 163–96, *Sage*, https://journals.sagepub.com/doi/10.1177/1469540508090089. Accessed September 1, 2018.

Index

Terms in square brackets indicate terms similar to the indexed one.

A

ABBA 45, 47, 51, 54–55

Abramović, Marina 140, 154–55, 159

African American 17, 20, 59, 62, 102, 106, 115–16, 118, 123, 126–27
  community 48, 124
  culture 67, 109, 113, 114

ageism 7, 41–42

Altman, Dennis 25, 37n29

androgyny [androgynous] 50, 64, 86, 130n17, 143, 147, 165

Angels in America 142

Auslander, Philip 21, 33n4, 45, 50–51, 135

B

Baker, William 6, 8, 38n36, 76–77, 80–81, 83–85, 88–91, 93–97

ballroom culture [ballroom scene] 35n21, 59–61, 66–68, 72n22, 123

Beyoncé 3, 6, 9, 22, 28, 97, 102–28, 137, 150, 162, 173, 182, 195, 197
  as Sasha Fierce 113–14
  Dreamgirls 105
  Formation Tour, The 28, 103, 119
  I Am… World Tour 106, 115
  Mrs. Carter Show Tour, The 109, 112, 119

Black
  Blackness 113, 119, 122, 125, 131n26

culture 44, 62, 104, 109, 113, 122, 124–27, 170n22

femininity 99n16, 106, 113–14, 119, 126, 130n14, 131n24

masculinity 119, 131n24

Bowie, David 35n15, 51, 55, 98n2, 98n3, 134, 158, 162, 165

burlesque and neo-burlesque 5, 8, 54, 56, 71n18, 77, 84–86, 97, 99n16, 99n17, 126, 129n11, 161, 164–65, 193n4

butch 59, 64, 151, 179

Butler, Judith 59–60, 62, 72n23, 170n19

C

camp
  Black camp 9, 109, 113, 124, 126–27, 197
  campification 49–50, 66, 137, 166, 193n1
  canon 17, 22, 180
  culture 2, 8, 12–13, 15, 18, 23, 30, 32, 36n25, 48, 84, 87–88, 103, 106, 124, 126, 129n9, 131n24, 167, 187, 195, 197
  metallic camp [metal camp] 152, 155, 162
  performance 8–9, 34n11, 47, 78, 109, 119, 186, 195
  praxis 31, 76, 96–97, 127, 138, 141, 149–50, 162, 166–67, 180, 185, 191–92, 195, 197

Chauncey, George 43, 177
Cleto, Fabio 11, 34n8, 90, 97n1, 162
Cher 3, 20, 83, 98n2, 165, 181, 196
cross-identification 18–19, 176, 180, 185
cultural appropriation 8, 20, 42–43, 46, 59,
    62, 67, 125, 197

D

Destiny's Child 103, 105, 110
Dietrich, Marlene 2, 12, 64–65, 90, 181
diva
    adoration or worship 3, 5, 10–11, 13–16,
        18–19, 22, 30-2, 33n2, 75, 77–78, 97,
        124, 187–88, 191–92, 195
    culture 3–4, 15, 176, 181, 192, 198
    disco diva 17–18, 35n16, 48, 105, 116–
        17
    film diva [cinema diva, Hollywood diva]
        13–14, 17, 124, 30–31, 124
    music diva 3, 14–15, 19, 30, 77, 176–
        77, 195–96
    opera diva 15–16, 18
    show 4–5, 27–30, 187, 189, 195–96
disco 8, 17–19, 35n16–17, 45–54, 56–
    57, 69n6, 70n14, 75, 79–82, 97, 117,
    138–39, 153, 161–62, 167, 170n21,
    197
    era 81, 117
    scene 5, 46, 138, 162
drag
    audience drag 10, 31–32, 171, 174, 176,
        182, 185–87, 190–92, 195, 197
    culture 10, 121, 164, 182–83, 195, 197
    performance 10, 14, 59, 184–85
Dyer, Richard 22, 79, 93–94

E

effeminacy [effeminate] 8, 26–27, 48, 50, 61,
    64, 88, 91, 124, 127, 143, 160, 176, 181,
    186, 190, 197

F

fan
    culture 24, 31–32, 167, 189, 191
    fanbase 80, 82–83, 87, 100, 104, 107, 128,
        134, 137, 156, 158, 191
    queer fan 4, 10–11, 22, 24, 32, 104, 173,
        187, 189–90
fandom 10, 22, 31, 75, 82, 103, 127, 134–35,
    174, 184, 186, 188, 191
    queer fandom 9, 22, 44, 59, 188
faux queens [bio queens] 182, 193
femininity
    glamorous femininity 4, 56–57, 84–85, 91,
        125, 140, 197
    hyperfemininity 79, 91
    performance (of) 8, 16, 56, 84, 86, 119,
        164, 182, 186, 193
femme 59, 64, 113, 115–16, 152, 155

G

Garland, Judy 1–2, 14, 22, 141–42, 188
gay
    and lesbian movement 12, 88
    culture 9, 12–13, 24–26, 32, 45, 74, 77,
        80, 88–89, 94–95, 97, 113–14, 127, 176,
        179, 181–83, 191
    identity 14, 35–37, 88
    men 1, 7–8, 12–17, 20, 26, 32, 34n14,
        36n27, 36n28, 43, 48, 61, 74–75, 77, 79,
        82, 87, 94, 100n25, 115, 119, 125–26,
        131n24, 181, 190
    propaganda 66
    sex 88
gender
    genderfuck 64–65
    genderqueer 19, 159, 131n25, 185
    identity 183
    performance (of) 8, 18, 20, 24, 38n35, 56,
        59–61, 91, 103, 113, 121–22, 125, 153,
        177, 181, 186, 190

INDEX

H

Hair 141–142, 162

Halberstam, Jack 29, 38n37, 134, 144

Halperin, David 2, 30, 88, 91

Harris, Daniel 2, 12–14, 32, 77, 188

Hawkins, Stan 20, 42, 53, 135

heterosexual

   culture 157, 179, 190

   heteronormative 11, 16, 19, 26, 29, 50, 61, 79, 87, 91, 96, 126– 27, 156, 158, 165, 178

   heterosexuality 48, 87, 96

HIV/AIDS 21–22, 41, 43, 49–50, 53, 100, 139, 191

homosexual

   culture 7, 11, 25, 179

   homoerotic 80, 82, 91–92, 154

   homosexuality 11–12, 15, 25–26, 29, 61, 66, 82, 88, 92, 124, 142, 156, 169n11, 177, 180, 188

hooks, bell 42, 59, 61–62, 67, 102, 120, 126

Horn, Katrin 135, 141–42

House [ballroom] 61–62, 67–68, 72, 177, 180, 192

I

Isherwood, Christopher 3, 12, 108

J

Jackson, Janet 27, 170n20

Jackson, Michael 27, 55, 98n2, 107, 129n10, 136, 138, 145, 193n1

Johnson, E. Patrick 119, 125, 131n24, 131n26

L

Lady Gaga 3, 6, 9–10, 22–23, 28–29, 67, 103, 128, 133–67, 172–73, 181, 186, 191, 195, 197–98

   ARTPOP 158–59, 161, 164, 169n16

   ArtRave: The ARTPOP Ball Tour 160–66

   as Jo Calderone 134, 145, 181

   Born This Way 133, 136, 144–47, 149–51, 154–55, 158

   Born This Way Ball 72n21, 139–40, 145– 48, 151–55, 166, 168n7

   Cheek to Cheek Tour 165, 167n2

   Fame, The 137, 158, 160

   Fame Ball, The 159, 160–61

   Fame Monster, The 137, 144– 45, 158

   Joanne 166–67

   Joanne World Tour 165–67

   Monster Ball Tour and *Monster Ball Tour 2.0* 135, 138–44, 153, 166, 168n5, 172

lesbian 12–13, 19–20, 37n31, 46, 48, 62, 65– 66, 121, 144, 153, 155, 179

   sex 64, 151

Lennox, Annie 19–20, 35n31, 98n2

LGBTQ+

   community 24, 65–66, 74, 125, 149

   culture 2, 25–26

   identity 25

   movement 7, 25, 90, 177, 183

   rights 134, 144

live

   concert [concert show, live show] 5–7, 38n34, 88, 173

   entertainment 171, 198

   liveness 5, 33n4

   performance 4–5, 10, 23–24, 41, 55–56, 86, 103, 113, 161, 164–65, 173, 196, 199

M

Madonna 3, 7, 8, 19, 20, 23, 28–29, 40–68, 75–78, 81–82, 103–04, 107, 114, 125, 134–36, 140, 145, 156, 162, 172–73, 175, 176, 184, 195–97

   Blond Ambition World Tour 41, 62, 76–77

   Confessions on a Dance Floor 45, 47, 51, 54–56, 70n14

   Confessions Tour 28, 44–57, 64, 81, 107

Girlie Show, The 54, 65, 71
Hard Candy 57, 72n24
Madonna: Truth or Dare 41, 62
MDNA Tour 46, 57, 64–65, 156
Rebel Heart Tour 46, 57, 65–66
Sticky & Sweet Tour 44, 56–57, 70n11, 140, 145
masculinity 19, 26–27, 48, 50–51, 61, 87, 91–95, 97, 100n25, 101n28, 110, 119, 127, 131n24, 176, 181, 197
  classical 93–95
  performance of masculinity 51, 91
  White 94, 127
masquerade 42, 56, 79, 114, 177
melodrama 16, 71n18, 79, 114, 136, 139, 148, 153, 155
Minaj, Nicki 15, 122
Minnelli, Liza 3, 56, 114
Minogue, Kylie 1–3, 5–8, 19, 22–23, 27, 51, 58, 63, 67, 74–97, 103–04, 107, 129n12, 135, 145, 162–63, 166, 173, 181, 195, 197–98
  Aphrodite: Les Folies Tour [Aphrodite Tour] 78, 89, 93–95, 101n26, 145
  Golden (Tour) 81–82, 166
  Kiss Me Once Tour 78, 95–96, 107
  KylieFever2002 129n12
  KylieX2008 [X Tour] 78, 80–82, 85, 94, 163
  Showgirl: The Greatest Hits Tour and *Showgirl: The Homecoming Tour* 2, 5, 63, 78, 83, 85
  White Diamond: A Personal Portrait of Kylie Minogue 76, 83–84
Monroe, Marilyn 2, 45, 56, 69n5, 72n19, 99n11, 165
Moore, Madison 182, 189–90
MTV 40, 44, 106, 134, 155, 175, 181
music
  bounce 29, 112, 123–24, 126

house 5, 8, 48, 57, 66, 116–17, 162
EDM [dance] 8, 48, 75, 80, 109, 133, 145, 161–64, 189
jazz 109, 165, 167
pop 17, 27, 76, 108
rap 29, 124
rock 4, 19, 27, 40, 47–48, 50–51, 97, 167, 174
television 19, 23, 44, 75
musical (show) [musical theater] 5, 9, 28, 90, 105, 112, 115, 124, 135–36, 139, 141, 148, 153, 155, 167n1, 180, 196–97

N
Newton, Esther 169n14, 178
nostalgia 6–7, 44–45, 54, 57–58, 80–82, 147, 167, 173, 197

P
Paglia, Camille 40–41
Paris Is Burning 60, 62, 68, 72n22, 72n23, 171, 190, 192
Perry, Katy 15, 27, 58, 72n21, 169n9, 170n20, 193n1
pop culture 2, 5, 9, 13, 23, 29, 31–32, 44, 66, 126, 136–37, 159, 174, 176, 181, 197
Pride 7, 12, 25–26, 29, 37n30, 37n31, 74, 134, 169n11, 176, 179
Prodigy, Jamel 6, 59, 67–68
prosumer [prosumption] 31–32, 39n39, 175, 183, 191

Q
queer
  audience 2–4, 8, 15–17, 19–24, 29–30, 32, 43, 58, 63, 65, 67, 80, 87, 103–04, 106, 118, 127–28, 141, 181–82, 187, 195–97
  community 1–2, 15, 21, 24–26, 29, 33, 47, 50, 113, 123, 134, 139, 176, 180, 192

INDEX

culture 1–4, 7–10, 13–15, 17, 20–21, 23–24, 26, 28, 32, 43–44, 58–61, 65, 67–68, 77–79, 82, 88, 103–4, 106, 118–19, 123–24, 126–27, 134, 137, 139, 143, 157, 174, 176–80, 182–83, 185–87, 190–92, 195–97

identity 13, 190, 195, 197

performance 10, 187

praxis 10, 20, 30, 66, 125, 195

queering 18, 31, 66, 85, 148, 180, 182, 186

sex 64, 144, 158, 189

sexuality 143, 174

R

rave 5, 46, 159, 161, 163–65

Rihanna 72n21, 129n10, 193n1

Robertson, Pamela 13, 34n11, 42–43, 56, 82, 98n9

role-play(ing) 19, 47, 64, 75, 115, 155, 159, 162, 183, 186, 196

Ross, Andrew 35n20, 52

Ross, Diana 3, 22, 48, 105, 117, 131n21, 196

RuPaul 171, 174, 180–81

RuPaul's Drag Race 181

S

Saturday Night Fever 45, 48, 53

Schneemann, Carolee 154–55

Shugart, Helene A. and Waggoner, Catherine E. 42–43, 111–12

Sontag, Susan 11–13, 34n10, 49, 76, 90, 108, 114

Stonewall (riots) 1, 13–14, 25, 48, 77, 94, 180

Summer, Donna 47–49, 117

S&M 8, 20, 44, 54, 63, 134

T

Tom of Finland 80, 82, 98n7

torchsinger [torch songstress] 16–17

touring 8, 24, 68, 145, 155, 165, 172, 186, 198

trans 104, 131, 177–79

transgender 7, 28, 61, 144, 159, 179–80

transphobic 189

transsexual 7, 134

V

vogue/voguing 6–8, 43, 55, 58–68, 125–26, 177, 180, 182, 192, 197

W

Warhol, Andy 81, 121, 134, 158–60, 169n16

White

culture 109, 113

Whiteness 9, 12, 26, 94, 97, 108

Wizard of Oz, The 1, 98, 141–42

233